Dynamic Learning:
Flash
CS3
Professional

with Video Tutorials and Lesson Files

Dynamic Learning:
Flash
CS3
Professional

with Video Tutorials and Lesson Files

Fred Gerantabee & AGI Creative Team

BEIJING · CAMBRIDGE · FARNHAM · KÖLN · PARIS · SEBASTOPOL · TAIPEI · TOKYO

Dynamic Learning: Flash CS3 Professional
By Fred Gerantabee & AGI Creative Team

Additional Writing: **Eric Rowse, Jennifer Smith, Jerron Smith, Jeremy Osborn, Sean McKnight**

Series Editor: **Christopher Smith**

Technical Editors: **Cathy Auclair, Jeff Ausura, Chad Chelius, Linda Forsvall, Haziel Olivera, Caitlin Smith**

Additional Editing: **Edie Freedman**

Video Project Manager: **Jeremy Osborn**

Cover Design: **Edie Freedman, O'Reilly Media**

Interior Design: **Ron Bilodeau, O'Reilly Media**

Graphic Production: **Lauren Mickol**

Additional Production: **Aquent Studios**

Indexing: **Caitlin Smith, Michele Filshie**

Video Editor: **Trevor Chamberlain**

Proofreading: **Jay Donahue**

Published by O'Reilly Media, Inc., 1005 Gravenstein Highway North, Sebastopol, CA 95472.

O'Reilly books may be purchased for educational, business, or sales promotional use. Online editions are also available for most titles (*safari.oreilly.com*). For more information, contact our corporate/institutional sales department: 800.998.9938 or *corporate@oreilly.com*.

Please report any errors by sending a message to errata@aquent.com.

Print History: July 2007, First Edition.
ISBN 10: 0-596-51058-6
ISBN 13: 978-0-596-51058-9
[F]

Printed in Canada.

Contents

Starting Up

Lesson 1: What's New in Adobe Flash CS3?   7

Lesson 2: Flash CS3 Jumpstart   17

Lesson 3: Getting Started with the Drawing Tools 51

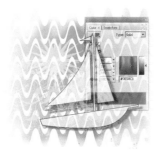

Lesson 4: Modifying and Transforming Graphics 95

Lesson 5: Using Symbols and the Library 123

Lesson 6: Creating Basic Animation 157

Lesson 7: Diving Deeper into Animation 187

Lesson 8: Customizing Your Workflow 221

Lesson 13: Introducing Movie Clips   357

Resources on the DVD

The *Dynamic Learning: Flash CS3 Professional* Digital Classroom DVD that is included with this book is loaded with useful information, video tutorials that accompany each lesson, and the lesson files that you'll need to complete the exercises contained in this book.

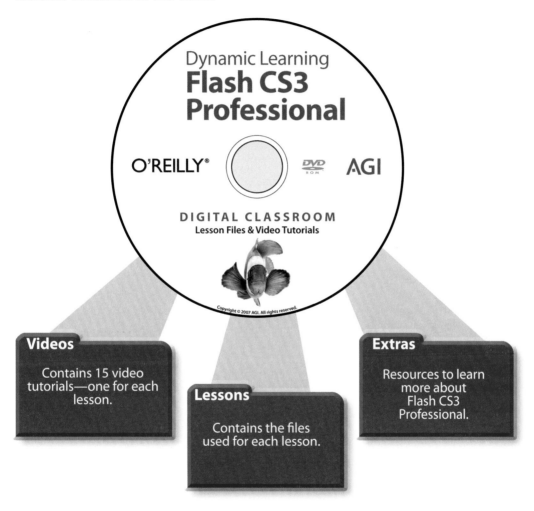

The included video tutorials play on both Windows and Mac OS computers using the free Adobe® Flash® player available at adobe.com/products/flashplayer.

Starting up

About Dynamic Learning

Adobe® Flash® CS3 Professional is the leading software application used to create and deliver interactive content. Adobe Flash CS3 Professional is the most advanced authoring environment for creating rich, interactive content for digital, web, and mobile platforms.

Dynamic Learning: Flash CS3 Professional is like having your own personal instructor guiding you through each lesson while you work at your own speed. This book includes 15 self-paced lessons that let you discover essential skills and explore the new features and capabilities of Flash CS3 Professional. Each lesson includes step-by-step instructions and lesson files, along with video tutorials that complement the topics covered in each lesson. These accompanying files are provided on the included *Dynamic Learning: Flash CS3 Professional* Digital Classroom DVD, developed by the same team of Adobe Certified Instructors and Flash experts who have created many of the official training titles for Adobe Systems.

Prerequisites

Before you start the lessons in *Dynamic Learning: Flash CS3 Professional,* you should have a working knowledge of your computer and its operating system. You should know how to use the directory system of your computer so that you can navigate through folders. You need to understand how to locate, save, and open files. You should also know how to use your mouse to access menus and commands.

Before starting the lessons files in *Dynamic Learning: Flash CS3 Professional*, make sure that you have installed Adobe Flash CS3 Professional. The software is sold separately, and not included with this book. You may use the 30-day trial version of Adobe Flash CS3 Professional available at the *Adobe.com* website, subject to the terms of its license agreement.

System requirements

Before starting the lessons in *Dynamic Learning: Flash CS3 Professional*, make sure that your computer is equipped for running Adobe Flash CS3 Professional, which you must purchase separately. The minimum system requirements for your computer to effectively use the software are listed below and on the following page.

System requirements for Adobe Flash CS3 Professional:

Windows OS

- Intel® Pentium® 4, Intel Centrino®, Intel Xeon®, or Intel Core™ Duo (or compatible) processor
- Microsoft® Windows® XP with Service Pack 2 or Windows Vista™ Home Premium, Business, Ultimate, or Enterprise (certified for 32-bit editions)
- 512MB of RAM (1GB recommended)

- 2.5GB of available hard-disk space (additional free space required during installation)
- 1,024x768 monitor resolution with 16-bit video card
- DVD-ROM drive
- QuickTime 7.1.2 software required for multimedia features
- Internet or phone connection required for product activation

Macintosh OS

- 1GHz PowerPC® G4 or G5 or multicore Intel® processor
- Mac OS X v.10.4.8 or later
- 512MB of RAM (1GB recommended)
- 2.5GB of available hard-disk space (additional free space required during installation)
- 1,024x768 monitor resolution with 16-bit video card
- DVD-ROM drive
- QuickTime 7.1.2 software required for multimedia features
- Internet or phone connection required for product activation

Starting Adobe Flash CS3 Professional

As with most software, Adobe Flash CS3 Professional is launched by locating the application in your Programs folder (Windows) or Applications folder (Mac OS). If necessary, follow these steps to start the Adobe Flash CS3 Professional application:

Windows

1 Choose Start > All Programs > Adobe Flash CS3 Professional.

2 Close the Welcome Screen when it appears. You are now ready to use Adobe Flash CS3 Professional.

Mac OS

1 Open the Applications folder, and then open the Adobe Flash CS3 Professional folder.

2 Double-click on the Adobe Flash CS3 Professional application icon.

3 Close the Welcome Screen when it appears. You are now ready to use Adobe Flash CS3 Professional.

Menus and commands are identified throughout the book by using the greater-than symbol (>). For example, the command to print a document would be identified as File > Print.

Fonts used in this book

Dynamic Learning: Flash CS3 Professional includes lessons that refer to fonts that were installed with your copy of Adobe Flash CS3 Professional. If you did not install the fonts, or have removed them from your computer, you may substitute different fonts for the exercises or re-install the software to access the fonts.

 If you receive a Missing Font Warning while working on the lessons, choose the Use Default button and proceed with the lesson.

Resetting the Flash workspace

To make certain that your panels and working environment are consistent, you should reset your workspace at the start of each lesson. To reset your workspace, choose Window > Workspace > Default.

Loading lesson files

The *Dynamic Learning: Flash CS3 Professional* Digital Classroom DVD includes files that accompany the exercises for each of the lessons. You may copy the entire lessons folder from the supplied DVD to your hard drive, or copy only the lesson folders for the individual lessons you wish to complete.

For each lesson in the book, the files are referenced by the file name of each file. The exact location of each file on your computer is not used, as you may have placed the files in a unique location on your hard drive. We suggest placing the lesson files in the My Documents folder (Windows) or at the top level of your hard drive (Mac OS).

Copying the lesson files to your hard drive:

1 Insert the *Dynamic Learning: Flash CS3 Professional* Digital Classroom DVD supplied with this book.

2 On your computer desktop, navigate to the DVD and locate the folder named fllessons.

3 You can install all of the files, or just specific lesson files. Do one of the following:
   • Install all lesson files by dragging the fllessons folder to your hard drive.
   • Install only some of the files by creating a new folder on your hard drive named fllessons. Open the fllessons folder on the supplied DVD, select the lesson you wish to complete, and drag the folder(s) to the fllessons folder you created on your hard drive.
   Macintosh users should see the important note on the next page.

Macintosh users may need to unlock the files after they are copied from the DVD. This only applies to MacOS computers. After copying the files from the DVD to your computer, select the fllessons folder, then choose File > Get Info. In the fllessons info window, click the You can drop-down menu labeled Read Only, which is located in the Ownership section of this window. From the You can drop-down menu, choose Read & Write. Click the arrow to the left of Details, then click the Apply to enclosed items... button at the bottom of the window. You may need to click the padlock icon before the Mac OS allows you to change these permissions. After making these changes, close the window.

Working with the video tutorials

Your *Dynamic Learning: Flash CS3 Professional* Digital Classroom DVD comes with video tutorials developed by the authors to help you understand the concepts explored in each lesson. Each tutorial is approximately five minutes long and demonstrates and explains the concepts and features covered in the lesson.

The videos are designed to supplement your understanding of the material in the chapter. We have selected exercises and examples that we feel will be most useful to you. You may want to view the entire video for each lesson before you begin that lesson. Additionally, at certain points in a lesson, you will encounter the DVD icon. The icon, with appropriate lesson number, indicates that an overview of the exercise being described can be found in the accompanying video.

DVD video icon.

Setting up for viewing the video tutorials

The DVD included with this book includes video tutorials for each lesson. Although you can view the lessons on your computer directly from the DVD, we recommend copying the folder labeled *Videos* from the *Dynamic Learning: Flash CS3 Professional* Digital Classroom DVD to your hard drive.

Copying the video tutorials to your hard drive:

1   Insert the *Dynamic Learning: Flash CS3 Professional* Digital Classroom DVD supplied with this book.

2   On your computer desktop, navigate to the DVD and locate the folder named Videos.

3   Drag the Videos folder to a location onto your hard drive.

Viewing the video tutorials with the Adobe Flash Player

To view the video tutorials, you need the Adobe Flash Player 8 or later (Adobe Flash Player 9). Earlier versions of the Flash Player will not play the videos correctly. If you're not sure that you have the latest version of the Flash Player, you can download it for free from the Adobe website: *http://www.adobe.com/support/flashplayer/downloads.html*

The accompanying video files use the Adobe Flash Video format to make universal viewing possible for users on both Windows and Mac OS computers. The most recent versions of the free Adobe Flash Player software generally improve playback performance of these video files.

Playing the video tutorials:

1   Make sure you have at least version 8 of the Adobe Flash Player.

2   On your computer desktop, navigate to the Videos folder on your hard drive or DVD.

3   Open the Videos folder and right-click (Windows) or Ctrl+click (Mac OS) on the video tutorial you wish to view.

4   Choose Open > Open With > Flash Player. If there is no Flash Player option available, you may need to install the latest version of Flash Player.

Macintosh users on the new Intel-based Mac OS computers may need to download the standalone Flash Player from Adobe.com to see this option. If the Flash Player is installed, you can just double-click the video tutorial file you wish to view.

5   The video tutorial opens, using the Flash Player, and begins to play. The Flash Player has a simple user interface that allows you to control the viewing experience, including stopping, pausing, playing, and restarting the video. You can also rewind or fast-forward, and adjust the playback volume.

*A. Go to beginning. **B**. Play/Pause. **C**. Fast-forward/rewind. **D**. Stop. **E**. Volume Off/On. **F**. Volume control.*

Playback volume is also affected by the settings in your operating system. Be certain to adjust the sound volume for your computer, in addition to the sound controls in the Player window.

Additional resources

The Dynamic Learning series goes beyond the training books. You can continue your learning online, with training videos, and at seminars and conferences.

Video training series

Expand your knowledge of the Adobe Creative Suite 3 applications with the Digital Classroom video training series that complements the skills you'll learn in this book. Learn more at *agitraining.com* or *oreilly.com*.

Seminars and conferences

The authors of the Dynamic Learning book series frequently conduct in-person seminars and speak at conferences, including the annual CRE8 Conference. Learn more at *agitraining.com* or *oreilly.com*.

Resources for educators

Visit *oreilly.com* to access resources for educators, including instructors' guides for incorporating Dynamic Learning into your curriculum.

Images and animations used in this book

The files provided on the DVD are to be used only in connection with the tutorials in this book. They are copyrighted, and may not be reproduced, copied, or used by you for any other work without first obtaining permission from the copyright owner.

What you'll learn in this lesson:

- Exploring the improved drawing tools

- Using Copy and Paste Motion

- Examining improved video import and export

- Using ActionScript 3.0 and Flash Player 9

- Previewing movies with Adobe Device Central

What's New in Adobe Flash CS3?

Adobe Flash is the premier program for designing rich, interactive content for the Web. It is also a leader in the creation of games, CD-ROMs, educational materials, and mobile phone content. Flash CS3 Professional contains many exciting new features and improvements to its existing capabilities, which you'll further explore in this lesson.

Starting up

This lesson does not require any lesson files from the included DVD. You can start Flash CS3 Professional and explore each new feature as it is discussed. If you haven't done so already, install Flash CS3 Professional and the Flash Video Encoder. Instructions for installation, system requirements, and using lesson files from the included DVD are in the Starting up section on page 1 of this book.

If you are new to Flash, or simply want to jump right into a lesson, move ahead to Lesson 2, "Flash CS3 Jumpstart." Like all of the other lessons in this book, the "Flash CS3 Jumpstart" lesson is a hands-on approach to learning Flash CS3 Professional.

See Lesson 1 in action!

Use the accompanying video to gain a better understanding of how to use some of the features discussed in this lesson. View the Lesson 1 video training file found in the Flash video tutorials on the included DVD.

Testing the waters

Flash CS3 Professional includes dynamic additions and updates that appeal to all types of Flash users, designers and developers alike. These include enhanced drawing capabilities, a new version of ActionScript, and a variety of improvements that make working with Flash easier and more enjoyable. Here's an overview of some of the updates you will find in Flash CS3:

Improved drawing tools

Flash CS3 Professional expands on its existing drawing tools with the redesigned Pen tool and new Smart Shapes tools. The Pen tool now works like the Pen tool found in Adobe Illustrator CS3. It provides improved handling and flexibility needed by professional illustrators, and also includes Add, Delete, and Convert Anchor Point tools, making it easier to create all types of drawings.

New to Flash CS3 Professional are the Smart Shapes tools, which offer a new level of flexibility for creating complex shapes. Without Smart Shapes tools, it can be cumbersome to create even simple shapes, like pie charts and bulls-eyes. These new tools make it easy to round corners, adjust angles, and define an inner radius for circles or ovals, allowing you to get exactly what you need with much less effort.

Learn more about the new drawing tools in Lesson 3, "Getting Started with the Drawing Tools."

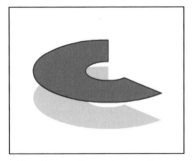

Unique shapes can be created more easily, thanks to the new Smart Shapes tools.

Copy and Paste Motion

There are many occasions when you need to have two or more objects on the Timeline animated in exactly the same way. In earlier versions of Flash, you had to repeat all of the hard work you put into one animation so a second animation would behave exactly the same as the first. Now, you can use the new Copy Motion feature to copy animation behavior from one object and apply it to another. With this feature, you can apply the same animation behavior to two or more completely different objects with just a few clicks of the mouse.

Copying and pasting motion is covered in Lesson 7, "Diving Deeper into Animation."

Reapply the same animation across multiple objects and layers with the new Copy and Paste Motion features.

Copy Motion as ActionScript 3.0

Bridging the long-standing gap between Flash designers and developers, Flash CS3 Professional adds the ability to capture timeline-based animation as ActionScript 3.0. While most designers prefer to create animation using the Timeline, many developers want the control and flexibility provided by programmed animation, using ActionScript. Any timeline-based animation can now be copied and pasted to the Actions panel for use with ActionScript 3.0's new Animator class. You can create intricate animation sequences in the Timeline, and then enhance them with ActionScript's dynamic elements and interactivity.

You'll discover more about converting motion to ActionScript in Lesson 10, "Introducing ActionScript."

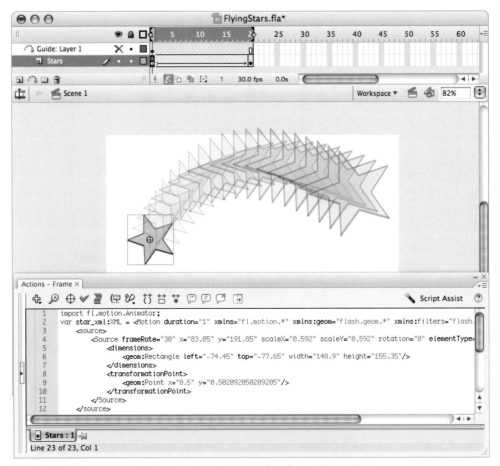

Animation created on the Timeline can be copied as ActionScript 3.0 for exchange with ActionScript programmers.

New Illustrator and Photoshop import options

Many designers prefer to develop graphics in Adobe Photoshop or Adobe Illustrator, and then import them into Flash. Those working with Flash CS3 Professional no longer need to reverse-engineer Photoshop and Illustrator file formats to make them work in Flash. The two programs' respective engineering teams have clearly collaborated to bridge the gap between the programs; you can now import Photoshop and Illustrator artwork into Flash files faster, more easily, and with a greater number of options, including the ability to work with layers from imported files.

The Illustrator Import Options panel lets you view and select the layers in an Illustrator document. The panel also gives users a great deal of control over the imported images and content; it lays out options to convert layer contents into symbols in your Flash library, distribute to keyframes and layers, and even merge layers in the original document as the file is imported.

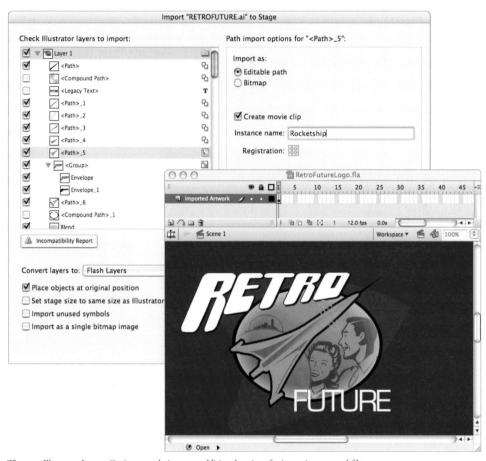

The new Illustrator Import Options panel gives you additional options for importing external files.

Users can now import Photoshop documents directly into Flash CS3 Professional in the native Photoshop file format. The Photoshop Import Options window includes the same features as the Illustrator Import Options, with full support for layer styles and blending modes. You'll learn more about importing Illustrator and Photoshop files in Lesson 9, "Working with Imported Files."

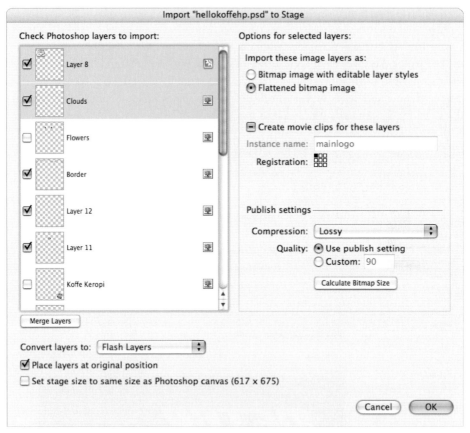

Photoshop layers can be imported to keyframes and movieclips, and merged on import.

Improved video import and export options

Flash provides full support for streaming an embedded video from a variety of popular formats. The Flash Video Encoder, which exists as a standalone application, is a significant improvement to Flash CS3 Professional. The scrubber bar, which is the bar above the Timeline that allows you to maneuver between the Timeline's frames, is bigger, as is the video preview window. If you work with video, you'll find it easier to encode using encoding profiles that can be saved and reused. You'll also find that encoding is a smoother experience now that the encoding options are more accessible.

Video export has also improved substantially with the Advanced QuickTime Export option. What you see in Flash is what you get in QuickTime, a program that adds full support for complex nested symbols, ActionScript code, and runtime effects such as Blur and Drop Shadow. You'll discover more of Flash's improved video options in Lesson 14, "Working with Video."

A wider view screen and slider for better video trims and more accurate frame-by-frame preview.

ActionScript 3.0 and Flash Player 9

ActionScript is the built-in programming language that extends Flash's capabilities beyond fancy animation and cool effects. ActionScript is the powerful, behind-the-scenes technology that makes buttons work, controls the playback of movies, captures user information in forms, connects Flash content to databases, and builds controls necessary for games and serious interactivity.

The newest versions of ActionScript and the Flash Player are designed to better work together, speeding up your workflow and improving your movies' performance.

The all-new ActionScript Virtual Machine 2 (AVM2) is dedicated to running ActionScript 3.0, making performance for demanding animations and scripting up to 10 times faster. If you've worked with previous versions of ActionScript, don't worry—ActionScript 1.0 and 2.0 are still supported through a second ActionScript Virtual Machine (AVM1), which runs side-by-side with the existing AVM2 to provide full backwards compatibility for movies built in previous versions of Flash.

Developers will also appreciate improved error reporting and debugging when troubleshooting ActionScript code.

While advanced ActionScript is beyond the scope of this book, you'll be introduced to the exciting capabilities of ActionScript in Lesson 10, "Introducing ActionScript," where you'll learn to control your animation and give life to buttons and navigation components. In Lesson 11, "Creating Button Symbols," you will then delve a little more deeply into ActionScript.

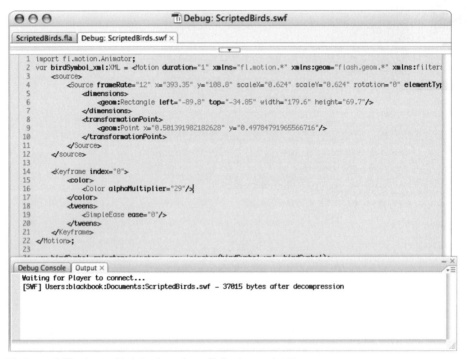

The improved debugging panel is designed to make troubleshooting more intuitive.

Adobe Device Central

Now you can more easily design interactive Flash content for mobile devices with Adobe Device Central, a new component integrated with various editions of Adobe Creative Suite 3. Adobe Device Central includes skins and profiles that emulate most popular mobile devices, so that you can see how your Flash content will actually look and perform. Device Central keeps you in the loop as new devices are released into the market. Adobe plans to release new skins and profiles on a quarterly basis.

Learn more about using Device Central in Lesson 15, "Delivering Your Final Movie."

*Adobe Device Central allows you to preview your
Flash content on specific mobile devices.*

Common Adobe Creative Suite 3 interface

Flash CS3 Professional features the slick new Adobe Creative Suite 3 interface, an intuitive space designed to give you all the screen space you need. The new Tools panel toggles between single- and double-column views, and you can collapse the panels into Icon view to access them easily and use very little screen space. This new common interface creates a better workflow and helps you transition easily between multiple CS3 applications.

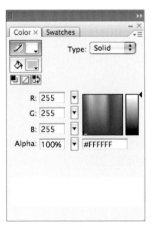

*The new CS3 interface allows you to minimize panels,
maximizing your screen space.*

And, you're off!

Now that you've had a glimpse of the new and improved Flash CS3 features, it's time to see them in action. Head now to Lesson 12, "Flash CS3 Jumpstart," where you'll dive right in and start working in Flash CS3 Professional. You'll find specific information about each of these new capabilities throughout the lessons in this book.

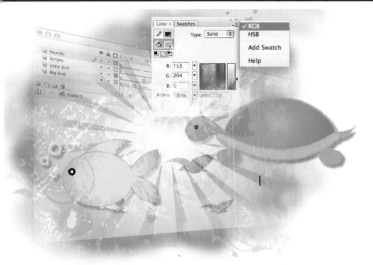

What you'll learn in this lesson:

- Using Flash's key features and capabilities

- Exploring the Flash Player

- Saving and opening documents

- Examining the Flash workspace

- Understanding illustration and animation essentials

Flash CS3 Jumpstart

This lesson takes you through the basics you'll need to get up and running with Flash CS3 Professional.

Starting up

In this lesson, you will set up a new Flash document and work with several prepared files to explore Flash's tools and features.

Before starting, make sure that your tools and panels are consistent by resetting your workspace. See "Resetting the Flash workspace" on page 3.

You will work with several files from the fl02lessons folder in this lesson. Make sure that you have loaded the fllessons folder onto your hard drive from the supplied DVD. See "Loading lesson files" on page 3.

See Lesson 2 in action!

Use the accompanying video to gain a better understanding of how to use some of the features shown in this lesson. Open the DynamicLearning_FlashCS3.suf file located in the Videos folder and select Lesson 2 to view the video training file for this lesson.

What is Flash?

You may have heard about Flash and seen it on eye-catching web sites, online games, and banner advertisements. But did you know that you can use Flash for more than creating animated graphics? With Flash CS3 Professional, you can also manipulate video and sound, and even connect to databases to build web-based applications, such as shopping carts, or display news feeds of continuously updated information.

There are four key feature areas in Flash CS3 Professional:

Drawing environment. Flash features a complete set of drawing tools to handle intricate illustration and typography. Like its cousin, Adobe Illustrator CS3, Flash is a native vector-drawing application where you'll create rich, detailed, and scalable digital illustrations. Flash now supports Illustrator and Photoshop files in their native file formats, .ai and .psd, making it easy to work with your favorite applications. All the content you create in Flash or these other programs can be brought to life through animation and interactivity.

Animation. Flash creates lightweight animation that incorporates images, sound, and video, and can be quickly downloaded via the Web. It has become a favorite—and essential—tool among web designers and developers who want to take their creativity to a whole new level. Flash animation is featured on websites, CD-ROMs, and interactive games, and has become very popular for developing interactive, web-based advertisements. Flash's compact files make it the ideal application for creating animated content, games, and applications for mobile phones and PDAs.

Flash supports traditional frame-by-frame animation as well as its own method of animation, known as tweening. With tweening, you specify an object to animate, create starting and ending frames, and Flash automatically creates the frames in between (hence "tween") to create slick motion, color, and transformation effects. You'll design your own Flash animations in Lesson 6, "Creating Basic Animation."

Flash's animation tweening generates slick animation between starting and ending frames.

Layout. The Flash Stage gives you the flexibility to create extraordinary web site layouts without the design restrictions typical of HTML-based web pages. You can position content anywhere on the Flash Stage with flexibility and precision, taking your layouts far beyond the limitations of static web pages. Flash movies can also include any typefaces you choose, allowing you to use fancy typography and unusual fonts freely on your web pages, which is typically difficult outside of Flash.

Programming. Hidden beneath the beauty of Flash CS3 Professional is the brain of ActionScript, a powerful, built-in scripting language that extends your capabilities beyond simple design and animation. With basic ActionScript, which you'll learn about in Lesson 10, "Introducing ActionScript," you can control movie playback or give functionality to buttons. If you venture deeper, ActionScript can turn Flash into a full-fledged, application-building environment to create shopping carts, music players, games, and mobile phone applications.

Flash can develop lightweight games for phones, PDAs, and other consumer devices.

About Flash Player

The Flash Player is a standalone application found most often as a plug-in to such popular browsers as Internet Explorer, Safari, and Firefox. The Flash Player is required to play compressed Flash movies (.swf files), much like a movie projector is needed to play film reels.

The Flash Player is much more than just a playback machine, however. It reads instructions written in ActionScript to add rich interactivity to your movies.

As of this writing, the Flash Player is installed on more than 96% of Internet-enabled computers, so a majority of your online audience is already equipped to view your Flash creations. For users who do not have Flash Player installed, it is available as a free download from the Adobe website, *adobe.com*.

Flash Player 9.0, including both a standalone application and browser plug-in, is automatically installed with the Flash CS3 Professional application.

Flash file types

You'll work with two types of files in Flash: .fla and .swf. Each one has a very specific purpose in the process of creating your Flash movie.

When you create and save a new document, Flash generates an .fla (Flash authoring) document. These are the working documents you'll use to design, edit, and store resources such as graphics, images, sound, and video. Additionally, each .fla document stores its own unique settings for final publishing. Because they are intended for designing and editing, .fla files can't be viewed by the Flash Player—they're used as the foundation to publish your final movie files in the .swf file format.

Shockwave Flash or .swf files are completed, compressed movie files exported from the Flash CS3 Professional application. These files, created from your original .fla authoring files, are the only format the Flash Player can display and play. Although you can import .swf files into the Flash CS3 Professional application, you cannot edit them; you will need to reopen the original .fla files to make changes or additions.

Now that you know what you're going to be working with, it's time to get your first Flash document started and begin exploring the Flash CS3 Professional workspace.

Creating a new document

Before you can draw or animate, you need to create a new document, or more specifically, an .fla file where all of your work takes place. You can create and open documents from the Welcome Screen or from the File menu at the top of the screen.

The Welcome Screen is the launch pad for creating and opening files, including handy, built-in sample templates for common document types, such as advertising banners and graphics for cell phones. The Welcome Screen appears when Flash is first launched or when no documents are open in the application.

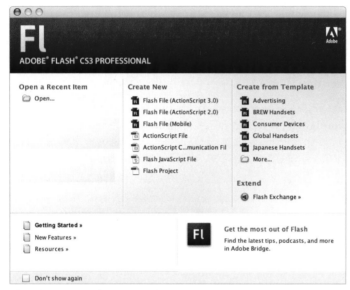

The Welcome Screen is the launch pad for new documents, including lots of templates for common projects.

To create a new .fla document using the Welcome Screen:

1   Open Flash CS3 Professional. If the application is already open, close any files that are currently open using File > Close All.

2   From the Create New column in the middle of the Welcome Screen, select Flash File (ActionScript 3.0). Your workspace, including the Stage, Timeline, and Tools panel, appears.

Alternatively, you can create a new .fla document using the File menu. If you already created a new document using the Welcome Screen, this is not necessary.

1   Choose File > New. The New Document dialog box appears.

2   Select Flash File (ActionScript 3.0), and press OK to create the new document. Your workspace appears.

Setting up your new document

Now that you've created your new Flash file, take a moment to specify some important settings for it. These settings, or *properties*, will prepare your document before you get to work.

1   Choose Modify > Document or use the keyboard shortcut Ctrl+J (Windows) or Command+J (Mac OS) to open the Document Properties dialog box.

2   In the Title field, enter **My Flash Movie**. The document title is visible only within the Flash CS3 Professional application, and a smart, short name can be helpful to identify the file's purpose.

3   Enter **This is my first Flash movie** in the Description field. A description, like the title, is optional. It is very useful for including notes about the document to anyone working on your project.

4   In the Width and Height fields, enter **500** and **300**, respectively, to set the size of your movie. These dimensions set the width and height of the Stage, measured in pixels. The size of the Stage is identical to the size of your final movie, so make sure the size accommodates the design you want to create.

5   Click on the Background Color swatch (▭) and the Swatches panel appears. This lets you choose the color of your Stage and, in turn, the background color for your final movie (.swf file) when it's published. Set the background color to white (#FFFFFF).

6   Enter **30** in the Frame rate field to set your movie's frame rate to 30 fps (frames per second). Frame rate determines the playback speed and performance of your movie. You'll learn more about fine-tuning your frame rate in Lesson 7, "Diving Deeper into Animation."

The Match to Printer option sets your new document to match the paper size of your default system printer. This option is typically set to Default, requiring you to specify the width and height, or use the default Dimensions settings stored in Flash.

7   From the Ruler units drop-down menu, choose Pixels to define the unit of measurement used throughout your Flash movie, including rulers, panels, and dialog boxes.

8   Press OK to exit the Document Properties dialog box and apply these settings. Leave the
new document open. You'll save it in the next part of this lesson.

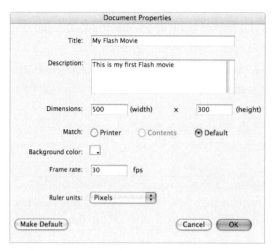

Use the Document Properties dialog box to specify settings.

 *If you are new to designing for the Web, the concept of pixels may feel a bit alien to you. It helps
to remember that there are generally 72 pixels in one inch if you're trying to calculate sizes. If you
prefer, you can use the Document Properties dialog box at any time to change the Ruler units for
your file to a different unit of measurement.*

Saving your Flash document

Your new document should be saved before starting any work or adding any content. By
default, the application saves documents in Flash CS3 (.fla) format.

1   Choose File > Save.

2   In the Save dialog box that appears, type **fl0201_work.fla** into the Name text field.
Navigate to the fl02lessons **folder, and press Save. Choose File > Close to close
the document.**

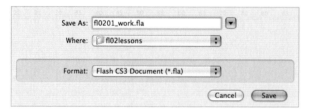

Use the Save dialog box to choose a name and location for your new file.

Always include the .fla extension at the end of your filename to make it easy to identify the file format.

To share your work with designers using earlier versions of Flash, you can choose to save your document in Flash 8 format. Flash CS3 Professional format files will not open in previous versions of Flash, unless you set the format to Flash 8 when saving the file. Flash CS3 Professional can open files created in older versions of Flash.

Get started with sample templates

Flash comes packed with a variety of sample templates that get you started with .fla files for web banners, graphics for mobile devices at common sizes, and even photo slideshows.

To get started with a sample template:

1 Choose File > New to open the New Document dialog box.

2 At the top of the window, click on the Templates tab to view the New from Template options. The template categories are displayed on the left.

3 Select Photo Slideshows, then select Modern Photo Slideshow, and press OK. A new, untitled document opens, based on the template, to which you can add your own content and make modifications.

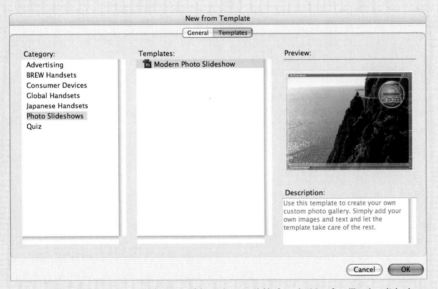

The Modern Photo Slideshow is one of many useful templates available from the New from Template dialog box.

Opening documents

Knowing how to open documents is as important as knowing how to save them. In addition to files created in Flash CS3 Professional, such as those included with this book, you can open documents created in previous versions of Flash. The steps are simple.

1   Choose File > Open. Use the Open dialog box to locate the fl0201_work.fla file you previously saved into the fl02lessons folder.

2   Select the fl0201_work.fla file, then press Open. Leave this file open. You will be using it in the next exercise.

The Open command works only with .fla files. To access files created in other applications, such as Photoshop or Illustrator, you must use the Import menu. Importing files from other applications is explored in detail in Lesson 9, "Working with Imported Files."

If you want to reopen a document on which you have recently worked, there's a shortcut. To list the last 10 documents you've opened, and to reopen one, choose File > Open Recent, then select the file you need.

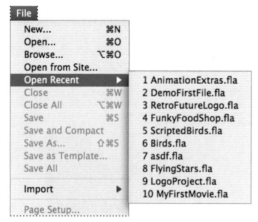

Choose File > Open Recent to access the last 10 documents opened in Flash.

You can also open files using the Open button (📂) at the bottom of the Open Recent Items column on the Welcome Screen. Above this icon, you'll see the last eight documents you worked on; this is a useful alternative to the Open Recent menu option.

The Flash workspace

Now that you know how to create, save, and open Flash documents, you're ready to get familiar with the workspace where you'll spend your time creating Flash content.

The Stage and work area

After you create a Flash document, the center of your screen, called the *Stage*, is where the action happens. The Stage is the visible area of your movie, where you place graphics and build animations. By default, the Flash Stage appears white, but, as you saw earlier, you can change this from the Document Properties dialog box using the Modify > Document command.

The gray area surrounding the Stage is the *work area*; artwork you place or create here is invisible in your final movie. Think of this area as *backstage*; for instance, you can animate a character to enter from the work area onto the Stage. The work area is also a good place to store objects that are not ready to appear in your movie.

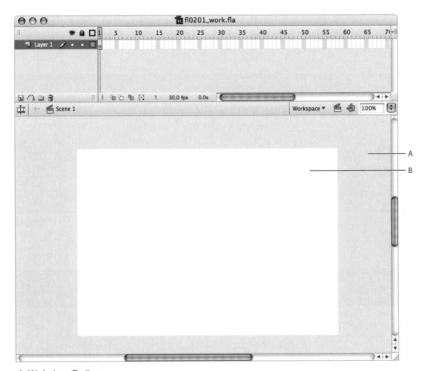

A. Work Area. *B*. Stage.

The Stage reflects the actual size of the movie you create when it is published. Artwork and objects can be placed outside the Stage in the work area, but items in the work area are not visible in your final movie.

The Flash Tools panel

The Flash Tools panel includes everything you need to create, select, or edit graphics on the Stage. The double arrows at the very top of the Tools panel toggle it between displaying single and double columns, making more room on your screen for other tasks.

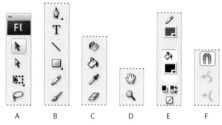

A   B   C   D   E   F

A. Selection tools.
B. Drawing and Text tools.
C. Color tools.
D. Navigation tools.
E. Stroke and Fill color selectors.
F. Tool Options.

Selection tools

ICON	TOOL NAME	USE	WHERE IT'S COVERED
	Selection	Moves selections or layers.	Lessons 2, 3
	Subselection	Selects and moves points on a path.	Lesson 3
	Free Transform	Resizes, rotates and skews objects.	Lesson 6
	Lasso	Makes selections.	Lesson 3

Drawing and Text tools

ICON	TOOL NAME	USE	WHERE IT'S COVERED
	Pen	Draws a vector path.	Lesson 3
T	Text	Creates a text box.	Lesson 3
	Line	Draws straight lines.	Lesson 3
	Shapes	Draws vector shapes.	Lesson 3
	Pencil	Draws freehand paths.	Lesson 3
	Brush	Draws freehand filled areas.	Lesson 4

Color tools

ICON	TOOL NAME	USE	WHERE IT'S COVERED
	Ink Bottle	Applies or modifies strokes.	Lesson 3, 4
	Paint Bucket	Applies or modifies fills.	Lesson 3, 4
	Eyedropper	Sample colors and styles.	Lesson 3, 4
	Eraser	Erases artwork.	Not referenced in this book

Navigation tools

ICON	TOOL NAME	USE	WHERE IT'S COVERED
	Hand	Navigates the page.	Lesson 8
	Zoom	Increases or decreases the relative size of the view.	Lesson 8

Stroke and Fill color selectors

ICON	TOOL NAME	USE	WHERE IT'S COVERED
	Stroke color	Selects Stroke (outline) color	Lesson 3
	Fill color	Selects Fill (inside) color	Lesson 3
	Default Stroke/Fill	Sets Stroke and Fill to default colors: black and white	Lesson 3
	Swap colors	Swaps Stroke and Fill colors	Lesson 3
	No color	Sets selected color to none	Lesson 3

Tool Options

ICON	TOOL NAME	USE	WHERE IT'S COVERED
	Snap to Objects	Enables snapping between objects on the Stage.	Lesson 5

The Property inspector

The Property inspector appears at the bottom of your Flash workspace. It displays properties and options for objects selected on the Stage, and also allows you to modify them. The Property inspector is contextual, so the information it displays is specific to the tool or object you select.

The Property inspector is an essential part of the Flash workflow; it can display and set an object's properties, including width, height, position, and fill color. Let's take a look at the Property inspector in action.

1   If the fl0201_work.fla file is not still open from the last exercise, choose File > Open to reopen it from inside the fl02lessons folder. Select the Rectangle tool (□) from the Tools panel.

2   At the bottom of the Tools panel, click the Fill Color swatch (🖉). When the Swatches panel appears, choose a yellow shade from the far right side of the Swatches panel.

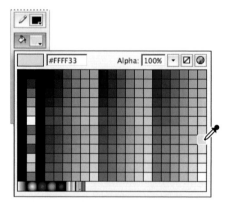

Choose fill and stroke colors using the swatches at the bottom of the Tools panel.

3   Move your cursor to the center of the Stage. Click and hold, then drag to draw a new rectangle. Release the mouse button after you have created a rectangle at the center of the Stage.

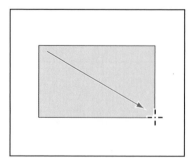

To draw shapes on the Stage, select a Shape tool, then click and drag.

4   If the Property inspector is not already open, choose Window > Properties > Properties to open it.

5   Choose the Selection tool (🅺) from the top of the Tools panel, and double-click the fill of the new shape to select it. Notice that the Property inspector now displays the selected shape's width (W) and height (H) in pixels. To the right of the width and height, the object's X and Y positions on the Stage are also displayed.

6   Double-click inside the width (W) text field to highlight the current value, then enter **250** to set the rectangle's width. Double-click inside the height (H) field and enter **150** to set the height.

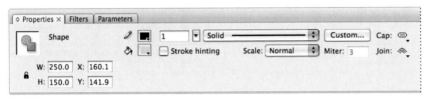

You can set properties for a selected shape using the Property inspector.

7   Choose the Text tool (T) from the Tools panel. Click above the new rectangle you created and enter the phrase "**Flash CS3**." Notice that the Property inspector now displays text options such as font and size.

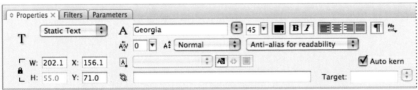

When text is selected, the Property inspector displays relevant options such as font and size.

8   Click and drag inside the new text box to select all of the text. In the Property inspector, locate the Font menu and choose Arial (or, if that's unavailable, Verdana). Use the slider to the right of the Font menu to set the type size to 45 or type **45** in the text field to the left of the slider.

9 In the Property inspector, click the Color swatch and choose a blue shade from the pop-up Swatches panel to change the color of your type.

10 Choose File > Save to save your work. Leave this file open; you'll need it for the next exercise.

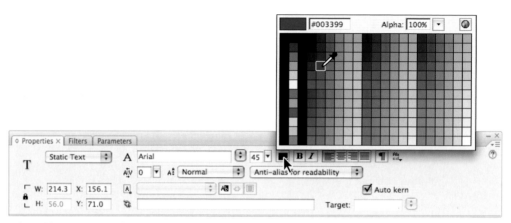

Select and format type directly from the Property inspector.

In addition to text and graphics, the Property inspector also works with the Timeline, allowing you to set options and view information for specific frames. You will use this essential tool throughout the lessons to modify objects on the Stage, and frames in the Timeline.

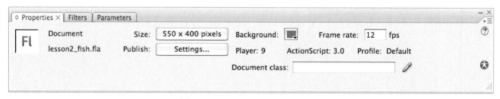

The Property inspector shows options for an active tool or information about a selected object.

Panels and panel groups

Panels appear on the right side of your workspace, and each one is dedicated to a specific task, such as setting colors, aligning multiple objects on the Stage, or transforming the dimensions of an object. The default workspace launches with three panels on the right side of the screen—Color, Swatches, and Library. You can toggle these on or off using the Window menu. New in CS3, you can collapse panel groups to space-saving icons, using the double arrows (»») in the top right corner of any panel group. You can also use these same arrows to expand panel groups back to full size.

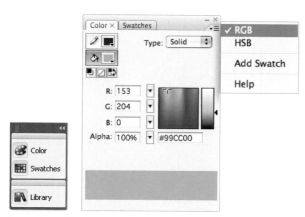

Icon mode and full-size panels.

Any fully expanded panel features its own panel menu. You can open a panel menu by clicking the menu icon (·≡) in the upper-right corner of each panel. These menus perform additional tasks or modify the panel's appearance. Many of the panel menu's options are also available as icons at the bottom of the panel.

Panels can be grouped in sets on the right side, of your display. You can also separate them and position each one freely on the screen. You can also group freely positioned panels together with other panels. The Color and Swatches panels are grouped together in the default workspace. If you need more room, you can collapse grouped panels on the right to display them in space-saving icon mode.

You'll explore the various panels in detail in upcoming lessons. For now, you'll concentrate on how to manipulate and customize the way panels display in your workspace.

1 Select Window > Workspace > Default to reset your workspace to its default layout. Locate the Color panel on the right side of the workspace.

2 At the top of the Color panel, click its title tab and drag the panel to the left, away from the Swatches panel, to ungroup it.

Drag a panel by its title tab to group, ungroup, or move it.

3 Click the title tab of the Swatches panel, and drag the panel on top of the Color panel to regroup the two panels.

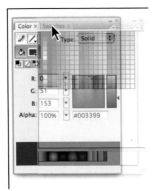

Drag one panel on top of another to group them.

4 To select both panels at once, click on the bar behind the panels' title tabs. Drag the entire panel group on top of the Library panel on the right to group all three.

5   Click the double arrows (►►) at the top of the panel group to collapse it to icon view.

6   Choose File > Close All to close the current document and any others that may be open.

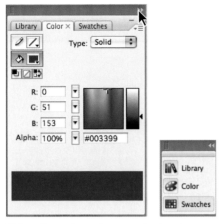

Collapse the panel group to space-saving icon view.

 Consider keeping frequently used panels available and docked in the master panel group on the right side. You can save configurations and locations of commonly used panels by creating your own custom Workspace Layouts, which you'll learn about in detail in Lesson 8, "Customizing Your Workflow."

The Timeline

The Flash Timeline is the heart of the action, where you create animations and sequence graphics with sound, video, and controls. The Timeline comprises frames, each one representing a point in time, just like a historical timeline. Graphics and animations are placed at specific points, or keyframes, along the Timeline to create sequences, slideshows, or movies. You can place ActionScript on individual keyframes to control playback and add interactivity, or place sounds along the Timeline to add sound effects, music, and dialogue.

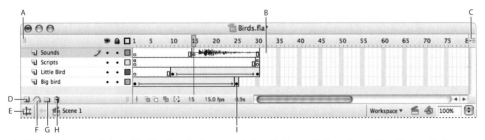

A. Click and drag to undock the Timeline from the document window. B. Frames. C. Frame/Layer View Options. D. Insert Layer. E. Hide/Show Timeline. F. Add Motion Guide. G. Insert Layer Folder. H. Delete Layer. I. Keyframe.

The Timeline also comprises layers; layers behave like transparent pieces of film stacked on top of one another. Each animation and piece of artwork can be placed on its own individual layer, which helps you organize and manage your work. If you've worked with other Adobe CS3 applications, such as Illustrator, Photoshop, or InDesign, you may already be familiar with the power and flexibility of layers. Use the View Options icon (·≡) in the upper-right corner to set the placement of the Timeline in your document, as well as to specify the width and height of the frames and layers displayed in the Timeline.

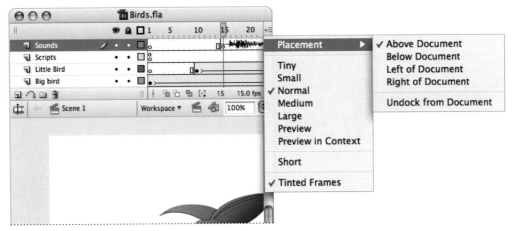

Change the Timeline settings according to how you'd like it to appear.

In this exercise, you'll explore a Timeline with multiple keyframes, animations, and layers to see how a typical Flash document looks.

1 Choose File > Open, and select the fl0203.fla document inside the fl02lessons folder. Press Open to open it for editing.

2 Examine the Timeline above the Stage. You'll see that it contains a layer, with a layer folder above it. Layer folders can contain layers and are used to organize the Timeline when layers start to add up. If necessary, click the arrow to the left of the Gears layer folder to expand it and reveal its contents. The three indented layers under the Gears name are the layers that are inside the folder.

Click the arrow to the left of a layer folder to expand it.

3   Each of the three layers contains a separate animation that is marked at the beginning and end with a keyframe. Keyframes are special frames that are created along the Timeline where you want to introduce or remove a graphic, start or end an animation, or trigger something to happen with ActionScript. An arrow between two keyframes indicates a tween, or animation. Press Enter (Windows) or Return (Mac OS) to play the Timeline.

4   Look at Layer 4 in the Timeline, which contains several consecutive keyframes. Click once on each keyframe to jump to that frame and see what it displays at that specific point in time.

5   To shuttle through the Timeline, grab the playhead at the top (indicated by the red marker), and drag it in either direction.

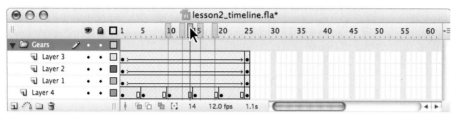

Shuttle back and forth in the Timeline by dragging the playhead.

 You can collapse or expand the Timeline using the Hide/Show Timeline icon (⊡) in the lower-left corner, below the Timeline.

6   Choose File > Close to close the current document. If prompted to save any changes, press Don't Save.

Tabbing between open documents

When you have more than one document open at a time, each document displays its own tab at the top of the document window. Click on a document's tab to switch to it and bring it forward for editing. To close the active document, you can choose File > Close, or use the small *x* that appears at the top of the document's tab. To close all open documents at once, choose File > Close All.

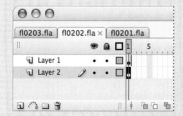

Tab easily between multiple documents at a time.

The Swatches panel

You'll see this swatch icon (■) quite a few times in Flash—it opens the Swatches panel, used to set colors for backgrounds, fills, outlines, and type. The Swatches panel is also a standalone panel, which you'll see grouped with the Color panel on the right side of your workspace. You can choose from 256 web-safe colors and seven preset gradients, or create your own. You will learn to add your own custom colors and gradients to the Swatches panel in Lesson 3, "Getting Started with the Drawing Tools."

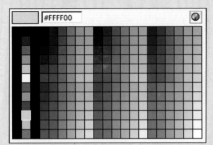

The Flash CS3 Swatches Panel.

The six-character code at the top of the Swatches panel is a *hexadecimal* code, the standard color-coding system for the Web. As you choose colors from the Swatches panel, you'll see the hexadecimal value for the selected color displayed at the top. The Color Picker in Adobe CS3 applications such as Illustrator and Photoshop also feature hexadecimal values, so you can easily match colors between applications by copying and pasting the code shown.

Practicing with the Flash tools

Now that you've had a tour of the Flash tools and workspace, it's time to take them for a test drive. In the following exercises, you'll complete the illustration shown in fl0202_fish.fla while getting the feel for the selection, drawing, and transformation tools. You'll also use Flash tweening to create your first animation.

The drawing and selection tools in action

Your first steps will be to create and modify shapes and freehand artwork with the drawing tools, and then fine-tune your work with the selection tools. The selection tools work as a team with the drawing tools to position and modify shapes, illustrations, and type.

1   If you haven't done so already, open the fl0202.fla file located in the fl02lessons folder.

2   Choose File > Save As; the Save As dialog box appears. In the Name text field, type **fl0202_work.fla**, then navigate to the fl02lessons folder and press Save.

3   Select the Selection tool (k) in the Tools panel. This versatile tool can select, move, and manipulate objects directly on the Stage.

4　On the Stage, click once on the fin above the fish's body to select it. Click and drag it downward until it joins with the body. Release the mouse button.

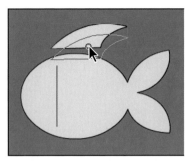

Use the Selection tool to select and move objects on the Stage.

5　You need to make a copy of this fin to use on the bottom of the fish. The easiest way is to clone it, or to drag a copy from the original. To do this, click the top fin once to select it, then, while holding the Alt (Windows) or Option (Mac OS) key, click and drag a copy away from the original fin.

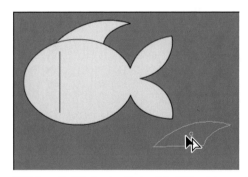

Hold down Alt (Windows) or Option (Mac OS) and drag an object to clone it.

6   Because the new copy will serve as the bottom fin, you'll need to flip it around so it's pointed in the proper direction. Click once to select the new fin copy, and choose Modify > Transform > Flip Vertical. This Transform menu command flips the fin so it's pointed the in the right direction.

The Transform menu features commands that flip, skew, and rotate a selected object.

7   Continuing to use the Selection tool, click and drag the new fin copy to the bottom of the fish's body, and leave it selected.

8   The new fin is almost there, but it's a bit big. There are several places within Flash where you can resize an object, including the Transform panel; choose Window > Transform to open it.

9   With the new fin selected, enter **60** in the horizontal and vertical Scale fields at the top of the panel and press Enter or Return to commit the change. The fin is reduced to 60% of its original size.

The Transform panel precisely resizes objects by a set percentage.

Notice the Constrain checkbox next to the Transform panel's Width and Height scale text fields. When you check this, you can enter a size in only one field and Flash will automatically resize the selected object proportionally.

10 To add an eye to your fish, select the Oval tool (○) on the Tools panel. You may need to click and hold on the Rectangle tool (□) to access this tool. At the bottom of the Tools panel, click on the Fill color swatch and choose black as the fill color.

11 Flash CS3's Smart Shapes feature lets you manipulate shapes even further; here, you'll add an inner radius to ovals to create ring-style shapes. If the Property inspector is not open, choose Window > Properties > Properties to open it. Enter **50** in the Inner radius text field and press Enter.

12 Select Layer 1 in the Timeline, and click and drag on the left side of the fish to draw a small oval, which will serve as the fish's eye.

To create perfect circles, hold down the Shift key while drawing ovals.

Use the Oval tool with an inner radius to add an eye to your fish.

Congratulations! You've designed your first graphic object in Flash. However, this fish is rather basic.

Using gradient and color tools

Now you'll add some depth and more vibrant color to your fish, using the gradient colors and artistic stroke styles.

1   Choose the Selection tool (k) from the Tools panel, and click once inside the body of the fish; a dotted pattern indicates the fill area is selected.

2   To change the body's color, click on the Fill color swatch at the bottom of the Tools panel. In the resulting Swatches panel, choose the orange/yellow gradient located at the bottom of the panel to apply it to the selected area. Deselect the fish by choosing Edit > Deselect All or by clicking offstage in the gray work area.

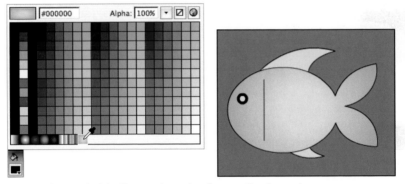

Give your fish more depth by filling it with a gradient from your Swatches panel..

3   The Eyedropper tool (✐) enables you to sample a color from one object and transfer it to another. You'll use it to apply the body color to the fish's fins. Using the Selection tool (k), hold down the Shift key and click once on each fin so both are selected at once. Select the Eyedropper tool from the Tools panel. Click once on the body of the fish to sample the new color and apply it to the selected fins.

4   Choose Edit > Deselect All to deselect all items on the Stage. In the Tools panel, select the Ink Bottle tool (⟆), which lets you change an object's stroke color. You'll use the Property inspector to set a stroke color and style to apply.

5   In the Property inspector, click the Stroke color swatch and type #FF6600 into the hexadecimal field at the top-left corner of the Swatches panel that appears. Press Enter to set this color, then close the Swatches panel.

6 Click on the Stroke Style menu that appears to the right of the color swatch. Choose the rough pencil style from the drop-down menu.

Choose a stroke color and style and apply them using the Ink Bottle tool.

7 Click on the edge of the fish body to apply the new stroke color and style. Click on the edge of the remaining two fins and the gill line to apply the same color and stroke style to all three. Choose Edit > Deselect All to deselect any active items on the Stage.

8 Choose the Selection tool from the top of the Tools panel. Move the pointer slightly to the right of the gill line without touching it; a small curve appears below your pointer. Click and drag slightly to the right to bend the gill line into a curve.

The Selection tool can bend straight lines or distort shapes.

9 Select the Oval tool (○) from the Tools panel. Click the Fill color swatch at the bottom of the Tools panel, and choose a light blue color. Click the Stroke color swatch and set your stroke color to No color (☑).

10 While holding down the Shift key, draw several ovals in front of the fish to create bubbles.

11 Choose File > Save to save your work.

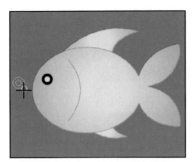

Use the Oval tool to draw bubbles in front of your fish.

12 Choose File > Open, select the fl0202_done.fla file in the fl02lessons folder, and press Open to open it. Compare your work against the completed file fl0202_done.fla. Choose File > Close All to close all currently open documents.

The finished illustration.

You're off to a good start with the drawing tools. You will work with these tools in more depth in Lesson 3, "Getting Started with the Drawing Tools."

Animation in action

Flash is known for powerful, yet easy-to-use animation that you create directly in the Timeline. The Timeline displays content over periods of time, represented on the Timeline in frames. Each frame can be set as a keyframe, where items can be placed and animation can start or end.

Flash can generate animation with little more than a starting point and ending point; this method is known as tweening. You tell Flash where you want an object to start and stop its animation, and it figures out the frames in between. To apply the same animation behavior to more than one object on the Stage, you'll use the new Copy Motion and Paste Motion features.

1   Choose File > Open and, when prompted, select the fl0201.fla file in the fl02lessons folder. Press Open. Two tortoises appear on the Stage. In the next steps, you'll apply an animation to one and then copy it to the other.

2   Click directly on the first frame in the Big Turtle layer in the Timeline; this will be the starting position for the first turtle. Click on Frame 60 on the same layer; on this frame, the turtle is positioned on the left side of the Stage. You'll need to create animation between these two frames to get the turtle moving.

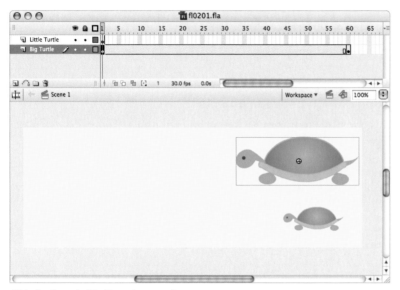

Click directly on the Timeline to jump to a frame.

3   Choose Window > Properties > Properties to open the Property inspector. Click directly on Frame 1 in the Big Turtle layer to select it. Click on the Tween menu in the Property inspector and choose Motion.

Select Motion from the Tween menu to create animation between two frames.

4 An arrow on a blue-shaded area appears between Frames 1 and 60 to let you know that Flash successfully created the tween animation. Press the Enter (Windows) or Return (Mac OS) key to start the Timeline and play your movie. The turtle should move across the screen—your first animation!

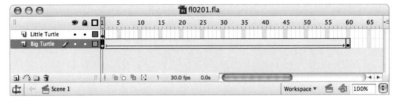

The arrow and blue-shaded area let you know that Flash created the animation.

Copying and pasting motion between objects

Now you'll put the second turtle in motion to follow his big brother. Rather than recreating the same animation, you can copy the tween from the first turtle and apply it to the second, using Copy Motion and Paste Motion.

1 Double-click the blue-shaded area between Frames 1 and 60 to highlight the entire tween (animation).

2 Right-click (Windows) or Ctrl+click (Mac OS) anywhere on the selected area. From the Timeline menu that appears, choose Copy Motion.

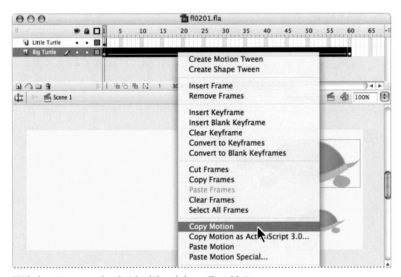

With the entire tween selected, right-click and choose Copy Motion.

3   On the Little Turtle layer, click on the first frame to select it. Right-click (Windows) or Ctrl+click (Mac OS) to open the Timeline menu. Choose Paste Motion Special, which enables you to choose specific aspects of the animation to apply before pasting.

4   In the Paste Motion Special dialog box that appears, uncheck the Horizontal scale and Vertical scale options. This ensures that the second turtle isn't resized to match the first. Leave the rest checked, and press OK. Flash applies a tween to the second turtle, as indicated by the arrow and shaded area.

Use Flash CS3's Paste Motion Special feature to paste animation behavior.

5   Press Enter (Windows) or Return (Mac OS) to play the animation.

6   Choose File > Open; locate the fl0201_done.fla file and press Open. Compare your work with the completed version of the lesson.

Tweening and animation are explored in more detail in Lesson 6, "Creating Basic Animation."

Getting help

If at any point you can't find a specific command, want to know how a tool works, or want to learn how to complete a certain task, you can always consult the Flash Help menu. The Help menu launches the Help viewer (an all-in-one glossary, troubleshooter, and reference manual), and also provides links to key Adobe forums and support centers.

The Flash Help viewer is a good source for quick answers.

1 Choose Help > Flash Help.

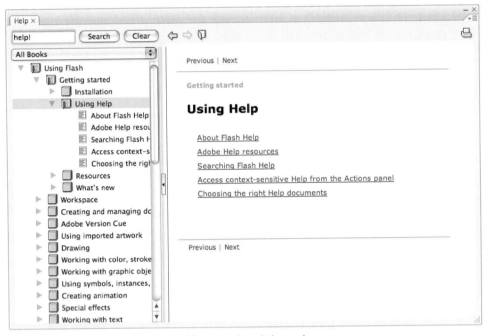

The Flash Help viewer acts as a reference manual for quick and easy lookups and answers.

2 When the panel appears, use the categorized list on the left, or type in a search term to get help on a specific topic or keyword.

Support forums

Adobe's Flash forums can be a rich source of answers, ideas, and tips from experts and other avid Flash users. You can search for answers to common questions or post your own topics and questions.

1 Choose Help > Flash Developer Center. The Support forum launches in your system's default browser.

2 In the search field in the upper right corner, enter terms you wish to explore, then press the Search button.

3 To post topics, questions, or replies, click the Your Account link at the top of the page to log in with your Adobe ID.

 You must register to post questions or replies to Adobe's Flash forums.

Moving forward

In the next chapter, you'll put pen to paper (or mouse to Stage, rather) to get your creativity flowing with the Flash drawing tools. Now that you've become familiar with the workspace, things should be just a bit easier. Don't hesitate to reference this chapter again to refresh your memory.

Self study

Create and save a new document in the fl02lessons folder. Use the Document Properties panel to set dimensions, background color, and frame rate. Experiment with the drawing tools you've learned so far to create artwork on the Stage, and use the Selection tool to move and adjust the artwork as needed.

To get a feel for the workspace, experiment with different panel setups and positions. The Workspace menu (Window > Workspace) features some presets that show how you can maximize the space in your work area.

Review

Questions

1 From what two locations can you open a document that was previously open?

2 What panel allows you to view information about a selected object, or set options for an active tool?

3 What method does Flash use to automatically create animation from a starting and ending point?

Answers

1 From File > Open Recent, or the Open a Recent Item column on the Welcome Screen.

2 The Property inspector.

3 Tweening.

Lesson 3

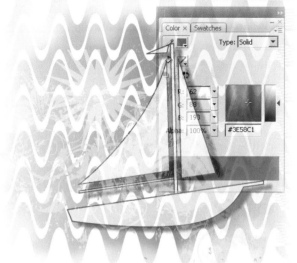

What you'll learn in this lesson:

- Working with shapes
- Using the Pencil tool
- Using the Line tool
- Using the Pen tool
- Importing and outlining a reference graphic

Getting Started with the Drawing Tools

Whether you prefer to draw freehand or trace an imported graphic, Flash's vector drawing tools can help you create sophisticated shapes. Once you understand how to use these tools, you'll be able to create or trace the vector shapes you need for your Flash projects.

Starting up

Before starting, make sure that your tools and panels are consistent by resetting your workspace. See "Resetting the Flash workspace" on page 3.

You will work with several files from the fl03lessons folder in this lesson. Make sure that you have loaded the fllessons folder onto your hard drive from the supplied DVD. See "Loading lesson files" on page 3.

See Lesson 3 in action!

Use the accompanying video to gain a better understanding of how to use some of the features shown in this lesson. Open the DynamicLearning_FlashCS3.swf file located in the Videos folder and select Lesson 3 to view the video training file for this lesson.

Drawing in Flash

Adobe Flash CS3 Professional has more powerful tools and features than ever to help you create shapes and lines. Whatever you create with the drawing tools can then be animated using the Timeline. In this lesson, you will experiment with two different drawing models that you can use to create artwork in Flash: the Merge Drawing model and the Object Drawing model.

Using the Merge Drawing model

The default model is the Merge Drawing model. At first, this model may be difficult for new users to grasp, especially those already familiar with the drawing tools in Adobe Illustrator. In this lesson, however, you'll see how the Merge Drawing model offers some unique benefits over traditional object drawing tools.

Opening the completed file

First, you will open the completed lesson file. The artwork may appear to be incredibly simple, but creating this artwork using the different drawing tools will familiarize you with how the Merge Drawing model works, and it also gives you the opportunity to create a symbol from your original art.

1   Launch Flash CS3 Professional if it is not already open.

2   Choose File > Browse to open Adobe Bridge. Use the Folders tab in the upper-left area of the Bridge workspace to navigate to the fl03lessons folder that you copied onto your computer. (Adobe Bridge is used to navigate and open files in this lesson, but if you prefer, you can choose File > Open.)

3   Once you have the fl03lessons folder open, double-click on the file named fl0301_done.fla to open it in Flash. A project file that includes a simple drawing of a truck appears.

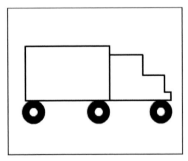

The finished drawing.

4   Press the Enter\Return key to play the animation of the truck driving across the Stage.

5   You can keep this file open for reference, or choose File > Close at this time. If asked if you want to save changes, choose No.

Drawing shapes

To create your own truck art you will explore the shape tools. Flash CS3 Professional offers five tools for making geometric shapes: Rectangle, Oval, Rectangle Primitive, Oval Primitive, and PolyStar.

Additional shape tools are hidden under the Rectangle tool.

In this lesson, you will create several of these geometric shapes using the shape tools.

1   Choose File > Browse to bring Adobe Bridge to the front. If you are not already viewing the contents of the fl03lessons folder, navigate to it now.

2   Double-click on the file named fl0301.fla to open it in Flash. A stage with prepared guides and references appears. Verify that the work layer is selected.

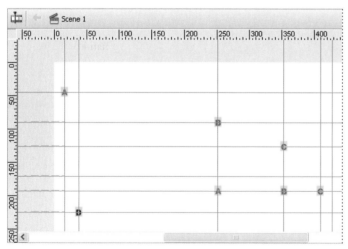

The start file includes guides and references.

3 Choose File > Save As to save a work file. The Save As dialog box appears.

4 In the Save As dialog box, type **fla0301_work.fla** in the Name text field. Make sure that you are in the fl03lessons folder, leave the format set to Flash CS3 Document, and press Save.

5 Make sure you have the default colors set to a white fill and a black stroke by clicking on the Black and white icon (⬛) at the bottom of the Tools panel.

Make sure you are using the default colors.

You'll now use several methods and tools to create shapes in Flash. These methods offer you the ability to control different attributes of the shapes as you create them. Note that you can use these methods with any of the shape tools.

6 Choose the Rectangle tool (▢) in the Tools panel.

7 Before creating your first shape, verify that you are not working in the Object Drawing model. You can tell if you are in the Object Drawing model by looking at the Object Drawing button at the bottom of the Tools panel. If a rounded corner border appears around the Object Drawing button, click on it to exit.

Object Drawing turned on   *Object Drawing button turned off*
(incorrect).   *(correct).*

8 If the Property inspector is not visible, choose Window > Properties > Properties or use the keyboard shortcut F3.

9   In the Stroke height text field, type **4**. This will make your stroke more visible when you start drawing.

Change the Stroke height.

10   Position your cursor over the topmost letter A on the Stage, then click and drag from the top red A to the red A located toward the lower-right area of the Stage. Release the mouse when you have reached the second A. The rectangle shape forms.

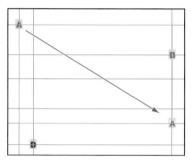

Click and drag to create a rectangle.

11   Using the same Rectangle tool, position the cursor over the topmost green B on the Stage. Hold down the Shift key, then click and drag, releasing when you reach the lower-left green B. By holding down the Shift key, you constrain the Rectangle tool to create a square.

12   Now create another rectangle by positioning the cursor over the topmost blue C and clicking and dragging to the lower-right blue C. You now have three shapes on the Stage.

13   Choose File > Save to save your work. Keep the file open for the next part of this lesson.

Eliminating strokes

In the Merge Drawing model, shapes are automatically merged when you overlap them. If you try to move a shape that is merged with another, the other shape is permanently altered. For example, if you drew a small circle on top of a larger circle, the two shapes would be merged. If you tried to move the smaller circle, the portion of that circle that overlaid the larger circle would be removed. You will take advantage of this feature to create the cab of the truck.

1 Choose the Selection tool (↖) and position your cursor over the line separating the second and third rectangle shapes (B and C).

2 When you see the cursor appear with the arc (↖), click on the stroke. It becomes highlighted, or stippled. You may have to move the guide slightly to do this.

3 Press the Delete key to delete just that stroke. Note that Flash, unlike other applications, recognized this stroke as an independent object, not part of the entire rectangle shape.

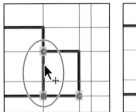 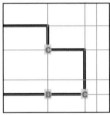

Delete the stroke separating   Result.
the 2nd and 3rd rectangles.

You'll now create the truck's front bumper, using the same merged shape technique.

4 Select the Rectangle tool (▢), then click and drag from within the third rectangle out to the guide on the right. The exact location where you start the rectangle shape is not important; just follow the guides to the right of the third shape for the width and height of the bumper.

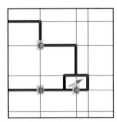

Create a rectangle for the bumper shape.

5 If necessary, use the Zoom tool (🔍) to zoom into the front area of the cab, then choose the Selection tool and select the left edge of the rectangle you just created to highlight the stroke of that edge. Press Delete to remove the stroke.

6 Click to select the stroke that creates the upper-left part of the rectangle and press the Delete key. You have now added a front bumper to the truck.

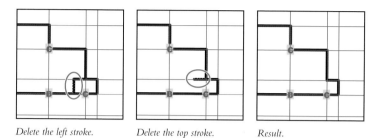

Delete the left stroke.   *Delete the top stroke.*   *Result.*

7 Choose File > Save to save this file. Keep the file open for the next part of this lesson.

Using the Oval Primitive tool

You will now create the wheels for the truck, using the Oval Primitive tool. Primitive objects (Rectangle Primitive or Oval Primitive tool) are graphic shapes that allow you to adjust their characteristics in the Property inspector. In the Property inspector, you can precisely control the size, corner radius, and other properties of the shape. Unlike merged objects, you can return at any time to primitive objects to change these attributes.

Before starting, you will turn off the default Snap to Guides feature. Snapping to guides and other objects can be helpful, but with the number of guides on the Stage you will have a little more control by turning them off.

1 With the fl0301_work.fla file still open, click and hold down on the Rectangle tool (▭) to select the hidden Oval Primitive tool (⊝).

2 Right-click (Windows) or Ctrl+click (Mac OS) anywhere on the Stage to display the contextual menu, select Snapping, then select Edit Snapping to open the Edit Snapping dialog box. Uncheck all checkboxes and press OK.

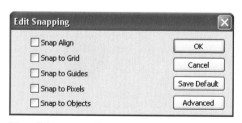

Turn off the Snapping feature.

3   Position your cursor so that it is centered over the crossed guides in front of the purple D on the Stage.

4   Hold down Alt+Shift (Windows) or Option+Shift (Mac OS) and click and drag from the center point until the top of the circle reaches the bottom of the truck.

By holding down the Alt/Option and Shift keys, you not only create a perfect circle, but also create the shape from the center click point. This can be helpful when you are creating shapes inside other shapes.

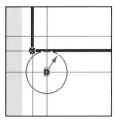

Hold down the Alt/Option and Shift keys to create the circle from the center.

Primitive objects display a center point as a reference, merged objects do not.

You will now use the Property inspector to adjust the color and inner radius of this circle.

5   If the Property inspector is not visible, choose Window > Properties > Properties.

6   Choose the Selection tool (◥) and click on the circle you just created to select it.

7   In the Property inspector, click on the Stroke color swatch and choose No color (☑) from the Swatches panel that appears.

8   Click on the Fill color swatch just below the Stroke color swatch. Choose black from the Swatches panel that appears.

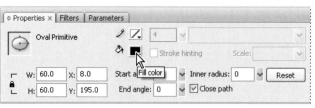

Change the Fill to black and the Stroke to No color.

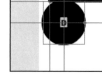

Result.

Understanding fills and strokes

When you create artwork in Flash, you have the opportunity to set both a fill and stroke for any active drawing tool.

 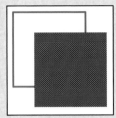

The fill (blue).   *The stroke (red).*

Fill refers to the area inside your shape; shapes can either be hollow (containing only an outline), or can be filled with a solid color, gradient, or bitmap. Fill color can be modified for any selected shape, or can be set before you begin drawing.

Stroke refers to the outline of your shape, and, like the fill color, can be set before or after you work with a drawing tool. In addition, strokes can be modified to use a variety of widths and styles to add character and distinction to your artwork. To select a stroke color, click and select a color using the Stroke color swatch located at the bottom of the Flash Tools panel.

Keep in mind that when a shape has both a stroke and a fill, these are considered separate graphic elements that can be selected and moved independently.

Fill and stroke colors can also be set from the Property inspector or Color panel when a tool or object is selected.

9 Using the Selection tool, click on the circle to make sure it is still selected. Then click and hold on the Inner radius slider in the Property inspector and slide upwards until you reach approximately 30, or type **30** into the Inner radius text field. Depending upon the size of your circle, you may want your inner radius set a little larger or smaller. Feel free to adjust the amount necessary to make your circle look like a tire.

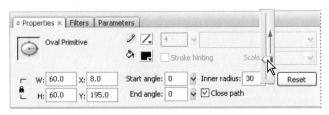 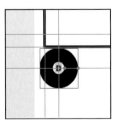

Change the Inner radius to 30.   *Result.*

10 Choose File > Save. Keep this file open for the next part of this lesson.

Cloning your shape

You will now duplicate, or clone, the circle shape several times to create the additional two wheels needed for this truck.

1 Choose View > Magnification > Fit in Window to see the entire document window.

2 With the Selection tool (♦), click on the circle you created to select it.

3 Hold down Alt (Windows) or Option (Mac OS), and drag the circle to the right. As you drag, notice that the cursor displays a plus sign (♦₀). The plus sign indicates that you are cloning the selected object. Release the mouse when the right side of the cloned circle is positioned at the back end of the truck's cab.

4 Now, hold down the Alt/Option key again while dragging the second circle to the right side of the cab, then release. There are now three wheels visible on the truck.

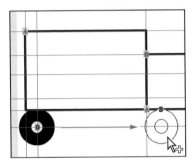 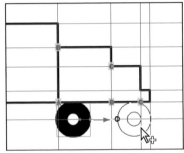

Clone the original circle you created to create two additional tires.

 You can hold down the Shift key while dragging and cloning to constrain the movement to a 45°, 90°, or 180° angle.

Creating a symbol from your artwork

You will now convert your truck to a symbol so that you can create a simple animation.

1 With the Selection tool active, choose Edit > Select All, or use the keyboard shortcut Ctrl+A (Windows) or Command+A (Mac OS).

2 Choose Modify > Convert to Symbol, or press F8. The Convert to Symbol dialog box appears.

3   Type **gotruck** in the Name text field and select Graphic as the Type, then press OK.

Select the truck art and convert it to a symbol.

Using a motion tween to create the animation

To add a little excitement to your artwork, you'll use a motion tween to make the truck move across the Stage. A motion tween allows you to define properties, such as position, and then change them over time. Since this lesson is focused on drawing, motion tweening is not covered here. Find out more about tweening in Lesson 6, "Creating Basic Animation."

Before creating the tween, you will discard the layer that was used for the letter guides and turn off the visibility of the guides.

1   If the Timeline is not visible, choose Window > Timeline.

On the left side of the Timeline are two layers that were used in this document: the work layer and the letters layer. You will discard the letters layer to declutter the Stage.

2   In the Timeline, click to select the layer named letters and then click on the Delete Layer button (🗑) at the bottom of the Timeline. The letters layer is deleted.

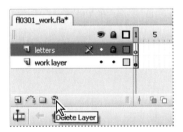

Delete the letters layer.

3   To clear the guides, choose View > Guides > Clear Guides. The guides are deleted from the document window.

4   In the Timeline, position your cursor over Frame 30. Right-click (Windows) or Ctrl+click (Mac OS) and choose Insert Keyframe. A keyframe is added at Frame 30.

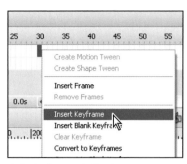

Add a keyframe to the Timeline.

5   Using the Selection tool (▲), click and drag the truck to the right side of the Stage.

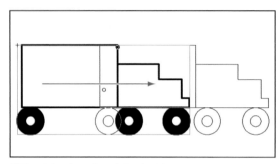

Click and drag the truck symbol to the right.

6   Click on Frame 1 in the Timeline (the original keyframe) to make sure that it is selected.

7   Right-click (Windows) or Ctrl+click (Mac OS) and select Create Motion Tween. An arrow appears between the keyframes.

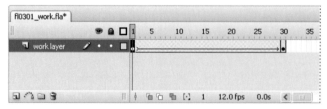

The Timeline after a Motion Tween is created.

8   Press the Enter (Windows) or Return (Mac OS) key to see your truck artwork animated.

9   Choose File > Save and File > Close.

Using the Object Drawing model

The Object Drawing model enables you to draw shapes as individual objects that remain independent of each other. For those of you familiar with Adobe Illustrator, you will recognise this method of drawing. In this lesson, you create a simple animation using artwork created in the Object Drawing model.

Using the PolyStar tool

1   Choose File > Browse to open Adobe Bridge. Use the Folders tab in the upper-left area of the Bridge workspace to navigate to the fl03lessons folder you copied onto your computer. Locate the file named fl0302_done.fla and double-click it to open it in Flash CS3 Professional. Artwork that can be used as a button appears. You will create a button with the artwork, using the Object Drawing model.

The completed lesson.

2   You can keep the file open for reference or choose File > Close to close the file now.

3   Choose File > New. The New Document dialog box appears.

4   Select Flash File (ActionScript 3.0) and press OK. A new document window is opened.

5   Choose File > Save. The Save As dialog box appears. Navigate to the fl03lessons folder and type **fl0302_work.fla** into the Name text field. Make sure the file type is Flash CS3, then press Save.

6   Since the last shape tool that you used was the Oval Primitive tool, you must click and hold onto that tool to select the hidden PolyStar tool (○).

7   With the PolyStar tool active, click on the Object Drawing button (◎) at the bottom of the Tools panel, or use the keyboard shortcut J. By pressing J, you enter or exit the Object Drawing model. As noted above, the Object Drawing model may be easier for some users to master, as it works very much like drawing programs such as Adobe Illustrator.

The Object Drawing model button.

8   If the Property inspector is not visible, choose Window > Properties > Properties.

9 Type **2** into the Stroke height text field in the Property inspector.

10 Click on the Stroke color swatch and choose any color that you like for the stroke. In the example, color #99CC33 was used.

11 Click on the Fill color swatch on the Property inspector and choose white from the Swatches panel.

12 Make sure that the Stroke type is set to Solid.

Select a 2-point solid stroke and white fill for the PolyStar tool.

13 Click on the Options button in the Property inspector; the Tool Settings dialog box appears. Choose star from the Style drop-down menu and type **20** into the Number of Sides text field. Press OK.

14 Click and drag on the Stage to create a 20-point star. Make it any size you like; if necessary, you can resize the artwork later.

Add additional points to the star.   *Result.*

Creating the rectangle shapes

Now you will create the rectangles that are behind the star in the completed lesson file. When you create additional shapes in the Object Drawing model, they stack on top of each other, as you would expect in a drawing program like Adobe Illustrator. Recall that when in the Merge Drawing model (creating the bumper of the truck), the objects that were stacked on top cut out the shapes below.

1 Click and hold on the PolyStar tool (○) to select the Rectangle tool (□).

2 Click outside and to the upper-left of the star and drag toward the lower right until you completely surround (cover) the star with the rectangle.

 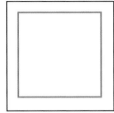

Click and drag the rectangle over the star.   *Result.*

3 Using the Selection tool (k), select the rectangle and then click on the Swap colors icon (⇄) at the bottom of the Tools panel. The fill color is now the stroke color and the stroke color is now the fill color.

The Swap colors button.

4 To verify that there is no stroke on your rectangle, click on the Stroke color swatch on the Property inspector and select No color (☑) from the Swatches panel that appears.

5 Make sure the solid rectangle is still selected, and choose Edit > Copy, or use the keyboard shortcut Ctrl+C (Windows) or Command+C (Mac OS), to copy the rectangle.

6 Paste the rectangle exactly on top of itself by choosing Edit > Paste in Place.

7   Select the Free Transform tool (⊞) from the Tools panel. A bounding box appears around the rectangle. Position the cursor on the top edge of the rectangle until you see the Skew cursor (↜) appear.

8   With the Skew cursor visible, click and drag toward the right to skew the rectangle. Any angle is okay for this lesson.

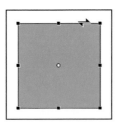 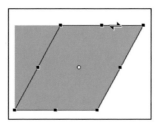

Position the cursor at the top   Click and drag to the right.
of the rectangle.

9   With the skewed rectangle still selected, click on the Fill color swatch in the Property inspector and choose a gray color. For this example, color #666666 was used.

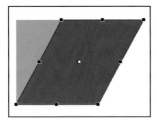

Color the rectangle gray.

10   Choose File > Save. Keep the file open for the next part of this lesson.

Rearranging the order of the objects

Since these shapes were created in the Object Drawing model, you can easily rearrange their stacking order.

1   Using the Selection tool (➤), click once on the gray rectangle and choose Modify > Arrange > Send to Back. Send to Back moves the gray rectangle to the very back of the stacking order. If the Arrange options are grayed out, you may have inadvertently double-clicked and entered the Object Drawing mode. Click off the shape to exit, and click once on the gray rectangle.

2   Using the Selection tool, select the green rectangle and choose Modify > Arrange > Send Backward. Send Backward sends the green rectangle backward, not to the very back, but behind the object directly underneath it, which is the star you created.

Rearrange the objects so the star is forward and the gray rectangle is in the back.

3   Choose File > Save. Keep the file open for the next part of this lesson.

Editing the drawing object

Even though you created the rectangle and star shapes using the Object Drawing model, you can still edit the shapes, as in the Merge Drawing model.

1   Using the Selection tool (➤), double-click on the star. The other shapes on the Stage are dimmed and inaccessible, but the star can be selected and edited, much like a shape created in the Merge Drawing model.

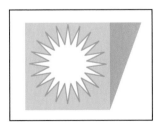

Edit the star shape.

2   Using the Selection tool, click outside the upper-left edge of the star and drag down toward the middle of the shape, essentially cutting it in half. Try to select a point exactly between the star points in the center of the star. If you need to reselect, simply click anywhere off the star and try again.

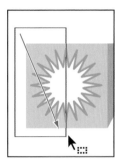

Click and drag to partially select the star.

3   With the Selection tool still active, click on the left side of the star and drag it to the left.

4   Double-click to select both the fill and stroke on the right side of the star and drag it to the right. Notice that by selecting the star in this edit mode you have separated the shape into two parts.

5   Using the Selection tool again, readjust the star so that the two halves are approximately in the center of the square. Don't forget to double-click to select both the fill and stroke when you make these adjustments.

6   Exit the Drawing Object edit mode by clicking on the left-facing arrow at the top of the Stage.

Exit the edit mode for the star by clicking on the arrow.

7   Choose File > Save. Keep this file open for the next part of this lesson.

Adding text to the artwork

You'll now add the final element to your artwork, the text. Flash provides many ways to work with text. For example, you can orient text horizontally or vertically and change attributes such as font, size, style, color, and line spacing.

1. Select the Text tool (T) from the Tools panel. The cursor turns into a text cursor (+). When you select the Text tool, the Property inspector offers the opportunity to change text attributes. You will make some changes in the Property inspector before typing your text.

2. In the Property inspector, press the arrow to the right of the Font drop-down menu and choose Arial Black. If you do not have Arial Black installed as a font on your system, choose Arial.

3. Press the arrow to the right of Font size and move the slider up until you are at about size 20, or type **20** into the Font size text field.

4. Click on the Text (fill) color swatch. When the Swatches panel appears, choose a gray color. In this example, color #666666 is used.

5. Click on the Align Center button. You will now type in some text and then return to the Property inspector to make some additional format changes.

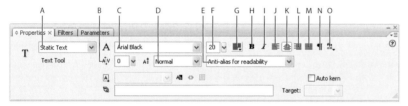

A. Text type. *B*. Letter spacing. *C*. Font. *D*. Character positioning. *E*. Font rendering method. *F*. Font size.
G. Text (fill) color. *H*. Bold. *I*. Italic. *J*. Align Left. *K*. Align Center. *L*. Align Right. *M*. Justify. *N*. Edit format options.
O. Change orientation of text.

6. Click once in the middle of the star, where it has been split in two. A text cursor appears. Don't worry if the placement is not exact, as the text can be repositioned later.

7. Type **About**, then press the Enter/Return key and type **Us**. Since there was no set size for your star and rectangle, your text may appear differently from what you see in this example. Feel free to adjust the text size.

Click once to create a text area.   Enter the text.

Now you will adjust the space between the lines of text. In page layout applications, this is referred to as leading; in Flash, this is called Line spacing.

8 Choose Edit > Select All, or use the keyboard shortcut Ctrl+A (Windows) or Command+A (Mac OS), to select the About Us text.

9 Access additional paragraph options, such as Line spacing, by clicking on the Edit format options button (¶) on the right side of the Property inspector. The Format Options dialog box appears.

10 Press the arrow to the right of Line spacing and drag the slider down until it is approximately at –10, or type **–10** into the Line spacing text field, then press OK (Windows) or Done (Mac OS). The lines of text are now closer together.

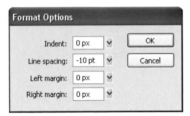

Change additional paragraph attributes using the Format Options dialog box.

Flash Player 8 supports negative leading, meaning that the amount of space between lines can be less than the height of the text. Negative leading can be useful when you want to put lines of text, such as headings, very close together.

As a final step in this exercise, you will use the Free Transform tool to reduce the height of the gray rectangle and make it look more like a drop shadow, rather than a separate shape.

11 Using the Selection tool (k), click anywhere on the gray rectangle.

12 Choose the Free Transform tool (⌖), then click on the top side of the gray rectangle and drag downwards to about a third of the distance from the top. No exact distance is required for this; you can use your own judgment to determine what works well as a drop shadow.

Click and drag with the Free Transform tool.

13 Choose File > Save. You are finished with this part of the lesson. Choose File > Close.

Adding strokes to text

As a default, text has a fill but no stroke. To add a stroke to text, you must use the Break Apart feature. To test this feature you will create a new document with two letters on it.

1   Choose File > Browse to open Adobe Bridge. Navigate to the fl03lessons folder, open it, then double-click on the file named fl0303_done.fla. The document appears with the word GO on the Stage.

The completed file.

2   You can keep this file open for reference, or choose File > Close at this time.

3   Choose File > New; the New Document dialog box appears. Select Flash File (ActionScript 3.0) and press OK. A new document window opens.

4   Choose File > Save; the Save As dialog box appears. Type **fl0303_work** into the Name text field, navigate to the fl03lessons folder, and press Save.

5   Select the Text tool (T). Click once on the Stage, then type **GO**. Any font, style, and size are fine for this part of the lesson.

6   Choose Edit > Select All, or use the keyboard shortcut Ctrl+A (Windows) or Command+A (Mac OS).

7   Click and hold on the arrow to the right of Font size in the Property inspector and drag upwards to the value of 70, or type **70** into the Font size text field.

8   Choose the Selection tool (⬀), and click on the text GO. Choose Modify > Break Apart. The Break Apart feature works much like the Create Outline feature works in Adobe Illustrator; the text is broken into individual letters. Choose Modify > Break Apart again to break the letters down into objects. You will now add a stroke to the letterforms you have created.

9   Select the Ink Bottle tool (⬙) from the Tools panel, then click on the Black and white button (▪) at the bottom of the Tools panel. This confirms that you have a black stroke and white fill set for the color of your object.

10   Position the ink bottle cursor so that the drip of ink (on the cursor) is on the outer edge of the G object, then click to apply a stroke.

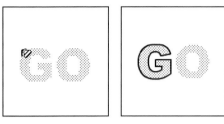

Click on the edge with   *A stroke is added to the letter.*
the Ink Bottle tool.

11   Using the Ink Bottle tool, click on the outside and inside edges of the O object. Strokes are added to edges of the O object.

12   Choose Edit > Select All, or use the keyboard shortcut Ctrl+A (Windows) or Command+A (Mac OS). Select the Selection tool (⬏) from the Tools panel.

13   Click on the Stroke color swatch in the Property inspector and choose the red radial-gradient swatch at the bottom of the Swatches panel that appears.

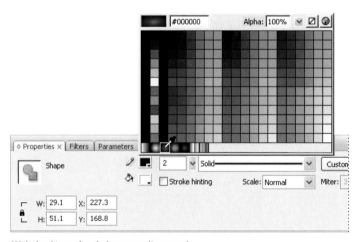

With the objects selected, choose a gradient swatch.

14 Type **4** into the Stroke height text field in the Property inspector and press Enter or Return. The stroke is now a 4-point gradient stroke.

The text with a stroke applied.

15 In the Property inspector, click and hold on the arrow to the right of the Stroke style drop-down menu and select the dotted style line (the fourth stroke style from the top). After you select the dotted line, click on a blank area of the Stage to deselect the G and O objects and see the stroke.

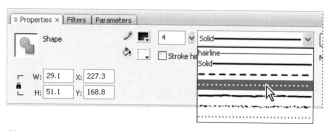

Choose the dotted line stroke.

Result.

16 Choose Edit > Select All and click on the Fill color swatch in the Property inspector. Choose the green radial-gradient from the Swatches panel that appears. The text now has a green radial-gradient fill.

17 Choose File > Save, then choose File > Close. You are finished with this part of the lesson.

Vector vs. raster graphics

The artwork you have created thus far has been vector art. Vector graphics are created using a series of mathematical calculations that describe how paths and shapes are formed, thereby making it easier to scale and use artwork at different resolutions.

In contrast, raster (or bitmap) graphics refer to graphics created with pixels. Raster graphics have a set pixel value and typically cannot be scaled or resized without degrading the quality of the artwork.

Vector artwork.   *Raster artwork.*

In this part of the lesson, you will have the opportunity to take raster artwork, like a scanned image, and recreate it using Flash's drawing tools, thereby creating scalable artwork.

Creating artwork using an imported graphic

In this exercise, you will place an image that you will use as a template for tracing.

1 Choose File > Browse to open Adobe Bridge. Use the Folders tab in the upper-left area of the Bridge workspace to navigate to the fl03lessons folder that you copied onto your hard drive. Double-click on the file named fl0304_done.fla to open it in Flash CS3. Artwork of a sailboat appears. You will create the same artwork using Flash's drawing tools.

2 You can keep this file open for reference or choose File > Close.

Importing raster graphics

You will now import a graphic into Flash CS3 Professional. You can import many types of files into Flash CS3 Professional, including native Photoshop files and other image formats, such as JPG, GIF and TIF files, among others.

1 Choose File > New; the New Document dialog box appears. Select Flash File (ActionScript 3.0) and press OK. A new document window opens.

In this part of the exercise, you will set up layers to help you build your artwork.

2 Choose File > Import > Import to Stage. A dialog box appears.

3   Navigate to the fl03lessons folder and locate the file named fl0304.tif. If you do not see the tif file in the dialog box, choose All Files from the Enable/Files of type drop-down menu. Double-click on the fl0304.tif file. Since the lesson file names are similar, you will be asked if you want to import a sequence of images; choose No. A raster image of a boat appears on the Stage.

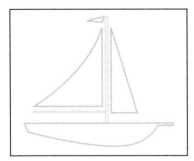

The imported image.

If the entire Stage is not displayed, you can choose View > Magnification > Fit in Window.

4   Choose File > Save. The Save As dialog box appears. Type **fl0304_work.fla** into the Name text field and navigate to the fl03lessons folder. Make sure the Flash CS3 Document format is selected, then press Save.

As a new document, this project contains one layer. Layers help you organize the artwork in your document. You will use layers in this exercise so that you can draw and edit objects on one layer without affecting objects on another layer.

5   With the Selection tool (↖), right-click (Windows) or Ctrl+click (Mac OS) on Layer 1 in the Timeline, and choose Guide from the contextual menu.

The layer is converted to a Guide.

The layer's icon changes from a bent-page icon to a T-square icon (⊤) to indicate that it is now a guide layer. Guide layers help you to align objects when you are drawing on other layers.

6   Choose Insert > Timeline > Layer to place a new layer over Layer 1. As a default, it is named Layer 2.

7 Select Layer 1 (the guide layer), and then click on the dot underneath the padlock icon (🔒) to the right. This locks the sailboat artwork down so that it is not inadvertently selected or repositioned.

Lock the Layer 1 layer.

8 Choose File > Save. Keep the file open for the next part of this lesson.

Drawing with the Pencil, Line, and Pen tools

Now that you have your workspace set up for drawing, you will use the Pencil, Line, and Pen tools to recreate the sailboat.

Using the Pencil tool

The Pencil tool draws paths (strokes) and never has a fill color.

1 Select Layer 2 to make sure that it is the active layer.

2 Choose the Pencil tool (✏️). Before using this tool, you must change some of the stroke attributes in the Property inspector. If the Property inspector is not open, choose Window > Properties > Properties.

3 Click on the Stroke color swatch in the Property inspector. When the Swatches panel appears, select a red color. For this example, color #FF0000 is selected.

4 Using the Stroke height slider, change the stroke to a value of 1, or type **1** into the Stroke height text field.

5 Click and hold on the Stroke style drop-down menu and choose Solid.

Adjust the attributes of the stroke before starting the drawing.

6   Select the Zoom tool (🔍), then click and drag to create a marquee surrounding the pennant at the top of the sailboat image. This zooms in so that you can see the image better.

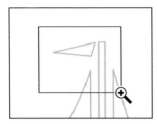

Click and drag with the Zoom tool.

7   Select the Pencil tool, then click and drag, following as closely as you can the pennant in the underlying image. Don't worry if it is not perfect; the pencil stroke you create smooths itself after you release the mouse.

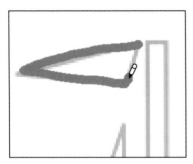

Click and drag with the Pencil tool.

8   Choose File > Save. Keep this file open for the next part of the lesson.

Adjusting your drawing preferences

Flash has preferences that affect how your drawing tools work. In this exercise, you will find out where they are located and make an adjustment.

1 Choose Edit > Preferences (Windows) or Flash > Preferences (Mac OS) and select Drawing from the list of categories on the left side.

2 Choose Tolerant from the Recognize shapes drop-down menu and press OK. The Tolerant setting changes the drawing preference so that shapes that are irregularly drawn are automatically converted into more standard shapes.

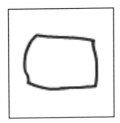 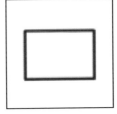

Shape drawn using the Pencil tool.

Shape automatically converted to a square.

Additional drawing preferences

Here is a brief description of the other drawing preferences that you can adjust:

Connect lines: Use the Connect lines setting to determine how close the end of a line that you are drawing must be before snapping to the nearest point on an existing line segment. The Connect Lines setting also controls how nearly horizontal or vertical a line must be drawn before Flash makes it exactly horizontal or vertical. The Snap To Objects option controls how close objects must be to snap to one another.

Smooth curves: The Smooth curves setting specifies the amount of smoothing applied to curved lines drawn with the Pencil tool when the drawing mode is set to Straighten or Smooth.

Recognize lines: The Recognize lines setting defines how nearly straight a line segment drawn with the Pencil tool must be before Flash recognizes it as a straight line and makes it perfectly straight.

Recognize shapes: The Recognize shapes setting controls how precisely you can draw circles, ovals, squares, rectangles, and 90° and 180° arcs to have them recognized as geometric shapes and automatically corrected.

The options are:

- Off—No change is made.

- Strict—Strict requires that the shape be drawn very close to straight.

- Normal—The default setting for the Recognize Shapes setting.

- Tolerant—Tolerant specifies that the shape can be somewhat rough; Flash will redraw the shape.

Click accuracy: The Click accuracy setting specifies how close an item must be to the pointer before Flash recognizes the item.

You can also use one of the three different Pencil modes to change the way you draw.

3   With the Pencil tool ( ) selected, press the Pencil mode button at the bottom of the Tools panel and select Straighten.

Select the Straighten Pencil mode.

4   Choose View > Magnification > Fit in Window so that you can see the entire Stage. You will now create a sun for your boat image.

5   Using the Pencil tool, click and drag to the right of the boat image to create a circle. Do the best you can; but Flash will adjust and correct your shape after you release the mouse. If you release your mouse, but your shape does not resemble a circle, press Ctrl+Z (Windows) or Command+Z (Mac OS) to undo the shape and try again.

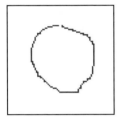   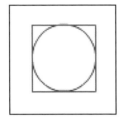

Draw the circle.   *Result.*

6   Once the circle is created, reposition it so it is in the upper-right area of the illustration. The point is to make it appear as though it is the sun in the sky.

7   Choose Edit > Preferences (Windows) or Flash > Preferences (Mac OS) and select Drawing from the list of categories on the left side. Select Smooth from the Smooth curves drop-down menu.

8 Select Off from the Recognize lines drop-down menu and make sure that Recognize shapes is set back to Normal. Press OK.

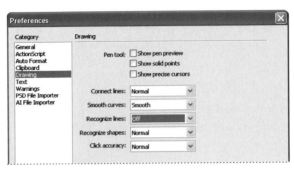

Change the preferences to create the rays of the sun.

9 With the Pencil tool selected, click and hold on the Pencil mode button at the bottom of the Tools panel and choose Smooth.

Select the Smooth Pencil mode.

10 Using the Pencil tool, do the best you can to create curvy line segments to be used as the rays of the sun. Notice that with the drawing preferences set, you need to exaggerate the curves for them to be recognized. Use Edit > Undo, or the keyboard shortcut Ctrl+Z (Windows) or Command+Z (Mac OS), as many times as needed to create line segments that you like.

Creating the rays of the sun.

11 Choose Edit > Preferences (Windows) or Flash > Preferences (Mac OS) and select Drawing from the list of categories on the left side. Set all drop-down menus back to Normal and press OK.

12 Choose File > Save. Keep this file open for the next part of this lesson. Drawing with the mouse can be awkward at first, so using the Pencil tool takes some practice. You will learn how to fine-tune lines in Lesson 4, "Modifying and Transforming Graphics."

Using the Line tool

You will now create the masts of the sailboat.

1 If you do not see the entire sailboat image, choose View > Magnification > Fit in Window. When using the drawing tools, you may notice that line segments you are creating snap toward guides and other lines. Though the snapping feature can be helpful, it can also be a nuisance. For this exercise, turn off the snapping feature by going to View > Snapping > Snap to Guides and deselecting it.

2 Select the Line tool (\) from the Tools panel. Click on the bottom-left corner of the mast and follow it up to the top while holding down the Shift key. Holding down the Shift key constrains the path you are creating to a straight line. When you release the mouse, you have created an individual line segment.

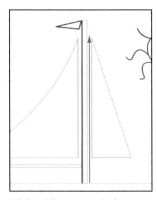

Click and drag to create the line.

3 Choose View > Magnification > 200%. Hold down the spacebar; the Hand cursor (✍) appears. Using the Hand cursor, click and drag to reposition the image area so that you can see the top of the mast better.

You will now delete your line segment so that you can use a feature that allows you to connect one line segment to another. It is important that you read through these steps first, and maybe even practice on a blank document before completing the rest of the exercise.

4 Using the Selection tool (▸), click on the straight line you created for the left side of the mast and press the Delete key. You will now create a series of merged line segments to make the mast.

5 Select the Line tool. Click on the bottom-left part of the mast, then drag to the top of the mast. Release the mouse, but DO NOT reposition the mouse.

6 Click with the mouse and drag from your ending point (top left of mast) to the top-right corner of the mast and release the mouse. Again, do not reposition the mouse. By not repositioning the mouse and clicking again, you keep the line segments connected.

7 Click again and drag toward the bottom right of the mast. Release the mouse, but do not change its position.

8 Click and drag the short distance from the lower left to return to your starting point. Do the best you can to line up the last point with the first one you created.

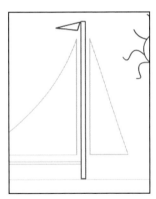

Move from one corner to another to create the mast.

9 Choose File > Save. Keep the file open for the next part of this lesson.

If the technique of creating connected lines is more frustrating than enlightening, use the Rectangle tool to create the mast.

Using the Pen tool

With patience and time, you can now trace any item with the Pencil or Line tools, but there's an easier way to make vector art: the Pen tool. The Pen tool mathematically creates shapes, using a series of anchor points and paths. You can easily manipulate Pen tool paths by adjusting the anchor points that you create.

1   Press Ctrl+4 (Windows) or Command+4 (Mac OS) to zoom to 400%, then select the Hand tool (🖑) from the Tools panel. Click and drag to reposition the image so that you can see the boom, the horizontal bar just below the large (main) sail.

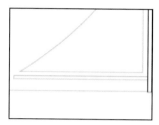

Zoom in and reposition the Stage to see the boom.

2   Select the Pen tool (◊) in the Tools panel. Click once in the bottom left corner of the boom. A very small circle (your first anchor point) appears where you clicked.

3   Hold down the Shift key and click on the top-left corner of the boom and then on the top-right and the lower-right corner.

By holding down the Shift key, you constrain the Pen tool to create straight lines.

4   Connect the last point with the first point by positioning the cursor near the first point. When a hollow circle appears, click. This creates a closed rectangle shape, forming the boom of the sailboat.

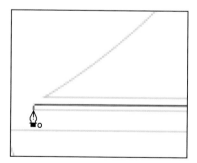

Create a closed shape using the Pen tool.

5   Choose File > Save. Keep this file open. You've mastered the Pen tool for straight lines. Now you'll try creating some curved lines with the help of Bézier curves.

Practice with curves

Before you start creating shapes with curves, you will complete a simple lesson on a separate document. Keep your sailboat document open, as you will return to it after this primer on creating curved paths using the Pen tool.

1 Choose File > Browse and navigate to the fl03lessons folder and double-click to open the file named pencurves.fla

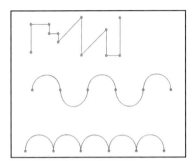

The practice pencurves.fla document.

2 Choose File > Save As. When the Save As dialog box appears, type **pencurves_work.fla** in the Name text field. Make sure that the location selected is the fl03lessons folder, and that the format is Flash CS3 document. Press Save.

 For this part of the lesson, a black stroke is used to help show the difference between the path that is being created and the underlying paths. You can continue to use red for your stroke.

3 Click once on the draw layer that appears in the layers section of the Timeline. This is to verify that you are creating your new paths on an empty layer.

You will first create a path with straight lines and then progress into creating curved paths using the Pen tool.

4 If the Pen tool (◊) is not selected, choose it now.

5 Press the Black and white button (◨) at the bottom of the Tools panel and, using the Stroke height slider in the Property inspector, set the width to 1 or type **1** in the Stroke height text field.

6 Click once on the lower-left point of the first straight line path that appears on the Stage, then hold down the Shift key and click from one circle to another (indicating anchor points) to complete the path. Notice that no matter at what angle you position the Pen cursor, you are snapped to 45°, 90°, or 180° angles.

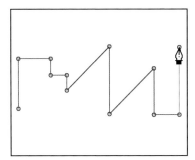

Hold down the Shift key while clicking from one point to another.

7 To deactivate the active path, hold down the Ctrl key (Windows) or Command key (Mac OS) and click off of the active path. If you do not deselect the path, the next point you create will connect to it.

8 Choose File > Save or use the keyboard shortcut Ctrl+S (Windows) or Command+S (Mac OS) to save the file. Keep the file open for the curves part of this lesson.

Using the Pen tool for curves

You will now create the curved pen paths.

1 With the Pen tool (◊) still selected, click the first circle (on the middle path) and immediately drag upwards. You have not created a path yet, just the direction line for your path.

2 Click and drag downwards on the second circle in the path. A path from one anchor point to another is formed. As you drag, you control the form of the curve.

You do not have to get the path right on the underlying path. You will adjust the path later using the Subselection tool (◊).

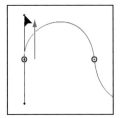 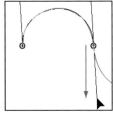

Click and drag up and then down to create your curve.

3 Repeat steps 1 and 2 by clicking and dragging up, then clicking and dragging down on each circle until the path is completed.

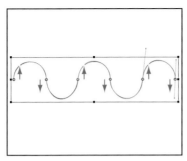

Click and drag up and down to create the curved path.

4 Select the Subselection tool (⬚) from the Tools panel and click on an anchor point to view and edit the position of the direction lines. If necessary, click on the direction points (at the ends of the direction lines) to refine your curve and more closely follow the curve of the underlying path.

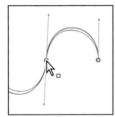
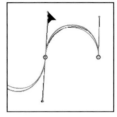

Select an anchor point.   *Click on direction point to adjust direction line.*

5 To deactivate the active path, hold down the Ctrl key (Windows) or Command key (Mac OS) and click off of it.

6 Choose File > Save. Keep the document open for the next part of this lesson.

Creating curves with corner points

In this next exercise, you will learn how to create repeating curves, using key modifiers while you form the path.

1 Using the Hand tool (✋), reposition the view of the Stage so that you can see the third path down on the page. You will recreate this path, starting out with the same technique used to make the last path.

2 Select the Pen tool (◊), then click on the first circle and immediately drag upwards. You have not created a path yet, just the direction line for the path.

Step 3 is tricky, so read over it carefully before you follow the instructions. The step requires you to click and drag to form a curved path, but before releasing, you need to hold down the Alt/Option key and drag in another direction. It may sound complicated, but it is a rather simple and smooth procedure once you do it a few times.

Press Ctrl+Z (Windows) or Command+Z (Mac OS) to undo as many times as you need to until you get this right. Don't worry about following the curve exactly, as you can adjust that later using the Subselection tool.

3   Click and drag downwards on the second circle in the path; your curve from one anchor point to another is formed. Do not release the mouse. Press the Alt (Windows) or Option (Mac OS) key and drag upwards. You have just created a corner point. Release the mouse and the Alt/Option key when the direction line you just made is slightly above the next curve.

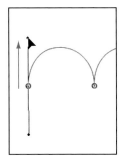
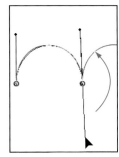
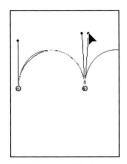

Click and drag up.　　*Click and drag down without releasing the mouse.*　　*Hold down Alt/Option and drag up to create a corner point.*

4   Move to the next circle in the path and click and drag downwards; the next curve is created. Again, do NOT release the mouse. Press the Alt (Windows) or Option (Mac OS) key and drag upwards.

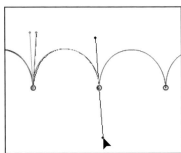

Click and drag down without releasing the mouse.　　*Hold down the Alt/Option key and drag up.*

5   Repeat this procedure to complete this curved path.

6 Select the Subselection tool (◊) from the Tools panel and click on an anchor point to view and edit the position of your direction lines. Click on the direction points (at the ends of the direction lines), if necessary, to refine your curve and more closely follow the curve of the underlying path.

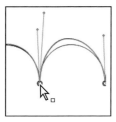 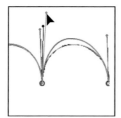

Select an anchor point.   *Edit the direction line.*

7 Choose File > Save and then File > Close.

Drawing the sailboat

You'll now use the Pen and Line tools to create the remainder of the sailboat.

1 Choose View > Magnification > 200%. Hold down the spacebar, then click and drag to reposition the image area so that you can better see the hull (the bottom of the sailboat).

2 Starting with the top-left corner of the hull, click once to place an anchor point.

3 Hold down the Shift key and position your mouse over the top-right corner of the hull, then click. A straight line creates the top of the hull.

 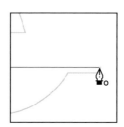

Click with the Pen tool to   *Shift+click on the far right*
start the path.   *corner of the hull.*

4   With the Pen tool still active, Shift+click on the lower-right corner point, then Shift+click on the point to the left, just before the curve of the hull begins.

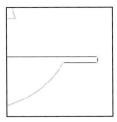

Shift+click to create the straight lines.

You are about to create a curved path. The positioning of the direction lines has much to do with controlling your path.

5   Click on the last anchor point you created. A caret (ʌ) symbol appears to the right of the Pen cursor when you are directly on top of that point. Click and drag a short distance along the side of the hull (following the direction of the hull) and release.

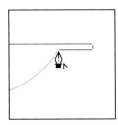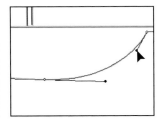

Click on the last anchor   *Drag to create a direction line.*
point created.

6   Click a short distance after the curve and drag to form the curve of the hull.

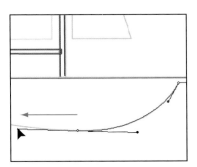

Click and drag to form the curve of the hull.

7 Click and drag on the lower-left corner of the hull to form the large curve.

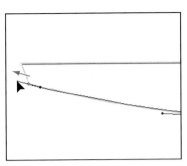

Click and drag to form the bottom of the hull.

8 If you were to click on another location on the Stage, you would create a curved path. This is due to the fact that you just clicked and dragged a curved path from the last anchor point. To eliminate the direction line on the last anchor point, simply position the Pen cursor over the last point. When you see the Pen cursor with the caret symbol, click. The direction line is eliminated.

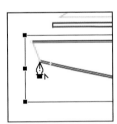

Click on the last anchor point to eliminate the direction line.

9 Position the Pen cursor over the original starting point. When you see the Close Path Pointer (⬩₀), click to close the path.

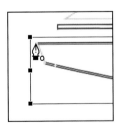

Close the path.

10 Choose File > Save. Keep the file open for the next part of this lesson.

Creating the sail shapes

The sail shapes will be handled the same way as the hull. Start with the large sail on the left side.

1 Using the Pen tool (✎), click the bottom-right corner of the larger sail.

2 Hold down the Shift key and click on the bottom-left point of the sail.

3 Now click and drag upwards on the last anchor point, making sure that you follow the direction of the sail.

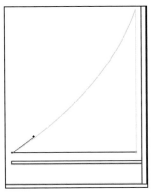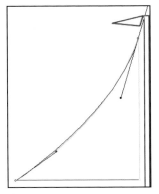

Drag when placing points to recreate the sail's curve.

4 Click once on the anchor point you just created at the top of the sail; this eliminates the direction line. Shift+click on the original starting point to close your shape.

You will now create the second, smaller sail. This should be much easier, as there are no curved paths.

5 Click once on the topmost point of the smaller sail, then click on the lower-right corner. Do not hold down the Shift key, as this is not a perfect 45° angle.

6 Shift+click on the left corner and then Shift+click back on the original starting point. The smaller sail is completed.

7 You have finished the sailboat. Choose File > Save to save the document. Keep the file open for the last part of this lesson, coloring the sailboat.

Saving custom colors

You will now fill some of the shapes you created with a custom color and gradient.

1 Choose Edit > Deselect All to make sure that no objects are selected.

2 If the Color panel is not visible, choose Window > Color. The Color panel appears. The System Color Picker lets you select a stroke or fill color visually.

3 Click on the System Color Picker and drag the crosshair pointer until you find the color you want. Any color you like is fine for this lesson. In this exercise, the crosshairs were dragged into the blue colors.

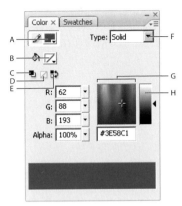

A. Current stroke color. *B*. Current fill color.
C. Black and white. *D*. No color. *E*. Swap colors.
F. Type of color. *G*. System Color Picker. *H*. Color ramp.

4 Click on the variation of the color that you selected in the color ramp to the right of the System Color Picker.

You will now save this color as a swatch so that you can reference it easily.

5 Click and hold on the Color panel menu and choose Add Swatch. The color is now stored as a custom color swatch in the Swatches panel.

6 Click in the Color ramp on a lighter or darker shade of your original selection, and choose Add Swatch from the Color panel menu to add a second color to the Swatches panel. In this example, both a lighter and a darker blue are added to the Swatches panel.

7 Click on the Swatches tab to reveal the Swatches panel, or choose Window > Swatches.

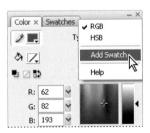

Add a color to the Swatches panel.

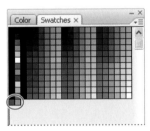

Colors in the Swatches panel.

Filling your shapes with color

In this part of the lesson, you will apply your saved colors to the fills of some of the shapes you have created.

1 Choose the Selection tool (k) and click on the large sail to select it.

2 Click and hold on the Fill color swatch at the bottom of the Tools panel and select the darker of your two saved color swatches.

3 Select the Paint Bucket tool (◈) from the Tools panel and click in the center of the large sail. The color is applied as the fill.

If the area does not fill with color, the shape may not be closed. To fix this, select the Zoom tool (⌕) from the Tools panel and zoom in to investigate the closing anchor points. If the two points aren't positioned exactly on top of each other, choose the Subselection tool (k) and click one of the points and move it. Zoom out and then try filling the region again.

4 Select the second sail, using the Selection tool.

5 Click and hold on the Fill color swatch at the bottom of the Tools panel and select the lighter of your two saved color swatches.

6 Select the Paint Bucket tool from the Tools panel and click in the center of the small sail. The color is applied as the fill.

7 Choose File > Save, then File > Close to close the file.

Congratulations! You have completed this lesson.

Self study

For more practice with the Pen and Line tools, import the fl0305.tif to the Stage in a new document.

Using the skills you have learned in this lesson, do your best to recreate this image. Fill the various shapes that you create with color.

Review

Questions

1 Which tool makes it easier to make changes to the corner radius after the shape has been created?

2 Which shape tool allows you to change the inner radius after the shape has been created?

3 How can you use an image as a base from which to draw?

4 Name and define the two drawing models in Flash CS3 Professional.

Answers

1 You can use the Property inspector to change the corner radius of a shape created with the Rectangle Primitive tool. Access the Rectangle Primitive tool by clicking and holding down on the Rectangle Shape tool. Then choose the Rectangle Primitive tool (or last shape tool used).

2 By using the Property inspector you can add an inner radius to a selected oval created with the Oval Primitive tool. Access the Oval Primitive tool by clicking and holding down on the Rectangle Shape tool (or last shape tool used).

3 To recreate a graphic more easily, you can import your image to the Stage and then lock the layer it is placed on.

a. Choose File > Import > Import to Stage and locate the image you wish to trace, then press Import.

b. Make the layer on which the image was imported into a guide layer. Do this by selecting the layer and Right-clicking (Windows) or Ctrl+clicking (Mac OS) and selecting Guide from the context menu. Guide layers are not exported and do not appear in a published .swf file. You may also choose to lock the guide layer so that you don't inadvertently reposition the image.

c. Create a new layer for your recreation of the artwork and start drawing.

4 The two drawing models in Flash CS3 Professional are:

Merge Drawing model: The Merge Drawing model is the default drawing model; it automatically merges shapes when you overlap them. If you select a shape that is merged with another and move it, the shape below it is permanently altered.

Object Drawing model: The Object Drawing model draws shapes as separate objects that do not automatically merge together when overlaid. Flash creates each shape as a separate object that you can individually manipulate.

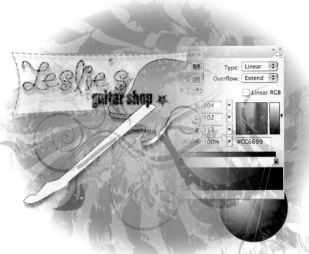

What you'll learn in this lesson:

- Using the Transform tool and panel

- Creating and transforming complex gradients

- Grouping and arranging artwork

- Sampling and unifying colors with the Eyedropper tool

Modifying and Transforming Graphics

In the previous chapter, you explored the Flash drawing tools and combined shapes, paths, and colors to create rich graphics on the Stage. Now it's time to take your graphics further by adding perspective, depth, and lighting effects using transformations and advanced color techniques.

Starting up

Before starting, make sure that your tools and panels are consistent by resetting your workspace. See "Resetting the Flash workspace" on page 3.

You will work with several files from the fl04lessons folder in this lesson. Make sure that you have loaded the fllessons folder onto your hard drive from the supplied DVD. See "Loading lesson files" on page 3.

See Lesson 4 in action!

Use the accompanying video to gain a better understanding of how to use some of the features shown in this lesson. Open the DynamicLearning_FlashCS3.swf file located in the Videos folder and select Lesson 4 to view the video training file for this lesson.

The project

In this lesson, you'll be updating a logo for Leslie's Guitar Shop, an online guitar shop for rockin' girls. To make the logo really stand out, you'll modify the existing graphics using the Transform tool and panel, and add complex gradients and color effects to create a 3-D look and feel.

Grouping and arranging artwork

As your graphics become more complex, you may want to break them down into several individual pieces for more flexibility and control. Arranging those pieces into a single piece of artwork becomes a little tricky, so you'll want to take advantage of Flash's ability to group and arrange graphics on the Stage. Grouping graphics lets you treat multiple items as if they were one object and, within that group, arrange the items in a specific stacking order to achieve the exact look you want.

Grouping and ungrouping graphics

Notice that the guitar has been created in two pieces. You'll need to keep these pieces together for the remainder of the lesson, and the best way to do this is to group them together. Grouping binds two or more independent items together so they can be moved, resized, and rotated together as one unit. The graphics are not actually merged—they are temporarily joined together until you decide to separate them again. This simplifies moving and adjusting artwork, especially when working with more complex graphics.

You'll join the guitar pieces so they can be modified as one unit.

In this lesson, you'll use color and transformation to spice up the artwork, giving Leslie's a new look. To get started, let's group the guitar and neck together so that they can be moved as one complete element.

1   Choose File > Open. Navigate to the fl04lessons folder and select fl0401.fla.

2   Press Open. On the Stage, you'll see the Leslie's logo, as well as an illustration of a guitar.

3   Choose File > Save As. Navigate to the fl04lessons folder and type **fl0401_work.fla** into the Name text field. Press Save.

4   Using the Selection tool (k), move the guitar body below the neck. The body should appear to be attached and slightly overlapping the neck at the top, right down the middle.

Use the Selection tool to move the guitar body right underneath the neck, as shown.

5   With the body of the guitar still selected, hold down the Shift key and click on the neck of the guitar so it is also selected.

   Both the neck and the body should now be selected; holding down the Shift key allows you to select multiple objects at once.

6 Choose Modify > Group to group the two selected graphics together. They now appear inside one bounding box, and will move together until they are ungrouped.

7 Click the new group once to select it and, if necessary, drag it upward so the entire guitar is within the Stage area.

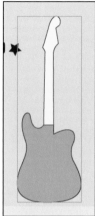

Grouped graphics appear inside a single bounding box.

Groups may contain other groups; to make a group from one or more grouped or non-grouped graphics, select the groups you wish to join together and choose Modify > Group. To ungroup graphics, select the group you want to break apart, and choose Modify > Ungroup or Modify > Break Apart. Both options leave behind the original graphic elements, which can be separated and moved independently.

Arranging grouped graphics

Once you've grouped the guitar's parts together, it's time to fine-tune the image's appearance by arranging the pieces in the proper stacking order. To make this look more realistic, you'll move the neck above the body. Although the guitar parts are contained within a group here, you can still arrange grouped or ungrouped drawing objects. To make any arrangements to a group, you will start by editing the group to access the individual parts of the artwork.

1 Double-click the guitar to edit the group, which consists of the neck and body. A Group icon (⊞) shown above the Stage (next to Scene 1) confirms that you're now inside the group and ready to edit. All other items on the main timeline appear dimmed out and cannot be selected.

2 Using the Selection tool (↖), click once on the body of the guitar to select it.

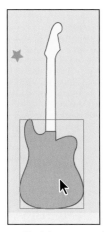

*Double-click a group on the Stage
to edit its individual elements.*

3 Choose Modify > Arrange > Send Backward. The guitar body moves backward in the stacking order and the neck now appears in front of the guitar body.

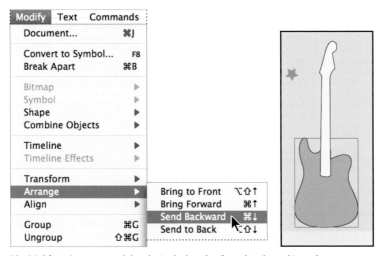

Use Modify > Arrange to send the selection backward or forward in the stacking order.

4 Exit the group by clicking the Scene 1 link below the Timeline.

Click Scene 1 to exit the group.

The Arrange option is available for artwork created in Object Drawing mode only. You can't arrange mergeable graphics even if they are contained within a group. If you want to arrange raw graphics, convert them to drawing objects first, using Modify > Combine Objects > Union. By default, mergeable graphics will appear behind Drawing Objects on the same layer.

Transforming graphics

Creating interesting and realistic artwork often involves transforming and fine-tuning existing illustrations. A transformation can be as simple as changing the width and height of a graphic, or as complex as skewing an object on a three-dimensional plane. There are several methods for applying transformations in Flash. In this lesson, you'll focus on the Transform tool, Transform panel, and Transform submenu, located under the Modify menu.

The Free Transform tool

When you need to resize or rotate objects, the Free Transform tool is often the easiest and most intuitive way to make adjustments. Since it relies on your eyes and hands rather than typing in exact values, it's a good choice for a quick-and-dirty manipulation on a graphic. You'll use this tool in the next exercise to rotate your guitar and get it ready for additional transformations.

1   Select the Free Transform tool (⛶) on the Tools panel, and then select the guitar on the Stage. A black bounding box with handles appears around the edge of the guitar.

2   Move your cursor above the top-right corner, outside the handle. The cursor changes to a rotating arrow icon (⟳). Click and drag the handle and rotate the guitar clockwise about 90° (to about 3 o'clock). Now your guitar is ready for some more transformations.

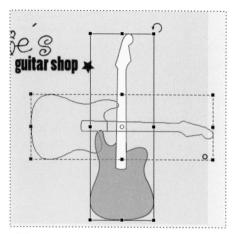

Click and drag any of the four corner handles to rotate an object clockwise or counterclockwise.

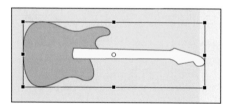

The completed rotation.

 To rotate a graphic in exact 45° increments, hold down the Shift key while dragging any corner handle.

Using the Free Transform tool

You can use the Free Transform tool to perform several different adjustments. Here are the ways it can be used to transform artwork:

Width and Height: Grab any of handles on the four sides of the black bounding box to resize width or height. To resize width and height simultaneously, use the handles on the four corners instead of the sides. To keep the width and height adjustments proportional, press the Shift key on your keyboard while making the adjustments.

Rotate: Move the cursor over and slightly outside of a corner handle until the cursor changes to a rotating arrow icon. Click and drag to rotate the object.

Flip: You can flip an object by grabbing one of the four side handles and pulling it across its opposing handle. To flip an object horizontally and vertically at the same time, click and drag a corner handle over its opposing corner handle.

Skew and Distort: To skew or freely distort an object, press and hold the Ctrl key (Windows) or Command key (Mac OS) while grabbing a handle. To skew, hold down the Ctrl/Command key and grab any one of the four side handles. To free distort, hold down the Ctrl/Command key and grab any one of the four corner handles.

The Transform submenu

The Transform submenu can be found under Modify > Transform, and provides an alternate to the Transform tool. It activates many of the Transform tool's modes and also performs some common tasks such as Flip, Rotate, and Scale. Now you will explore the Transform submenu and apply some additional changes to the guitar graphic.

1   Using the Selection tool (▸), click once to select the guitar. Remember the guitar is a group you created earlier and is composed of two parts—the body and neck.

2   Choose Modify > Transform > Flip Horizontal. This flips the guitar so that the neck is pointing toward the left side of the Stage.

3 With the guitar still selected, choose Modify > Transform > Flip Vertical. This flips the guitar upside-down. Keep the guitar selected.

Select Flip Horizontal to flip the guitar on its x-axis. Flip Vertical flips the guitar upside-down.

4 Choose Modify > Transform > Scale and Rotate. This opens the Scale and Rotate dialog box, where you can specify exact values for scaling and rotation. You'll make some adjustments to get your guitar closer to the desired result.

5 In the Scale text field, type **120,** then type in **–45** in the Rotation text field. Entering a negative number performs a counterclockwise rotation. Press OK to confirm the changes.

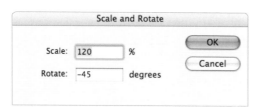

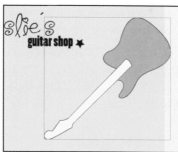

The Scale and Rotate command opens a dialog box where you can specify exact values to adjust an object.

Here the Transform submenu allowed you to make adjustments with a high degree of precision. In the next few steps, you'll explore the Transform panel, which also lets you adjust the size, skew, and rotation of objects on the Stage with the same precision.

The Transform panel

When you need to apply more precise transformations, the Transform panel gives you the ability to specify exact values for width, height, rotation, and skew. You will find many similarities between this panel and its cousins in the Tools panel and Modify menus. The panel performs many of the same functions with exact precision. It also indicates any transformations that have already been applied to a selected object. Open the Transform panel by choosing Window > Transform.

Skewing graphics

The concept of skewing involves taking an image and moving it horizontally or vertically on a perceived angle. A good way of illustrating this is to take a photograph, hold it directly facing you, and then tilt it back and sideways so that the viewing angle is not directly head-on. Skewing can be accomplished from the Transform panel.

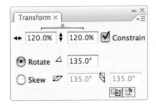

Open the Transform panel by choosing Open > Transform.

1   Using the Selection tool (⬚), click once to select the guitar. Choose Window > Transform to open the Transform panel.

2   Select the Skew option radio button. The horizontal and vertical fields to its right become active, allowing you to enter specific values.

3   Enter **–130** in the left (horizontal) text field, and **–160** in the right (vertical) text field, then press Enter (Windows) or Return (Mac OS). Notice that the guitar now appears to be positioned at a slight angle. Keep the guitar selected. To finish up, we'll position the guitar and place it behind the rest of our logo.

Specify exact values for Horizontal and Vertical Skew to finish the transformation.

4 In the Property inspector, enter **45** in the X text field, and **25** in the Y text field. This positions the guitar near the top of the Stage and above the text.

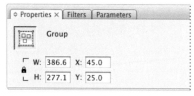

Use the Property inspector to shift the guitar into position with the rest of the logo.

5 With the guitar selected, choose Modify > Arrange > Send to Back. This moves the guitar behind the text.

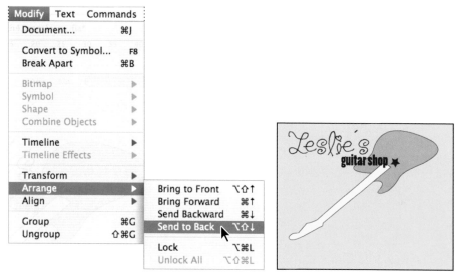

The Arrange menu is used to move the guitar behind the text.

As you've discovered, there are several ways to apply transformations to a graphic. Depending upon how you like to work and the level of precision required, you may use different methods of transforming objects.

Modifying Fill and Stroke colors

Flash CS3 Professional gives you several tools for working with color, making it easy and intuitive to tweak and blend colors to perfect your artwork. Get things started with basic colors, and then enhance graphics with gradients and artistic strokes to add creative effects and depth to your artwork.

Working with gradients

The Swatches panel is where colors are saved for reuse in Flash. It includes solid colors along with a handful of gradient swatches. Gradients are gradual blends between two or more colors, often used for artistic effects or to simulate lighting or textured surfaces.

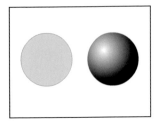

On the left: ball, circle, or gray pancake?
On the right, the same shape with a gradient applied.

You can create your own gradients and add them to the Swatches panel so you can easily reuse them. Flash also provides you with a special tool for manipulating gradients that you've already applied—the Gradient Transform tool. You'll find it underneath the Free Transform tool that you used earlier in this lesson. Click and hold on the Free Transform tool in the Tools panel, and you'll see the Gradient Transform tool underneath.

Click and hold the Transform tool to reveal the Gradient Transform tool.

For the Leslie's Guitar Shop logo, you'll use gradients to spice up your guitar and add some dimension to the overall piece. Because you can easily apply and design gradients on an active selection, you'll edit the guitar group so you can focus exclusively on the guitar body.

1 Using the Selection tool (▲), double-click the guitar to edit the group. Once inside the group, click once on the guitar's body.

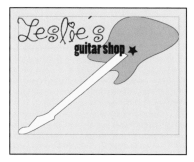 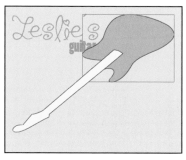

Double-click the group that forms the whole guitar to then select only the body of the guitar.

2 Choose Window > Color to access the Color panel if it's not already visible. The Color panel displays the stroke and fill colors of the selected object—in this case, the body of the guitar. Press the Fill color button, indicated by the paint bucket, in the top-left corner. This ensures that any color changes you apply are made to the fill of the guitar.

3 Under the Type drop-down menu, located in the top-right corner, switch the fill style from Solid to Linear. This switches to the default white-to-black gradient, and two sliders appear on the color ramp at the bottom of the panel. The guitar body changes to reflect the gradient colors.

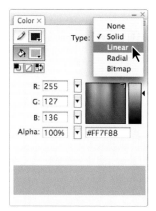 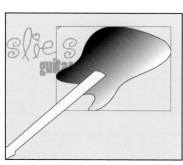 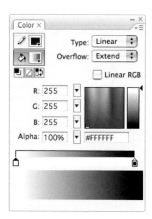

Switch fill style from Solid to Linear (or Radial) to create a gradient. The default gradient is white-to-black.

4   To edit the colors in your gradient, you'll establish start and stop colors for the gradient. These are represented by the two sliders on the color ramp. Double-click the left slider to open the Swatches panel. Select the purple color labeled #CC6699.

It may be easiest to type the color code directly into the hexadecimal field at the top of the Swatches panel.

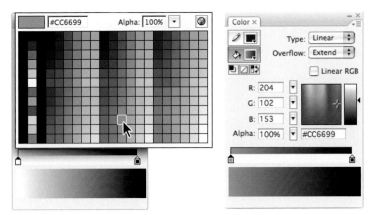

Double-click the color slider to modify the colors.   *The purple color replaces the default white color.*

5   Repeating the process you used in the previous step, double-click the right slider on the color ramp and select the light purple color labeled #CC99CC. You've now created a new gradient, which is applied to the guitar body.

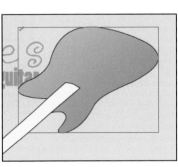

The finished gradient now fills the guitar body.

6 To save the gradient so you can reuse it later, click in the top-right corner of the Color panel to open the panel menu, and choose Add Swatch. The gradient is now added to your existing color swatch presets. You will not receive confirmation that the swatch is added; it will simply appear in the Swatches panel at next use.

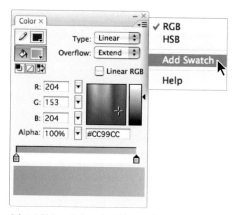

Select Add Swatch from the Color panel's menu to save your gradient.

Transforming gradients

A gradient can make a big creative difference, but you can take it even further using the Gradient Transform tool. Regardless of what type of gradient you've created, there are three aspects of each gradient that can be modified to give it a different feel: the intensity, size, and direction of the gradients. The Gradient Transform tool allows you to modify all three of these so you can get your gradient fill to look just the way you want it to. You'll explore this tool using the gradient you just created for the guitar body.

1 If necessary, double-click the guitar to edit the group. Using the Selection tool (↖), click once to select only the body of the guitar.

2 In the Tools panel, select the Gradient Transform tool (▦). Remember that it is hidden underneath the Free Transform tool (✥) in the Tools panel. You'll see a unique bounding box appear that follows the direction of the body of the guitar.

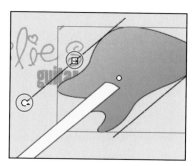

Use the handles to adjust the gradient.

3   On the bounding box, move your cursor over the circular handle until it changes to a rotating arrow icon (↺). This circular handle controls the angle and direction of the gradient.

4   Click and drag the handle in a counterclockwise motion and rotate it until the darkest part of the gradient appears at the top.

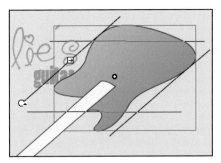

You can also change the direction of the gradient.

5   To simulate light hitting the guitar from the front, you'll make some changes so that the majority of the guitar reveals the lighter part of the gradient, with the darkest part of the guitar in the far back. To make this adjustment, you'll need to change the balance between the two colors.

Notice a center point in the middle of the selection area. Move your cursor over this center point, but do not click. Place your cursor over the center point until the cursor changes to a four-way arrow (✛). Click and drag up toward the top to shift the gradient so that the lighter of the two colors is more prominent.

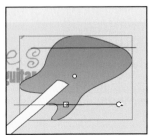 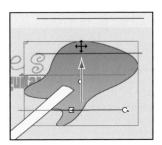 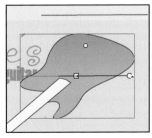

Moving the center point of the bounding box changes the balance between the colors being blended.

6   To finish this off, you'll adjust the intensity of the gradient so that the blend between the colors is less gradual. On the gradient's bounding box, locate the square handle with an arrow inside; this controls the gradient's size and intensity.

7 Click and drag the square handle so that the two sides of the bounding box move closer together. This narrows the size of the gradient, forcing the color blend to occur over a shorter distance.

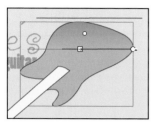

The finished product.

Creating complex gradients

While the gradient you created in the last step included only two colors, gradients can incorporate several colors to create more complex blends. In some cases, you may need four or more colors to accurately depict lighting on an irregular surface. For the guitar, you'll create a more realistic appearance by enhancing the existing gradients.

You'll start by duplicating the body and then moving the duplicate slightly away from the original. You will then create a special gradient to fill the side of the guitar.

1 If necessary, use the Selection tool (↖) and double-click the guitar to enter and edit its group. Using the Selection tool, click once to select only the body of the guitar.

Now you'll make an exact copy of the guitar body by cloning it. The cloning technique is an easy way to create a copy from any object you have selected on the Stage.

2 Press and hold the Alt key (Windows) or Option key (Mac OS). Using the Selection tool, click the body of the guitar and drag it slightly downwards. Release the mouse button to create a copy that is placed on top of the original. Leave the new copy of the guitar body selected.

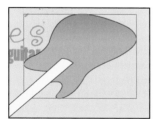 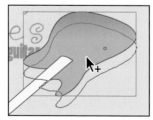 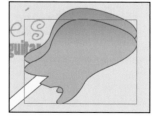

Hold down Alt/Option.   *Drag the guitar.*   *Result.*

3 With the copy of the guitar body selected, choose Modify > Arrange > Send to Back to move the duplicate behind the original. Position it slightly below the original.

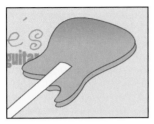

Send the duplicate behind the original.

Modifying gradient colors

Next, you will create a gradient that illustrates the contours along the sides of the guitar. To do this you will once again work with the Color panel. If necessary, open the Color panel by choosing Window > Color.

1 With the Color panel visible, click to select the copy of the guitar body that you just created. The Color panel shows that it's using the same gradient you created earlier. To follow the curves and contours of the side of the guitar body, you'll create a gradient that contains four shades: two for the darkest parts and two for the lightest.

2 In the Color panel, click just below the color ramp in the middle of the panel. A new color slider is created. Repeat this process by clicking slightly to the right of the slider you created in the previous step, adding another slider. When you're done, you should have a total of four sliders.

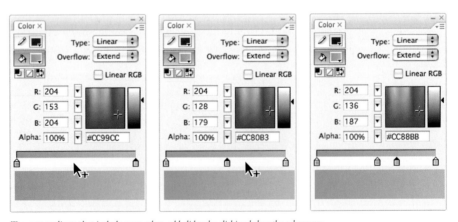

To create gradients that include more colors, add sliders by clicking below the color ramp.

3 You'll now set colors for the two new sliders. Double-click the first slider you created in the center to open the Swatches panel. Click to select the white swatch labeled #FFFFFF and set the slider to white. Repeat this process for the second slider you created, choosing the light purple color labeled #CC99CC.

4 The right-most slider contains the same dark color as the first slider on the left. Double-click the slider on the far right and choose the color purple labeled #CC6699. You now have a four-color gradient that you can use to add contours to the body of the guitar.

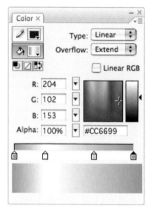

Creating a four-color gradient.

5 Using the Selection tool (▶), select the duplicate of the guitar body. Switch to the Gradient Transform tool (⬛). Grab the circular handle and rotate the gradient 90° counterclockwise, so that the colors are moving from left to right (matching the color ramp).

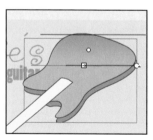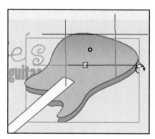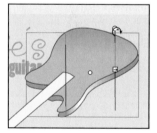

Shift the direction of the gradient so that it flows from left to right.

6 Select the center point of the gradient transform bounding box, and then click and drag to move the gradient slightly to the left. The white portion of the gradient should align with the body extension of the guitar (the fin-like part above where the neck meets the body). Use the gradient resize handle to make the gradient slightly smaller horizontally.

7 Fine-tune the gradient by moving the sliders on the color ramp. This will place the colors appropriately across the spectrum.

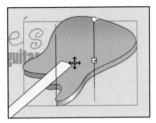

Reposition the gradient fill using the center anchor.

 To remove sliders from the color ramp, click and drag the slider you want to remove downwards, off the Color panel.

8 Click the Scene 1 link below the Timeline to return to the main stage.

The finished guitar.

You've done great work so far, taking a two-dimensional guitar and giving it a three-dimensional appearance using gradients. You're ready to move on to the rest of the logo. Next you'll explore working with strokes, selections, and the Eyedropper to manipulate colors and make intricate adjustments.

Adding and modifying stroke styles and colors

The stroke of an object can be more than just a border—it can be styled to enhance the look of shapes, illustrations, and even type. The Property inspector gives you an easy way to apply interesting effects to existing strokes, or you can add strokes using the Ink Bottle tool. To add more to the Leslie's Guitar Shop logo, you'll focus on the type portion of the logo, and apply stroke effects to make it stand out.

You'll start by adding a stroke to an existing shape.

1   Using the Selection tool (↖), select the guitar shop portion of the logo. Click the Stroke color swatch at the bottom of the Tools panel and choose the stroke color purple #CC3399. The stroke is applied to all of the characters in the words "guitar shop."

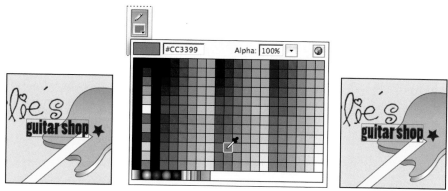

Select a stroke color from the Tools panel and apply it to a selected object.

2   If necessary, open the Property inspector by choosing Window > Properties > Properties, or use the keyboard shortcut Ctrl+F3 (Windows) or Command+F3 (Mac OS). Notice that the stroke and fill color swatches are displayed in the Property inspector, along with options for stroke width and style.

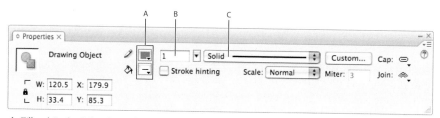

A. *Fill and Stroke Colors*. *B*. *Stroke height*. *C*. *Stroke style*.

3   Set the Stroke height to 5 pixels by typing **5** into the Stroke height text field or using the sliding adjustment. The stroke may appear large, but you'll fix it in the next step.

4   Using the Style drop-down menu on the Property inspector, select the charcoal pencil-style stroke to apply it to the type. The charcoal stroke creates an edgy accent around the type.

Change the width and style to create a new look for the type.

Using the Eyedropper tool to sample colors and styles

If you've worked hard to get a specific look for a shape or text, you may want to reuse the color or styles on other objects or text. Using the Eyedropper tool, you can sample colors and styles from one object to another. This speeds up your workflow and ensures consistency across your artwork.

Unifying colors and styles across graphics and type

To sample a color from one object to another, select the target object that you wish to format, then select the Eyedropper tool from the Tools panel. Using the Eyedropper tool, click the source object from which you want to sample attributes. After you click the source, the colors and styles will be sampled from either the stroke or fill, depending on which part of the object you clicked.

Next, you'll sample the style you just applied to the guitar shop text and apply it to the star positioned to its right.

1   Select the star to the right of the guitar shop text, then choose the Eyedropper tool (✐) from the Tools panel.

2   Click anywhere on the guitar shop portion of the logo. The style from guitar shop is applied to the star you selected.

Sampling colors and styles from one object to another is easy with the Eyedropper tool.

If you find yourself frequently using the Eyedropper to sample a custom color you've created, consider saving the color as a swatch using Add Swatch from the Color panel's menu.

Creating complex selections

As artwork begins to occupy the small space on the Stage, you may find it tricky to select what you want without accidentally selecting other items. The Selection tool is great for drawing selection areas around objects when you have room to spare, but it can be more difficult when you need to select unconnected or ungrouped pieces of complex art. The Leslie's portion of the logo is neither a group nor a single drawing object. Each character is a separate graphic that borders closely on other items on the Stage, making it more difficult to select. In the next section, you'll learn how to make these complex selections.

The Lasso tool

When you need to select multiple items that are ungrouped, or items with an irregular shape, consider using the Lasso tool. This freehand selection tool lets you specify the exact selection area by dragging and drawing around the objects you want to include. The Lasso tool is on the Tools panel, and is a great alternative to the Selection tool.

You'll use the Lasso tool to select and group together the individual characters that make up the word "Leslie's" in your logo.

1   Choose the Lasso tool (⌒) from the Tools panel.

2   Click and hold the mouse just to the left and above the word "Leslie's," and start dragging a selection area around all of the characters. Move slowly and keep a bit of distance from the edges to avoid chopping up any of the letters.

Draw a complete selection area around some tight spots using the Lasso tool.

 To make intricate selections easier, try using the Zoom tool (⌕) to enlarge an area or object on the Stage.

3   Draw a selection around the entire word *Leslie's*. When you get back to the starting point for the selection, overlap the area where you started and release the mouse to close the selection path. All the letters will be selected. If you missed anything or overshot the selection area, repeat steps 1 through 3.

4   To keep the characters together for future tasks, convert them to a single Drawing Object by selecting Modify > Combine Objects > Union.

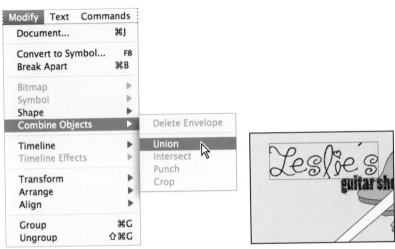

Combine the characters into a single Drawing Object to make them easier to select.

Finishing the logo

Now it's time to combine some of the concepts you've learned to finish up the Leslie's Guitar Shop logo. To spice up the Leslie's text, you'll take the same approach you used with the "guitar shop" text. You'll apply a fancy stroke to make it stand out and then create a cool border that will frame the whole piece.

1   Use the Selection tool (⬀) to select the word Leslie's. Remember that you converted this to a single Drawing Object in the last exercise.

2   On the Tools panel, select the orange labeled #FF6600 from the Stroke color swatch. The Property inspector displays the same stroke style that you used earlier on the words guitar shop. By default, Flash uses the last settings you applied.

3 In the Property inspector, select the dashed stroke style from the drop-down menu. The dashed stroke is applied to the outlines of each character in the word Leslie's.

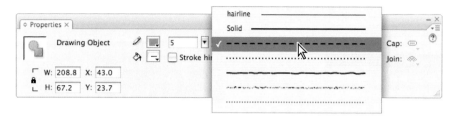

Specify a new stroke style for Leslie's.

4 In the Property inspector, reduce the stroke width from 5 pixels to 2 pixels using the stroke slider or entering the value directly in the stroke width field and pressing Enter/Return. This makes the logo more readable.

The finished logo.

Adding a frame

Finally, you'll use a simple shape tool you worked with in the last chapter, the Rectangle tool, to frame the logo. You'll put the Selection tool's creative side to use, making the frame as funky as the rest of the logo. It's also time to explore the Selection tool's modification possibilities—it doesn't just select and move, but can also be used to bend lines and shapes in interesting ways.

1 Select the Rectangle tool (□) from the Tools panel. Use the Fill color swatch on the bottom of the Tools panel to set the fill color to No color (☑) and use the Stroke color swatch to choose the orange color (#FF6600) for your stroke. This is the same orange you used in the previous exercises in this lesson.

2 Click and drag a rectangle around the text portion of the logo on the Stage. Switch to the Selection tool (k) and double-click the stroke of the new rectangle to select the entire shape.

3   In the Property inspector, make sure that the padlock (🔒) located to the left of the W (width) and H (height) text fields is not selected. Enter **350** in the width (W) text field and **120** in the height (H) text field to resize the new box.

Use the Rectangle Tool to create a decorative frame.

4   With the Selection tool active, click on the Stage or work area to deselect any selected objects. Move your cursor along the left edge of the new rectangle until the cursor displays a curved line underneath. Click and then drag to the right, bending the line.

5   Repeat the previous step for the remaining three sides of the rectangle until all the sides are curved inward. You've created an interesting shape that frames your logo and completes the job.

Curve all sides inward using the Selection tool.

6   If necessary, click to select the entire frame and send it behind the text and guitar by choosing Modify > Arrange > Send To Back.

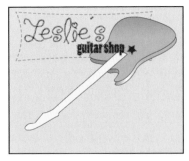

Send the frame to the back of the stacking order.

Congratulations! You have finished the lesson and learned many ways to transform and modify graphics.

Self study

Design a logo for yourself, a friend, or a local business using the techniques you've learned so far. Use groups to build and arrange your logo, which should include a graphic and at least one line of text.

Use the Color panel to create and apply a new gradient (use at least three colors) to your logo, and add the gradient to your Swatches panel.

Experiment with different stroke styles and settings using the Stroke options in the Property inspector to add style to your logo.

Review

Questions

1   How are groups created and edited on the Stage?

2   What three methods can be used to transform a selected graphic on the Stage?

3   What selection tool can be used to make complex selections around intricate artwork on the Stage?

Answers

1   To create a group, select two or more objects on the Stage and choose Modify > Group. To edit a group, double-click it on the Stage.

2   The Free Transform tool, the Transform panel, and the Transform submenu (located under Modify).

3   The Lasso tool.

What you'll learn in this lesson:

- Working with the Library panel
- Adding symbols to the library
- Creating and managing artwork using symbols
- Editing and swapping symbols for easy updates
- Organizing the library

Using Symbols and the Library

Within each Flash CS3 Professional document, you'll find a powerful tool designed to help you effectively build and design your movies: the library. The library stores and manages symbols— reusable graphics, buttons, and animations—as well as imported photos, sounds, and video. In this lesson, you'll explore the advantages of using symbols and the library.

Starting up

Before starting, make sure that your tools and panels are consistent by resetting your workspace. See "Resetting the Flash workspace" on page 3.

You will work with several files from the fl05lessons folder in this lesson. Make sure that you have loaded the fllessons folder onto your hard drive from the supplied DVD. See "Loading lesson files" on page 3.

See Lesson 5 in action!

Use the accompanying video to gain a better understanding of how to use some of the features shown in this lesson. Open the DynamicLearning_FlashCS3.swf file located in the Videos folder and select Lesson 5 to view the video training file for this lesson.

The project

You'll be learning to create symbols from existing artwork and reuse those symbols throughout your movie to build a web banner for a department store's winter sale. After you build a layout for this season, you'll be able to easily modify it for other seasonal campaigns using the symbol's powerful swap and editing capabilities. Each exercise will introduce you to a new concept as you creatively evolve your ad campaign.

What are symbols?

As you create graphics on the Stage, you'll realize that you want to reuse those graphics several times throughout your movie. Although you could copy and paste the artwork as many times as necessary, keeping track of each copy would be difficult because there's no way of letting Flash know they are related. Modifications, such as an overall color or shape change, would need to be applied to each copy individually, taking up creative time and opening the door to inconsistencies in your movie.

A better choice is to use symbols: reusable graphics, images, and animations stored in your document's library. You can create symbols from any graphics or imported images on the Stage, or from animations on the Timeline. A symbol is the original from which all copies are made; each copy of a symbol (called an instance) remains linked to the master symbol in the library. Changes made to the original symbol in your library affect all instances of that symbol throughout your movie.

As described in detail in the sidebar "Symbol-ism: the symbol types," Flash uses three types of symbols:

*   Graphic
*   Button
*   Movie clip

This lesson focuses on graphic symbols only, and you'll be converting existing graphics to symbols, as well as creating new symbols from the ground up. Lesson 11, "Creating Button Symbols," will explore buttons, while Lesson 13, "Introducing Movie Clips," covers the creation and use of movie clips—powerful symbols that can contain entire animations.

Symbol-ism: the symbol types

Each symbol type has different attributes and a unique purpose within your movie. Everything from basic graphics to full-blown animations can be stored as symbols in the library, making it easy to manage and build even the most complex movies. Each symbol is represented in the library and in the Property inspector by a unique icon, so you can easily identify which symbol belongs to which category. Here's a closer look at what makes each unique:

Graphic (▨): Graphic symbols are the most basic of the three types and can contain graphics, type, imported artwork, or bitmaps. Use graphic symbols to store your artwork in the library or to get graphics ready for animation. Graphic symbols can contain other graphics, so you can make more elaborate symbols by converting groups of graphics symbols into a single, new graphic symbol.

Button (🖰): These symbols are designed for use as controls, and they contain multiple states that react to a user's mouse interaction including clicks and rollovers. You'll learn how to create and work with buttons in Lesson 11, "Creating Button Symbols."

Movie clip (▣): Movie clips can best be described as super-symbols. They can contain anything from other symbols to full animations, even sounds and video. In addition, movie clip symbols have their own independent timelines, so they are capable of housing elaborate animations that can be treated as movies themselves. You'll learn to create and work with movie clips in Lesson 13, "Introducing Movie Clips."

A look at the Library panel

Each Flash document contains its own library that stores symbols as well as assets; images, sounds, and video files that you've imported into your Flash document can all be found in the library. The library's contents are displayed and managed in the Library panel. This powerful organizational tool lets you view, sort, edit, and return information on symbols. Located on the right side of the screen in the default workspace, the Library panel is the store-all management system for symbols and imported assets. For a detailed list of the panel's features, see the sidebar "Library panel options."

The Library panel opens up further possibilities by letting you export symbols for direct interaction with ActionScript, or share library items across multiple .fla documents. To open the Library panel, choose Window > Library or use the keyboard shortcut Ctrl+L (Windows) or Command+L (Mac OS).

The Library panel is invaluable for managing symbols and imported assets.

Creating symbols

The first step toward taking advantage of symbols is to add some to the library. You can create symbols from existing artwork on the Stage, or you can create blank symbols with the option to add content afterwards.

Converting a graphic to a symbol

If you haven't already done so, open the fl0501.fla file located in the fl05lessons folder, and select File > Save As. The Save As dialog box appears. In the Name text field, type **fl0501_work.fla**, and press Save.

On the Stage you'll find all the artwork you need to construct an ad banner for the fictional department store Spacey's. This document was created using the 500x500 (Popup) sample template found in the New Document dialog box under Templates > Advertising, which you learned about in Lesson 2, "Flash CS3 Jumpstart."

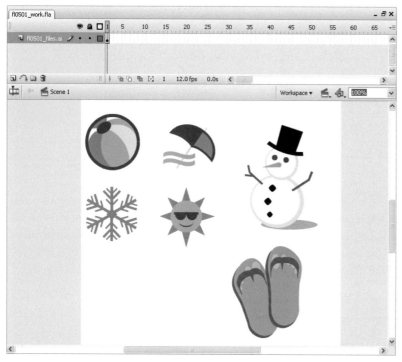

The lesson file contains all the raw artwork you need to get your ad banner started.

In this exercise, you'll convert the six drawings on the Stage to symbols so you can store them in the library and reuse them several times throughout your movie.

1 Select the snowflake on the Stage by forming a selection area around the entire drawing with the Selection tool (⬚).

2 Choose Modify > Convert to Symbol, or use the keyboard shortcut F8 to open the Convert to Symbol dialog box.

Choose Modify > Convert to Symbol to save any artwork on the Stage as a symbol in your library.

3   Assign the name **Snowflake** to the new symbol by typing it in the Name text field. You can name symbols just about anything you want, but try to keep names short and intuitive so you can easily figure out what's what when viewing the Library panel.

4   Click the radio button to choose Graphic from the three symbol types shown.

5   Set the registration point for the new symbol by clicking the box in the center of the small grid shown on the right. Registration points serve as the "handles" by which you rotate and position symbols on the Stage. Registration point locations will vary based on the shape of the artwork you're creating; here a centered point works best.

The finished Convert to Symbol dialog box.

6   Press OK. The new symbol appears in the Library panel, and the snowflake image remains exactly where you left it on the Stage. Select the snowflake and look at the Property inspector; a special Graphic icon (⬚) on the left-hand side will confirm that the artwork is now an instance of the newly created Snowflake symbol. After it is converted to a graphic symbol, the snowflake should have a registration point in its center and a blue bounding box surrounding it.

The snowflake raw artwork.   *The artwork as a symbol.*

The Graphic icon and label verify that you have converted your symbol properly.

7 Repeat steps 1 through 6 for the snowman, beachball, umbrella, and sun designs on the Stage, using the corresponding names respectively. Leave the sandals design unconverted for now. When you're done, look at the Library panel and you'll see that the artwork pieces have been added to your library as graphic symbols.

8 Choose File > Save to save your work, and keep the document open.

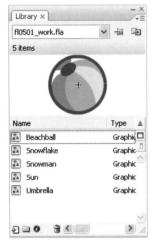

The new symbols in the library.

Don't confuse symbols with Drawing Objects. Although both appear inside of bounding boxes, only symbols are stored in the library and have all the advantages discussed in this lesson. If you're unsure, select the artwork and use the Property inspector to verify that what you're looking at is truly a symbol instance, and not a Drawing Object.

What's the point of registration points?

The registration point on a selected symbol instance.

The registration point as a crosshair inside the symbol's Edit mode.

A symbol's registration point determines the measurement point by which the symbol is positioned on the Stage.

You specify a registration point when you first convert an object to a symbol, and you should choose a point subjectively based on the shape of the object. It is common to set a centered registration point for objects that are round or symmetrical (such as the beachball), or a top-left registration point for text or symbols that have no real point of symmetry (such as the snowman). When you edit your symbol, you can change the registration point by moving the artwork around relative to the crosshair that appears on the Stage in the symbol's Edit mode.

Change the registration point.

Creating blank symbols

You can create symbols of any type even when existing artwork isn't available. To do this, you can form an empty symbol, and add content later by drawing, pasting, or importing artwork into the new symbol. Here's how:

1 Select the entire drawing of the sandals on the Stage using the Selection tool (⬆).

You can also draw a selection area around the sandals using the Lasso tool (⌀)to make sure you get all of its pieces.

Use the Selection tool to select the sandals drawing.

2 Choose Edit > Cut to cut the artwork from the Stage and place it on the clipboard.

3 Choose Insert > New Symbol to open the Create New Symbol dialog box, which looks identical to the Convert to Symbol dialog box you used in the last exercise.

Enter **Sandals** in the Name text field to name the new symbol.

4 Click the radio button to select Graphic from the three symbol types shown. Press OK to create the new symbol.

The Create New Symbol dialog box.

5 The new Sandals symbol appears in the Library panel, and you are presented with a blank stage. You are now in Edit mode for the new symbol, where you can draw, paste, or import content for your symbol.

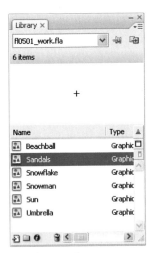

The Library now features your new sandals symbol.

6 Select Edit > Paste in Center to paste the sandals artwork from the clipboard onto the symbol's stage. This artwork is now included in your symbol, confirmed by the updated preview in the Library panel.

Paste the sandals onto the Stage in Edit mode.

7 Exit Edit mode by selecting the Scene 1 link below the Timeline.

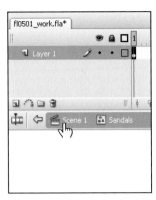

Select Scene 1 above the Stage to exit the symbol's Edit mode.

8 Choose File > Save to save your work.

You'll notice that the Create New Symbol dialog box didn't give you the option to specify a registration point. This is done when you paste, draw, or import artwork and position it relative to the crosshair in the symbol's Edit mode.

Whether you create blank symbols or convert existing artwork to symbols is completely up to you. Some designers prefer to have something tangible to work with before they create a symbol; others like to get symbols defined ahead of time.

Building artwork with symbol instances

With all the artwork added to the library as graphic symbols, you're ready to start building the layout for the banner advertisement. You'll find that working with symbols will be essential as the theme for your banner evolves. You'll soon discover how to easily place, swap, and update symbol instances to build and change the look and feel of your banner in a snap.

Positioning and snapping in symbol instances

To get the Spacey's ad banner started, you'll create a patterned background using some of your new symbols. The lesson is already sized and has visual guides to help you. To more accurately position symbols on the Stage, you'll use snapping. Snapping enables a magnet-like behavior, causing objects you move around the Stage to "snap" in place to guides, grids, or other objects when they are moved within a close-enough range of those objects.

1 Choose View > Snapping to open the Snapping submenu, and make sure the Snap to Grid and Snap to Guides options are checked.

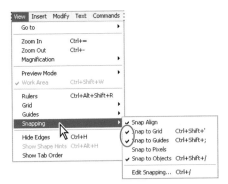

Set up your Snap options under View > Snapping.

2 Choose View > Grid > Show Grid to display the grid; in this document, it's set with the gridlines 50 pixels apart. You can store unique grid settings with each document.

3 Choose View > Guides > Show Guides. Vertical and horizontal guides appear, each one centered within the gridlines. These will help center and position symbols inside each box formed by the grid.

The visible grid and guides will help you align artwork on the Stage.

4 Choose Edit > Select All, and press Backspace (Windows) or Delete (Mac OS) to delete any existing symbol instances from the Stage. Now you have a clean start for the layout.

5   With the Library panel open, locate and drag an instance of the Snowflake symbol from the library onto the Stage.

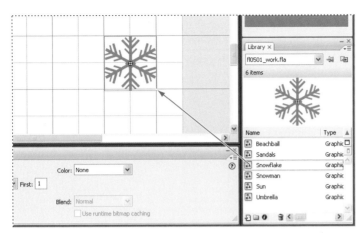

To place a symbol, drag it from the Library panel onto the Stage.

6   Using the snapping action behavior to help you, position the Snowflake symbol in the upper-left box.

7   To finish the background pattern, drag 12 more Snowflake instances onto the Stage. Place one in every other box checkerboard style, with the second row starting on the second box.

8   Choose File > Save to save your work.

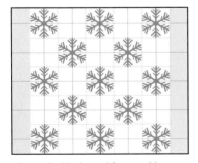

The completed background for your ad banner.

Editing and duplicating symbols

The beauty of working with symbols is that modifications to the master symbol automatically transfer to all instances throughout your movie. If you're not quite happy with the snowflake, for example, adjust it once and the entire background changes, because all symbol instances are linked. You can update symbols in two places: from the master symbol in the Library panel or from any instance of that symbol on the Stage. In this exercise you'll explore both methods.

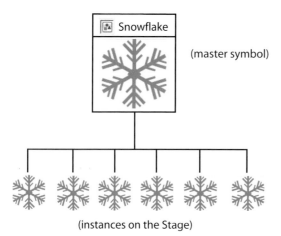

(master symbol)

(instances on the Stage)

A master symbol controls all its instances throughout a movie.

To edit a symbol directly from the Library panel:

1   Double-click the Snowflake symbol in the Library panel to enter the symbol's Edit mode.

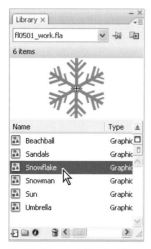

Double-click a symbol in the Library panel to edit it.

It now appears on the Stage in raw form, as it was before you added it to the library.

Inside the Snowflake symbol's Edit mode.

2 Select the snowflake with the Selection tool (k), if it is not already selected. From the Fill color swatch in the Tool panel, select the light blue color labeled #CCCCFF.

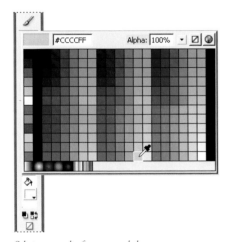

Select a new color for your symbol.

3   Exit the symbol's Edit mode by clicking the Scene 1 link below the Timeline. Flash returns you to the main stage. All 13 instances of the Snowflake symbol on the Stage should now reflect the color change that you applied.

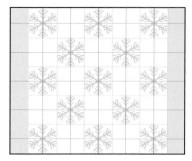

All snowflakes adopt changes made to the master symbol.

Editing symbols in place

The advantage to editing symbols directly from the Library panel is that you can focus on the symbol itself without the interference of other artwork on the Stage. Sometimes, however, you need to modify a symbol to better fit with the artwork surrounding it. In these cases, you can edit the symbol in-place on the Stage to see it in context as you make changes.

To edit a symbol in place on the Stage:

1   Double-click one of the Snowflake instances on the Stage. The other instances *dim out* because they are no longer selectable. The snowflake you chose, however, is editable as raw artwork, just as it was in the previous exercise.

2   In the Property inspector, enter **80** in both the width (W) and height (H) text fields to set the width and height of the snowflake to 80 pixels. Notice that changes also affect the dimmed instances that are visible in the background and that changing the size of the symbol affects its alignment relative to your grid. To compensate for this, use the Property inspector to set the X and Y positions of the graphic to **–40** each, which shifts the symbol instances enough to keep them in each of their respective grid boxes.

Reposition the snowflake symbol to compensate for its size change.

3 Exit the symbol's Edit mode by clicking the Scene 1 link above the Stage. Back on the main stage, you can see the changes you applied in context, exactly as you saw them when you were editing.

4 Choose File > Save to save your work.

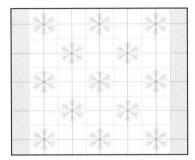

Edit in Place allows you to see a symbol in the context of other items onstage.

Modifying individual symbol instances

What if you don't want a whole new look, you just need to make a minor tweak to a single symbol instance? The link between the master symbol and its instances may seem constraining at times. The good news is that it doesn't have to be: Every instance of a symbol can be modified to take on its own color, dimensions, rotation, and transparency.

To resize or rotate a symbol instance, for example, select the instance on the Stage and use the Transform tool, Property inspector, or Transform panel. See how this works in your ad banner.

1 Using the Selection tool (⬉), select a single instance of your Snowflake symbol on the Stage, and choose Window > Transform to open the Transform panel, which allows you to enter exact values and resize and rotate a single instance of the Snowflake symbol.

2 In the Transform panel, make sure the Constrain option is checked, and enter **80%** in either the vertical or horizontal scaling boxes at the top of the pane. Press Enter (Windows) or Return (Mac OS).

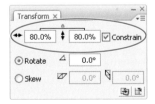

Resize and rotate a single instance of the Snowflake symbol.

3 Enter **45** in the Rotate text field to rotate your snowflake, then press the Enter (Windows) or Return (Mac OS) key to apply the transformations. This, combined with the scaling in step 2, creates a nice variation from the other instances on the Stage.

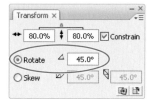

Set the rotation in degrees for the Snowflake symbol.

Modifying instance color

To modify the color of a symbol instance, you will use the Color drop-down menu on the Property inspector, which lets you create interesting variations by applying color tints, brightness, and transparency. Try it on one of the ad banner's Snowflake symbols:

1 Select the instance of the Snowflake on the upper-left corner of the Stage. Make sure the Property inspector is visible.

2 From the Color drop-down menu on the right side of the Property inspector, choose Tint. This will produce several options, including a color swatch and tint amount (percentage).

You can apply a unique color tint to any instance of a symbol using the Property inspector.

3 From the color swatch, choose a blue (to match the example, use #0066CC). Set the tint amount to 100% by using the slider or entering **100** in the tint percentage text field. The symbol instance is now a darker blue, leaving the other instances and the master symbol unaffected. As you see, you can achieve some creative variations among your snowflake instances without modifying the original symbol in the library.

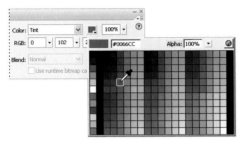

Choose a color and tint percentage with the Color menu's Tint option.

In the next exercise, you'll modify the background of your banner by changing the color and transparency of different symbol instances to create variety and texture.

Fine-tuning your background

You can take advantage of the unique characteristics that can be assigned to each symbol instance to add depth to your background. To make the snowflakes less obstructive to the type and additional artwork you'll add later, you can reduce the transparency (referred to as alpha) of all instances on the Stage. You can also use the Property inspector to apply varying color tints to selected instances.

1 Choose Edit > Select All to select all instances of the Snowflake symbol on the Stage.

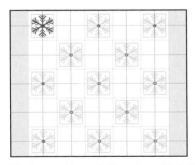

To select everything on the Stage, choose Edit > Select All.

2 On the right side of the Property inspector, select Alpha from the Color drop-down menu. The Alpha percentage and slider should appear, enabling you to set the transparency (in percent) of your symbols.

The Alpha option is found in the Color menu in the Property inspector.

3 Using the Alpha slider, change the transparency of the selected symbols to 40%. Or, if you prefer, enter **40** in the text field next to the slider. Notice that the symbols immediately become more transparent on the Stage.

Set the Alpha amount to 40% to decrease the opacity of the symbol instances.

4 Choose Edit > Deselect All. Select only the Snowflake instance in the lower-left corner. Adjust the Alpha setting on the Property inspector to 90% to darken this instance of the snowflake, setting it apart from the others.

Set the opacity amount to 90% to darken the instance and make it stand out.

Duplicating symbols

Sometimes a variation on a theme is the best way to explore other possible design ideas. Perhaps you want to apply changes to a symbol beyond simply color or size (for instance, changing its actual shape). Rather than make edits that compromise the original symbol, consider making a duplicate of the symbol in the Library panel. Duplicating makes an exact copy of a symbol, and the new copy becomes its own symbol that's not associated with the original. Try creating a variation on the Snowflake symbol by duplicating it in the Library panel and making changes to the new copy.

1   Select the Snowflake symbol in the Library panel.

2   Choose Duplicate from the Library panel's menu. The Duplicate Symbol dialog box appears, prompting you to rename the symbol and, if desired, change the symbol type.

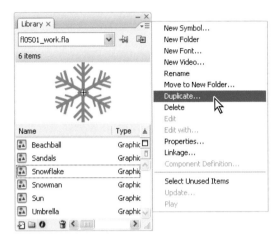

Duplicate the symbol through the Library panel's panel menu.

3   Name the symbol Snowflake 2. Leave the type as Graphic, and press OK. Flash adds the new symbol to the library. You can now use this symbol like any other, and it has no relationship to the original from which it was created.

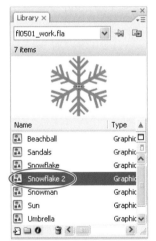

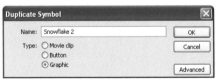

Snowflake 2 is a modified copy of the Snowflake symbol.

4 Double-click the new symbol in the Library panel to edit it. Add a different color, or use the Ink Bottle to apply an interesting outline (stroke) to it. Click on Scene 1 to exit the Edit mode for this symbol and return to the main stage. Notice that the modifications made to Snowflake 2 don't affect instances of the original Snowflake symbol on the Stage.

5 Choose File > Save to save your work.

Make some changes to distinguish Snowflake 2 from the original.

A duplicated symbol has no relationship to the symbol from which it was created. Modifications made to the duplicate will have no effect on the original or any of its instances. They are regarded as completely different symbols.

Adding graphics and text to your banner

With your background complete, you're ready to add the headline text and feature graphics to advertise your sale. For your feature graphic, you'll use the snowman drawing you added to the library earlier in the chapter. For the type, you'll use the Text tool and skills you learned in Lesson 3, "Getting Started with the Drawing Tools."

1 Drag a copy of the Snowman symbol from the Library panel onto the right side of the Stage.

2 If necessary, open the Property inspector by pressing Ctrl+F3 (Windows) or Command+F3 (Mac OS). Click the padlock icon (🔒) next to the X and Y fields to keep any adjustments to either the width or height proportional.

The Padlock icon keeps your symbol proportional.

3 Enter **350** in the H (height) field to resize the snowman. Enter **350** for the X position, and **300** for Y position.

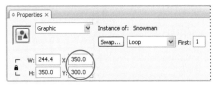

Use the Property inspector to reposition and resize the snowman.

4 Select the Text tool (T) on the Tools panel. Text-related options such as Font and Font size (in points) appear in the Property inspector. Choose Times New Roman (or equivalent) for the font, and enter **40** in the Font size text field (or use the slider). For now, set your type color to black using the Text (fill) color swatch.

Use the Text tool and the Property inspector to specify type options before creating it on the Stage.

5 Click on the left side of the stage, and type the words **SPACEY'S winter sale**, as shown below.

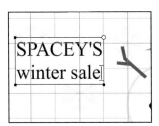

Type the words "SPACEY'S winter sale" on the Stage.

6 Use the Text tool to select only the words *winter sale* inside the text area.

7 In the Property inspector, set the color of the selected text to blue. To match the example, use the color labeled #336699. Click on the Italic button (also in the Property inspector) to change the style of the selected text to italics.

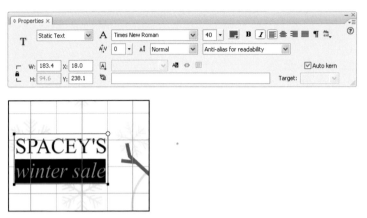

Use the Property inspector to fine-tune the color and style of the selected text.

Your banner should be complete for the winter sale; use View > Guides > Show Guides to toggle the guides off and View > Grid > Show Grid to hide your grid. Creating and using symbols in this lesson allowed you to place and modify as many instances as you needed to complete your layout. In the next exercise, you'll discover how symbols can streamline your creative process even further.

Your completed banner, constructed using symbol instances.

Swapping symbols

Sometimes when you think you're finished, you're not—requirements change, new products are introduced, or those bright ideas you had in a late-night design session look dim the next morning. Symbols make such revisions easier; instead of starting from scratch, use the Property inspector to swap any instance of a symbol with an instance of another symbol in the Library panel.

Consider your Spacey's winter sale banner, for example. If Spacey's wants a summer sale banner based on your successful winter design, you can easily reinvent your banner with a few quick symbol swaps.

1   Click once on the instance of the Snowflake symbol in the upper-left corner to select it. Make sure your Property inspector is visible.

2   Click the Swap button in your Property inspector. The Swap Symbol dialog box appears, displaying all the symbols currently in the library. The swap button lets you swap any symbol instance on the Stage with another symbol from the library.

Swap any symbol instance on the Stage with another symbol from the library.

3   Select the Beachball symbol from the list and press OK, or double-click the Beachball symbol. A beachball replaces the snowflake in the upper-left corner. Swapped symbols inherit position as well as transformations.

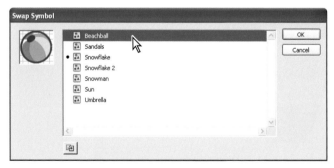

Select a different symbol from the library with which you can replace the current instance.

4   Repeat steps 1 through 3 for all remaining instances of the Snowflake symbol that appear in your background. If you'd like to change it up, try swapping some instances with the Sun or Umbrella symbols instead. Replacing each Snowflake instance with other symbols in the library changes the whole theme. The best part is that positioning and other unique properties applied to the Snowflake instances (such as Alpha) are maintained, even when a new symbol takes their place.

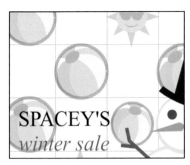

Swap out all the Snowflake instances.

5   Select the Snowman symbol on the Stage. This is currently your feature graphic, which you need to replace with something that matches the new theme.

6   Click the Swap button to open the Swap Symbol dialog box, and double-click the Sandals symbol in the list that appears. An instance of the Sandals symbol replaces the Snowman. There is no need to resize the sandals, because the new symbol instance inherits size properties from the previous one.

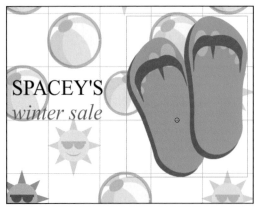

Away goes winter as you replace the Snowman with the Sandals symbol using the Swap button.

7   Select the Text tool (T) from the Tools panel, and select the words *winter sale* inside the text frame to edit them.

8 Replace the word *winter* by entering **summer**, and set the type color to orange (use #FF9900) using the Property inspector.

9 Press the Escape key to commit the text changes. Choose File > Save to save your work.

Your new summer sale banner.

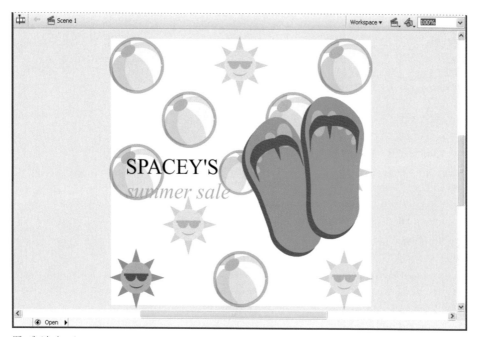

The finished project.

Swapping symbols is not only great for use for a single instance, but also can be taken further to change the feel of an entire movie or layout.

Managing the Library

As you use symbols more and more, you may find the Library panel getting a bit crowded. Even with the panel's sorting abilities, you'll definitely need to get a handle on things with a bit of organization. The Library panel features several ways to clean house and make sense of your assets.

Library panel options

As you've seen, the Library panel houses some additional features, and if you take a closer look at the Library panel, you'll see features that help organize, sort, and view your symbols and assets.

A. Library selector. B. Preview window. C. Properties. D. New Folder. E. New Symbol. F. Panel menu. G. New library panel. H. Pin current library. I. Column labels. J. Delete.

Library selector: Allows you to navigate through the libraries of all currently open documents.

Preview window: Displays your symbol so you can see what it looks like. This is helpful if you have symbols with vague or similar names.

Properties: Opens up the Symbol Properties dialog box for the currently highlighted symbol. From Symbol Properties you can switch the symbol's type or assign it a new name.

New Folder: Creates a folder in the Library panel into which symbols can be sorted. Folders can go several levels deep, making fine-tuned organization possible.

New Symbol: Creates a new symbol in the library and is the same command as Insert > New Symbol or New Symbol from the Library panel's menu.

Panel menu: This menu features additional options for working with symbols or modifying the display of the Library panel. This contains advanced options for linking symbols to ActionScript or setting up shared libraries.

New library panel: Opens a duplicate Library panel. Use this if you want to display libraries from multiple open documents at once, or to create several different views of the library you're working on.

Pin current library: Keeps the current library in view, even when switching between other open documents. The default behavior is for the Library panel to display the library for the currently active document only. This is useful if you'd like to copy symbols between movies and need to keep a previous library view available while you switch documents.

Column labels: Shown at the top of the library items list, these headers let you sort your symbols by Name, Type, Linkage, Last Modified Date, or Use Count. Click the column header to sort ascending (arrow points up) or descending (arrow points down).

Delete: Deletes the currently selected symbol from the library. Choose Select Unused Items from the panel menu to highlight items that are not currently used by your movie or another symbol in the library.

Organizing symbols with folders

Whether for papers in a file cabinet or files on your computer's hard drive, folders play an essential role in categorizing and organizing content. Flash's Library panel can use folders to organize symbols, sounds, and imported assets such as bitmap images and video.

You can create folders using the New Folder icon (🗀) or by choosing New Folder from the Library panel's menu. For very flexible organizational possibilities, you can also nest folders inside of other folders. Practice organizing your banner project's symbols.

1   Open the Library panel by selecting Window > Library, or pressing Ctrl+L (Windows) or Command+L (Mac OS).

2   Click the New Folder icon in the lower-left corner to create a new folder in the Library panel. In the highlighted text field next to the new folder icon, enter the phrase **Winter Graphics** to replace the default name, Untitled Folder 1. Press Enter/Return.

Add a new folder for sorting symbols.

3   Click and drag the Snowflake symbol into the new Winter Graphics folder. Flash sorts it into the folder, and in indented view, it appears indented under the new folder. Collapsed view will hide the sorted symbols within their folders.

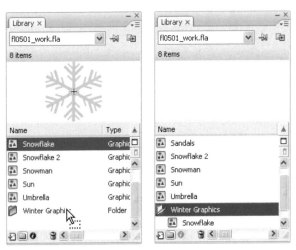

Drag symbols to sort them into folders.

4   Repeat step 3 to add the Snowman symbol to the Winter Graphics folder.

The Move to New Folder command

A convenient alternative to these steps is the Move to New Folder command under the Library panel menu. Move to New Folder creates, names, and moves any selected items to a new folder in one step. Sort the summer-themed graphics into a new folder to try it out.

1   Hold down the Ctrl key (Windows) or Command key (Mac OS), and select the Beachball, Sun, and Sandals symbols together.

2   Choose Move to New Folder from the Library panel's menu.

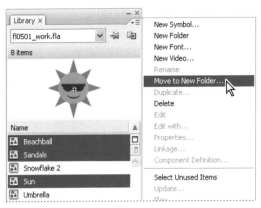

Move To Folder creates, names, and sorts selected items in the Library panel into a new folder.

3 Flash displays a prompt instructing you to assign a name to the new folder. Enter the name Summer Graphics in the field, and press OK. The selected symbols now appear inside a new folder.

*Name the new folder **Summer Graphics**.*

4 Double-click a folder, or use the Library panel menu's Collapse Folder option to hide the sorted symbols in the new folder.

5 Choose File > Save to save your work.

The Summer Graphics folder, shown collapsed.

Deleting items from the library

Over the life of a project, many symbols and assets may accumulate in the Library panel, some of which may not even be in use. If sorting your symbols is not enough to tackle this scenario, you can consider selecting and trashing unused items to eliminate clutter and reduce the size of your .fla file.

To ensure that you don't accidentally delete items that are active, use the Select Unused Items option, found in the Library panel's menu. This selects any items in the Library panel that are not currently in use by your movie.

Deleting unused symbols from the library is simple.

1   Open the Library panel, and choose Select Unused Items from its panel menu. Use this feature before you delete anything to avoid accidentally trashing items you need.

2   You should see the Umbrella, Snowflake, Snowflake 2, and Snowman symbols highlighted in the Library panel. Some of these symbols were never used; others, such as the Snowman, were retired when you changed the theme of your banner.

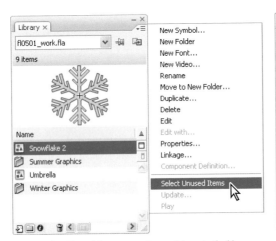 

Choose Select Unused Items to reveal unused items in the library.

3   Delete the selected symbols by clicking the Delete icon (🗑) at the bottom of the Library panel.

4   Choose File > Save to save your work, and choose File > Close to close the document.

Symbols that include other symbols create dependencies; one symbol can't be deleted without affecting the other. If a graphic symbol is composed of other graphic symbols, it requires those symbols to remain in one piece, like bricks that make up a wall. Always use the Delete Unused Items option to be sure; it accounts for symbols that are in use by other symbols.

Controlling library views

The Library panel's menu features some additional options you can use to adjust the appearance of contents in the library. If you combine this with the panel's sorting capabilities, managing and organizing the library will be easy, even with the most extensive Flash movies.

Collapsed and expanded views can be easily shown and hidden using the panel menu.

To expand all folders and view their contents, for example, choose Expand All Folders from the Library panel's menu. To expand a single folder, select a folder and choose Expand Folder from the panel menu or double-click the folder.

To collapse all folders and hide their contents, choose Collapse All Folders from the Library panel's menu. To collapse a single folder, select a folder and choose Collapse Folder from the panel menu or double-click the folder.

Wrapping up

In this lesson, you've learned about the power of symbols, and how you can reuse, swap, and easily update artwork used throughout your movie. As you'll see in later lessons, symbols also play an essential role in creating animation and adding interactivity in the form of buttons and movie clips.

Self study

Create new artwork in a fresh Flash file, and convert it to one or more graphic symbols. Use the new symbols to create a layout, and use the swap technique to substitute one symbol for another. Experiment with a variety of color and transformation modifications with each instance.

Review

Questions

1 What are the three symbol types that Flash supports?

2 True or False: You cannot modify the color or size of a symbol instance without changing all other instances of that same symbol.

3 What behavior allows objects on the Stage to magnetically move toward each other or toward visual aids in the work area?

Answers

1 Graphics, Buttons, and movie clips.

2 False. Each instance of a symbol on the Stage can have unique transformation, scaling, or color effects applied.

3 Snapping. This behavior can be fine-tuned or enabled/disabled by choosing View > Snapping.

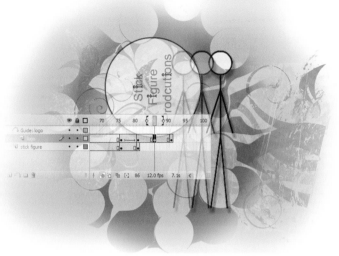

What you'll learn in this lesson:

- Using the Timeline
- Understanding the difference between frames and keyframes
- Setting up frame-by-frame animation
- Taking advantage of tweening
- Using motion guides
- Testing your movie

Creating Basic Animation

Adobe Flash is widely regarded as the tool of choice for animation for the Web. With its ability to manipulate graphics in a variety of ways, the possibilities are endless when it comes to creating exciting, eye-catching animations for your projects.

Starting up

Before starting, make sure that your tools and panels are consistent by resetting your workspace. See "Resetting the Flash workspace" on page 3.

You will work with several files from the fl06lessons folder in this lesson. Make sure that you have loaded the fl06lessons folder onto your hard drive from the supplied DVD. See "Loading lesson files" on page 3.

See Lesson 6 in action!

Use the accompanying video to gain a better understanding of how to use some of the features shown in this lesson. Open the DynamicLearning_FlashCS3.swf file located in the Videos folder and select Lesson 6 to view the video training file for this lesson.

The project

To see a completed example of the animated web banner you'll be creating, launch Flash and open the fl0601_done.swf file. Close the Flash Player and return to Flash CS3 Professional when you're done.

A look at the Timeline

Your primary workspace in Flash is the Timeline, which consists of two main areas: layers and frames. Layers allow you to organize your graphics, text, and symbols separately from one another, thereby giving you greater control over your project elements. Frames and keyframes allow you to designate when, and how long, graphics and animation are visible on the Stage in your movie. Creating a new project is a good way to examine the Timeline, so give it a try.

1   Choose File > New and, in the resulting New Document dialog box, select the tab marked Templates. You'll find a number of templates that you can modify to suit your needs.

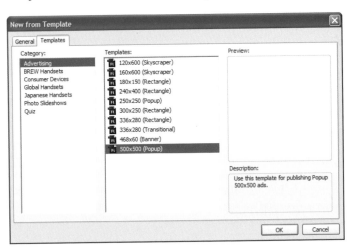

You can construct a project from built-in Flash templates.

2   From the Advertising category, select the 500x500 (Popup) template, and press OK. The new document and your workspace appear. The Timeline sits above the Stage at the top of the screen.

You can also access the Timeline by choosing Window > Timeline.

3 To see the properties of a layer, double-click on the Layer icon (⟋) to the left of the layer named Content. From the resulting Layer Properties dialog box, you can rename the selected layer, change the type of layer it is, and more. Press Cancel, as you'll be renaming this layer a bit later.

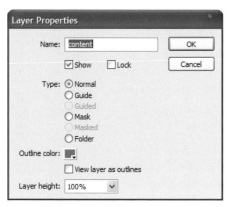

The Layer Properties dialog box.

4 You can magnify the view of the frames to see them at a larger size or to see more of them at a time. Click the Panel menu (·≡) button at the top-right corner of the Timeline. From this menu, you can magnify the Timeline to display the frames at different sizes. You also have the option of determining where the Timeline is located in proportion to the Stage by making a selection from the Placement options.

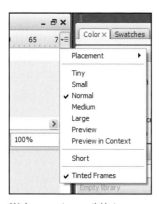

Workspace options available in the Timeline's Panel menu.

Importing a library

One of the benefits of using Flash is the ability to share collections of resources—images, sounds, symbols, and video files—between different projects. These collections are organized and stored in libraries and managed with the Library panel. You can compile your own library of elements, or you can import libraries from coworkers, earlier projects, or other sources.

To access the graphics you'll be animating for your Web banner, you need to open a pre-assembled library.

1   Choose File > Import > Open External Library.

Access the Open External Library option through the File menu.

2   Open the fl06lessons folder, select the fl06_library.fla file, and press Open. A new Library panel opens as a floating window. Drag the new Library panel into the Library panel on the right side of the screen.

3   Click and select the various items in the newly opened Library panel to preview them. You'll be setting some of these in motion in the next exercise.

4   Save your file by choosing File > Save As. Navigate to the fl06lessons folder and type **fl0601_work.fla** in the name text field. Press Save. A warning may appear indicating that you are converting a Flash 8 or older document to Flash CS3 format, press Save.

To learn more about working with libraries and the Library panel, see Lesson 5, "Using Symbols and the Library."

Building your frame-by-frame animation

For this project, you'll animate a stick figure running away from a persistent company logo. Organization is essential for using Flash efficiently. Taking a little time to label things clearly and arrange your workspace can save you a lot of time down the road.

Organizing the Timeline

Before you start to animate, you'll change a layer name and the size of the Stage so you can more easily see what's going on.

1 Double-click on the layer name content. In the text field that appears, rename the layer **stick figure,** and press Enter (Windows) or Return (Mac OS) to commit the change. In trying to be descriptive, sometimes you can end up with layer names so long that they run out of space and get cut off in the Timeline. Next, you will fix this.

Remember, another way to rename a layer is to open the Layer Properties dialog box by double-clicking the Layer icon (⤵) next to the layer name.

2 Move your cursor to the line that separates the layers and frames; the cursor changes to a double arrow. Click and drag the line to the right to expand the amount of room for the layer area of the Timeline.

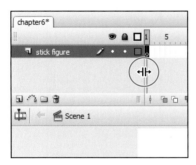

The double-arrow cursor helps you customize the Timeline.

3 To change the size of the Stage overall, click on the Magnification menu in the upper-right corner of the Stage and choose Fit in Window. For more precision, you can type a percentage in the window instead.

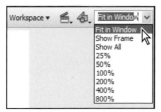

The Magnification menu adjusts the size of the Stage.

First steps to animation: placing elements

Now that you have the resources you need, you're done organizing. It's time to put the stick figure on the Stage to get him ready to run.

1 Open the Library panel and drag the graphic symbol item named stick still 1 from the panel to the Stage. Using the Selection tool (↖), select and move the stick figure to the right side of the Stage. Now, you'll add the logo that will chase the stick figure around.

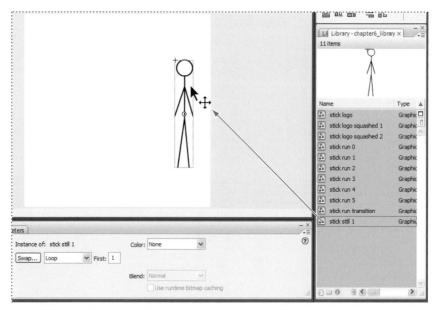

Drag and drop an instance of stick still 1 from the Library panel onto the Stage.

2 Add a new layer by clicking the Insert Layer button (⊐|) at the bottom-left corner of the layer area of the Timeline. Double-click the title area of your new layer to edit it, and rename the layer **logo**.

*Rename your new layer **logo**.*

3 Keep the logo layer selected. Drag an instance of the graphic symbol named stick logo from the Library panel to the left side of your Stage.

Remember to keep an eye on which layer you have selected. When placing items on the Stage, they end up on this layer.

4 The starting point of each image needs to be established; this is the first thing people will see when they view the banner. Because it starts its movement offstage, drag your circle (stick logo) to the gray work area. If you want to be precise, you can enter the desired position of the stick logo symbol using the X and Y values in the Property inspector. In the example, the stick logo symbol is placed at X: −122.7, Y: 296.1.

Understanding frames and keyframes

The stick figure is alone on the Stage to start the animation, then the logo suddenly rolls onto the Stage to chase him. At the moment, however, the stick figure is on the Stage for one frame only—not much time to build tension. You need to give the figure more time onstage before the chase begins.

The Timeline is composed of frames that move from left to right; each frame represents a different point in time. To have an object appear (or disappear) at a specific point in time, you'll need to place it in a special type of frame known as a keyframe. Keyframes are created at specific points along the Timeline where something significant needs to happen, such as the appearance of an object or the beginning or end of an animation sequence.

Frames can be added to extend keyframes, and in turn specify how long an object stays on the Stage. By default, each new layer is created with a single keyframe on Frame 1. In this exercise, you'll add frames to give the stick figure more stage time before the chase begins.

1   On the Timeline, click and select Frame 10 of the stick figure layer, and choose Insert > Timeline > Frame. Notice that the length of the stick figure layer is now ten frames. This ten-frame span gives the stick figure a little time to breathe before he has to make a run for it.

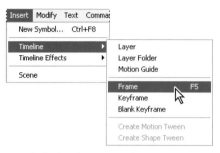

Extend a keyframe by inserting a frame.

 To add frames, you can also right-click (Windows) or Ctrl+click (Mac OS) in a frame and choose Insert Frame.

2   You don't need the logo to show up until Frame 10, but currently it's on Frame 1. You'll need to change the point at which the logo appears by moving the keyframe it's on.

 Each layer starts with a blank keyframe, which is a keyframe with no graphics or information placed on it. When you start to add graphics to the Stage, the blank keyframe changes to a regular keyframe. Blank keyframes are represented by a hollow circle (○), and regular keyframes are represented by a filled black circle (•).

3   Click and select the keyframe in Frame 1 of the logo layer. Keep your mouse pointer over the keyframe until you see a small box below your pointer. Click and hold down the mouse button, then drag the keyframe to Frame 10. The logo is ready to roll onto the Stage to start chasing the stick figure, but it's on the last frame of the animation. Both the stick figure's and the logo's layers need more frames to keep them onstage longer.

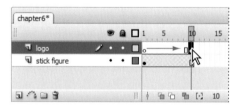

Click and drag to move a keyframe.

4 You can add frames to multiple layers at once to save time: select Frame 20 of the logo layer, then hold down Shift and select Frame 20 of the stick figure layer. With both layers selected, choose Insert > Timeline > Frame.

As an alternative to holding the Shift key, you can click and drag through multiple layer frames to select more than one at a time.

The key to keyframes

Used for animation in many programs, keyframes indicate change over time. You can use keyframes to animate properties such as position, rotation, color, and size. You can also use keyframes in conjunction with tweening, Flash's built-in method of creating animation automatically from little more than starting and ending keyframes.

With motion tweening, you specify an element's position on the starting and ending keyframes. Flash then automatically creates the frames in between, freeing you from having to animate every single frame by hand. In addition to starting and ending keyframes, motion tweens require the use of two instances of the same symbol. Note that motion tweens can't work with raw graphics, drawing objects, or unmatched symbol instances.

You'll use keyframes and then a motion tween to get the logo moving toward the stick figure.

1 On the Timeline, select Frame 20 of the logo layer.

2 Choose Insert > Timeline > Keyframe. This creates a new keyframe that contains another instance of the stick logo symbol. By default, Flash always copies the contents of the preceding keyframe to any new keyframe on the same layer.

3 With the keyframe at Frame 20 still selected, drag the instance of the stick logo and place it near the stick figure.

4 Press Enter (Windows) or Return (Mac OS) to play back the Timeline so far; the logo suddenly jumps from one spot to another when the playhead reaches Frame 20.

5 Select the keyframe at Frame 10 of the logo layer. In the Property inspector, click the Tween drop-down menu and select Motion. In the Timeline, you'll see an arrow and a shaded area between the two keyframes in the logo layer. The arrow indicates that a successful tween has been created between Frames 10 and 20.

Select Motion from the Tween drop-down menu in the Property inspector.

6 Press the Enter (Windows) or Return (Mac OS) key to play back the Timeline. You'll see the logo now slides to its spot near the stick figure instead of just popping in.

7 Select the keyframe at Frame 10 (where your tween begins) and note the new options available in the Property inspector. After you add a tween, Flash automatically adds controls that allow you to further enhance your animations. In the next exercise, you'll use a number of these controls to modify how the logo moves on the Stage.

With a tween selected, the Property inspector allows you to fine-tune and enhance your animation.

Ease In, Ease Out, and Rotate

Even if you're not aiming for a highly stylized animation, you generally want your objects to move the way things would move in real life. For example, if you're working with a graphic or symbol that's circular, you might want it to roll like a wheel. The pacing of the movement also has an impact, as objects in the real world rarely move at a constant speed. You might want an object to speed up or slow down while it's moving. Adjusting the Property inspector's Ease In and Ease Out values is a simple way to give your animated objects a more natural feel when they're moving onstage.

You'll modify both the pacing and rotation of the logo animation to make it look more like a wheel rolling into place and then stopping. Let's start with the pacing of the movement:

1 Select the keyframe at Frame 10 of the logo layer, where your tween begins.

2 Select the Ease option in the Property inspector and drag the slider up until the value reads 100 and the word "out" appears next to the menu.

Drag the Ease slider in the Property inspector up to 100.

3 Press Enter (Windows) or Return (Mac OS) to preview the animation. Notice how the logo moves onstage and gradually slows down just before it stops by the stick figure—a much more natural movement.

4 If it's not still selected, select the keyframe at Frame 10 of the logo layer.

5 In the Property inspector, click the Rotate drop-down menu and choose CW (as in clockwise). This option allows you to set a rotation direction.

Set the Rotate option to CW.

6 Once again, press Enter (Windows) or Return (Mac OS) to preview the animation. The logo now rolls into place instead of sliding across the Stage.

 A positive (1 to 100) Ease value slows an animation down as it reaches its end. In contrast, a negative (-1 to -100) value slows the animation down at the beginning so it picks up speed toward the end.

7 Select the keyframe at Frame 10 of the logo layer and take note of the text-entry box next to the Rotate menu in the Property inspector. The value of 1 prompts the logo to rotate once. To increase the number of times the image rotates between keyframes, type a higher value in the box.

8 Choose File > Save to save your file.

Testing with Test Movie

Up until now you've been viewing your animation within Flash, which is acceptable but not always the best representation of your final movie. The Flash preview can play a bit slowly and sometimes stutter, especially if your project is complex. To see a more accurate preview of your movie, you can use the Test Movie command, which exports a finished .swf file of your current movie and displays it immediately in the Flash Player.

Since your end users will always view your finished movie in the Flash Player (via their Web browser or desktop), this lets you see how your work truly performs.

1 Choose Control > Test Movie. Flash exports your movie, and opens it in Flash Player.

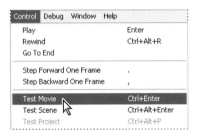

Preview you movie by choosing Control > Test Movie.

2 In the Flash Player window, open the Control menu to see the options for stopping, rewinding, and playing your movie.

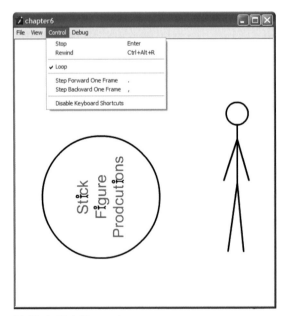

Modify the Flash Player settings.

3 Close the Flash Player window and return to Flash.

The Flash Player preview is the real deal; with accurate playback speeds, what you see is what your viewers will see. Preview your project at different points with Test Movie if you have a lot of animation and you need an accurate idea of how things will move when you're finished.

Frame-by-frame animation versus tweening

Flash offers two methods to animate your objects: frame-by-frame and tweening. Which method is "best" boils down to what you're trying to achieve visually. Although tweening is well-suited for sliding objects from one location to another (like the project's rolling logo), it's not going to work for the running stick figure. Frame-by-frame animation usually yields better results for complex motion such as walking and talking. When creating a frame-by-frame animation, you must design graphics at different points of movement to create the appearance of motion you're trying to simulate. Understanding the type of movement you want to achieve helps define your method of animation.

For the next part of the project, you'll work with both styles of animation, matching the proper style with the task at hand.

Timing and Onion Skins

Timing is a crucial element in animation. As the one creating the project, you know what's about to happen, but your audience needs time to view and absorb what's going on. To help them, you'll add some pauses to the animation rather than just generating a continuous stream of movement.

To figure out where pauses would be most effective and how the action should progress, create a storyboard. Rough out your animation on paper before you get into Flash. Not only does this help you to flush out the design, but it also give you an idea of the prep work required before you can animate. Storyboarding the example project reveals that you'll need graphics of the stick figure in various running positions. They're waiting in the library. You'll put those poses to work now, using the frame-by-frame method.

1 Shift+click Frame 25 on both layers of the Timeline and choose Insert > Timeline > Keyframe to insert a brief pause before the chase begins.

2 Select Frame 26 of the stick figure layer, and choose Insert > Timeline > Blank Keyframe. The blank keyframe contains no information; it acts as a placeholder where you can add content later on. Right now, however, you can't see any graphics, including the position of the stick figure that you placed on the Stage earlier. The next step provides a solution.

3   Press the Onion Skin button (🗃) on the Timeline to turn on Onion Skin view, which lets you reveal the contents of multiple frames at once and see how your graphics are placed in conjunction with other objects already on the Stage. By showing you what you're doing relative to what you've done, Onion Skin view can help you consistently place your artwork while building a frame-by-frame sequence.

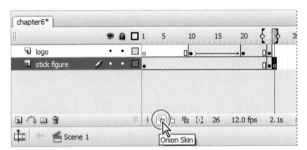

The Onion Skin feature allows you to see more than one frame image at a time.

4   With Frame 26 selected, examine the Timeline. Although Frame 26 itself is empty, you can still see the logo and the stick figure. Notice the frame number display in the Timeline. The brackets on the frame ruler by the number 25 indicate the frame range of the Onion Skin. Any images within the frame range of the Onion Skin are displayed onstage with a slight transparency. You can click and drag the left and right range brackets to extend or reduce the number of viewable frames. Note that you cannot drag the right bracket farther than the last available keyframe on the Timeline.

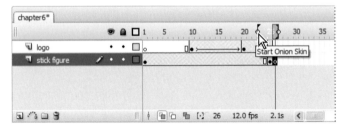

The Onion Skin's frame range selector.

5 With Frame 26 of the stick figure layer selected, drag an instance of the stick run 0 symbol from the Library panel to the Stage. Position it to the right of the original stick figure.

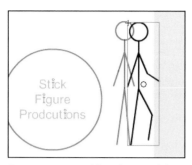

Position an instance of the stick run symbol
next to the original stick figure.

6 Select Frame 27 of the stick figure layer, and choose Insert > Timeline > Blank Keyframe.

The Onion Skin range may change when new frames are entered in the Timeline. You may have to readjust the range of the Onion Skin to accommodate your needs.

7 Drag an instance of the stick run 1 symbol from the Library panel, and place it on Frame 27 to the right of stick run 0 (the stick figure before it) and halfway offstage. Choose Control > Test Movie to preview your work and you'll see your runner in motion—your first frame-by-frame animation.

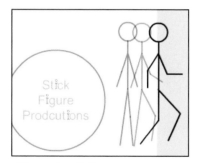

Animating frame by frame.

Combining tweening with frame-by-frame animation

In this exercise, you'll practice what you've learned so far by combining frame-by-frame animation and tweening. The goal is to make the logo follow the stick figure offstage. You can deselect the Onion Skin button, if you like; you won't need it for this exercise.

1   Select Frame 27 of the logo layer, and choose Insert > Timeline > Keyframe to insert a keyframe.

2   Select Frame 32 of the logo layer, and insert a second keyframe.

3   On Frame 32, drag the instance of the logo to the gray work area on the right.

Holding down the Shift key as you drag an image constrains the movement to a straight line and keeps the image moving in a consistent direction rather than drifting slightly diagonally.

4   Select the keyframe at Frame 27 of the logo layer.

    In the Property inspector, choose Motion from the Tween menu.

To create a tween, you can also Right-click (Windows) or Ctrl+click (Mac OS) in the frame and choose Create Motion Tween from the contextual menu.

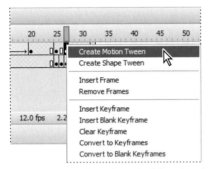

Access the contextual menu by Right-clicking (Windows)
or Ctrl+clicking (Mac OS).

5   With Frame 27 of the logo layer still selected, in the Property inspector, set the Ease value to –100 by clicking its slider and moving it all the way down. This sets the logo's motion to start slowly and then pick up speed.

6   Also in the Property inspector, choose CW from the Rotate drop-down menu so the logo rolls counter clockwise off the Stage.

7   Choose File > Save to save the latest changes to your work.

8   Choose Control > Test Movie to preview the animation. Close the Flash Player when you're finished previewing and return to Flash.

Transforming graphics

You can change the size and shape of graphics very easily in Flash. Since all artwork created within Flash is vector-based, you have lots of flexibility to transform graphics without such side effects as pixellation and jagged edges. In addition, Flash's transformation tools enable you to scale, rotate, and skew images. Using keyframes and tweens, you can make these transformations happen over a series of frames, taking your animation to a whole new level.

Scaling the size of an element is one way to establish distance. In this exercise, you'll change the size of the stick figure and the logo to make both appear as if they've moved away from the viewer.

1   Select Frame 28 of the stick figure layer, and choose Insert > Timeline > Blank Keyframe. You'll add a range of blank keyframes to the Timeline so that you can start to add fresh graphics to your project rather than extending the duration of the other items already in the Timeline.

2   While holding down the Shift key, select Frame 33 on both layers, and choose Insert > Timeline > Blank Keyframe to insert another blank keyframe.

Insert blank keyframes on both layers.

3   Select Frame 33 of the stick figure layer, and drag stick run 2 from the Library panel onto the Stage.

4   Choose Modify > Transform > Flip Horizontal to change the direction in which the stick figure is running.

Choose Transform > Flip Horizontal from the Modify menu.

5   Re-select the stick figure on the Stage, if necessary. Choose Modify > Transform > Scale and Rotate. In the Scale field, enter **35** to scale the figure to 35% of its original size and press OK.

6   Position the stick figure toward the top-right corner of the Stage.

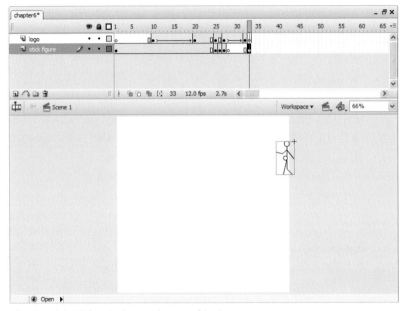

Place the scaled stick figure in the top-right corner of the Stage.

Streamline your methodology

Parts of the animation process can be very repetitive, so learning keyboard shortcuts can be a time-saver. The more you work with shortcuts, the more you'll refine your techniques—you may even begin to wonder how you made progress without them. As you continue to run the stick figure across the Stage with frame-by-frame animation, practice your shortcuts.

To customize the keyboard shortcuts to your own style, choose Edit > Keyboard Shortcuts. For more information, see Lesson 8, "Customizing Your Workflow."

1   Click the Onion Skin button (🖼) below the Timeline to enable it if it's not already active; you'll use it to determine proper positioning as you create your animation.

2   Right-click (Windows) or Ctrl+click (Mac OS) Frame 34 of the stick figure layer, and choose Insert Blank Keyframe from the contextual menu, or use the keyboard shortcut F7.

3   Drag an instance of the stick run 1 symbol from the Library panel to the Stage, and choose Modify > Transform > Flip Horizontal.

4 Press Ctrl+Alt+S (Windows) or Command+Option+S (Mac OS) to open the Scale and Rotate dialog box.

5 Confirm that Flash saved the Scale value from the last time you opened this window (it should read 35), and press OK.

6 Using Onion Skin view, position the new stick figure to the left of the instance in Frame 33.

Use Onion Skin view to position the stick figure in Frame 34.

7 Starting with Frame 35 in the stick figure layer, repeat steps 2 through 6, placing an instance of stick run transition in the next frame, followed by stick run 2, stick run transition again, then stick run 3.

Putting each one in its own blank frame, continue cycling through the numbered figures in the Library panel, with each one separated by one frame of stick run transition, until the stick figure is finished running from one side of the Stage to the other. Be sure to make the stick figure run completely offstage into the work area.

While you're placing your stick figures, take note of the X and Y values in the Property inspector. Each stick figure should have a different X value (horizontal position on-screen) but the same Y value, to ensure that the animation moves in a straight line across the Stage.

Use the Property inspector to maintain a consistent vertical position for all of the stick figures.

The stick run transition image was drawn as a transitional image to be used between the other running images. If you examine the other images, you'll see that each is in a different state of running. This image acts as a bridge from one running image to the next to keep the movement looking smooth.

When finished, the Timeline should look similar to the Timeline below.

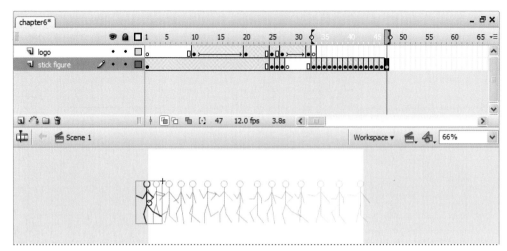

The succession of stick figure instances as seen in the Onion Skin view.

The number of frames you need to finish the animation may vary from the example. We used a total of 15 frames, starting at Frame 33 and ending at Frame 47.

8 Choose File > Save to save your animation. Press Ctrl+Enter (Windows) or Command+Return (Mac OS) to test the movie. Close Flash Player and return to Flash when you're finished previewing the animation.

Motion guides

Because the logo is circular, logically it might move like a wheel or a ball. The logo is already rolling to start things off, but what if you wanted it to bounce after the stick figure?

One very effective way of animating an object along a path that has a specific shape is through the use of motion guides.

A motion guide is a special type of layer that allows you to set a specific path for a motion tween to follow. By default, motion tweens create a linear path of motion. You can change this behavior by creating your own path with the drawing tools and placing it on a motion guide layer.

To make the logo appear to bounce after the stick figure, you'll draw the bounce path first and then convert it into a motion guide for the logo to travel along.

1 Select the logo layer, and click the Add Motion Guide button ( ) below the Timeline. A new layer appears above the logo layer with a special icon; you'll create a path on this guide layer that the tween on your logo layer will follow.

Guide layers are not exported with your final movie and don't appear anywhere other than in the Flash authoring environment.

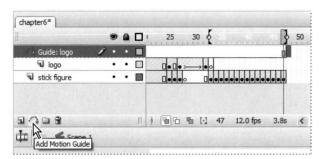

Create a guide layer above the logo layer.

2 Right-click (Windows) or Ctrl+click (Mac OS) Frame 48 of the guide layer and insert a blank keyframe.

3 Select the Pencil tool ( ) in the Tools panel. From the options at the bottom of the Tools panel, set the mode to Smooth. Make sure you choose a stroke color (at the bottom of the Tools panel) before you begin drawing.

Smooth a path after it's been drawn.

4 With Frame 48 of the guide layer selected, draw a path that portrays a bouncing motion for a ball. Start drawing in the work area to the right and continue it across the Stage.

Don't worry if the bouncing ball path that you drew isn't as smooth as you'd like it. After you draw the path, double-click the path with the Selection tool to select it. Repeatedly click the Smooth button (at the bottom of the Tools panel) to smooth the path out.

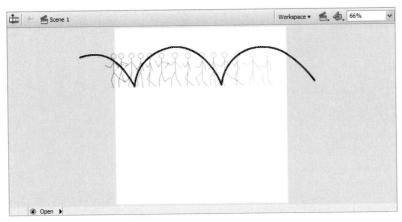

The path guides the movement of the image.

5 Right-click (Windows) or Ctrl+click (Mac OS) Frame 48 of the logo layer and insert a blank keyframe.

6 Drag an instance of the stick logo from the Library panel onto the Stage and with the instance selected, press Ctrl+Alt+S (Windows) or Command+Option+S (Mac OS) to open the Scale and Rotate dialog box. Check that the Scale value is still at 35% and press OK.

7 Choose View > Snapping > Snap to Objects. If it's not already selected, select the instance of the stick logo you just placed. Drag the logo by its center point to the start of the path you drew (at the right side of the screen). Make sure the center of the logo lines up with the very end of the path—when it does, you should see it snap into place on the end of the line.

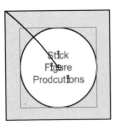

Drag the logo until it snaps into place at the end of the line.

8 Insert a new keyframe on Frame 60 of both the guide layer and the logo layer, by choosing Insert > Timeline > Keyframe.

9 Select the keyframe at Frame 60 of the logo layer. With the Selection tool (↖), select the logo on the Stage and drag it to the other end of the bouncing path. Line up the logo's center with the other end of the path.

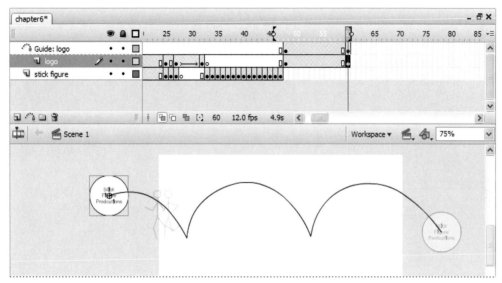

On Frame 60, drag the logo until it snaps to the other end of your guide.

10 Right-click (Windows) or Ctrl+click (Mac OS) the keyframe at Frame 48 of the logo layer and choose Create Motion Tween from the contextual menu.

11 Choose Control > Test Movie to preview the animation. The logo should move along the bouncing path. If the logo is not following the path, return to the starting and ending keyframes of your tween, where you aligned the logo with the path. Magnify the view and make sure that the center point of the logo is lined up with the very end of the path.

Final animation steps

In these last exercises, you'll finish animating the stick figure and spice up the logo to finish your movie.

The stick figure will make one last run, only to find that his fate is sealed. The logo will appear once more and cycle through some colors as text appears. Animating color is an effective way to grab a viewer's attention. Finally, the company's tagline will appear onstage.

To finish the figure animation:

1 Add a blank keyframe to Frames 48 and 61 of the stick figure layer.

2 If it's not already selected, select the blank keyframe at Frame 61 and drag an instance of the stick run 3 symbol from the Library panel onto the Stage.

3 Press Ctrl+Alt+S (Windows) or Command+Option+S (Mac OS). In the Scale and Rotate dialog box, set the Scale to **60%**, and press OK.

4 Position the stick figure on the left side of the Stage, half onstage, half in the work area.

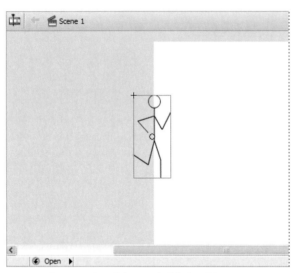

In Frame 61, position the stick figure at the left edge of the Stage.

5 Insert a blank keyframe in Frame 62 of the stick figure layer. Select one of the stick run symbols from the Library panel (stick run 0 – 5) and drag an instance of it to the Stage.

6 Press Ctrl+Alt+S (Windows) or Command+Option+S (Mac OS) to scale the new stick figure; leave the value for Scale at 60%, and press OK.

7 If it's not already enabled, press the Onion Skin button (⊕) below the Timeline. As you saw earlier, the Onion Skin view helps you to position sequential frames of animation.

Set the stick figure instance slightly to the right of the one on Frame 61. Don't forget about the Y value in the Property inspector; make sure it is consistent from stick figure to stick figure to ensure movement in a consistent direction.

8   Repeat steps 5 through 7 until the stick figure reaches the middle of the Stage. Insert one more blank keyframe and drag an instance of stick still 1 from the Library panel onto the Stage to finish the sequence.

Add an instance of stick still 1 to complete the sequence.

9   Insert a frame at Frame 75 of the stick figure layer to create a pause.

10 Preview the animation by pressing Ctrl+Enter (Windows) or Command+Return (Mac OS). This key combination is the same as choosing Control > Test Movie. Close the Flash Player and return to Flash.

The logo catches up

The stick figure is finished running, so now it's time for the logo to return. You'll bring the logo back in and animate it so that it finally catches the stick figure by landing on top of it.

1   Start by inserting two blank keyframes on the logo layer, one on Frame 61, the other on Frame 76.

2   On the stick figure layer, insert a keyframe on Frame 76 and a blank keyframe on Frame 81.

3   If you disabled Onion Skin view, click the Onion Skin button (⊞) back on so you can see the position of the stick figure on the Stage.

4   With the keyframe on Frame 81 of the stick figure layer selected, drag an instance of the stick squashed symbol from the Library panel and place it on the Stage. You'll want to position it in the same area as the stick figure in Frame 75.

5   Scale the stick squashed instance by pressing Ctrl+Alt+S (Windows) or Command+Option+S (Mac OS). Leave the scale value at 60%, and press OK.

6   Select the Free Transform tool (⊠) in the Tools panel.

7   Move your pointer above the upper-left corner of the instance and look for the curved arrow (↻). When you see it, click and drag to rotate the stick figure so it looks like it's lying flat on the floor. Position the stick figure as shown in the figure below.

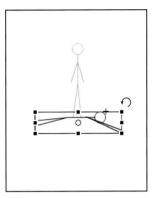

Rotate the stick figure to a lying position.

8 Switch to the Selection tool (⬚) and select the blank keyframe on Frame 76 of the logo layer. Drag an instance of the stick logo symbol from the Library panel and place it on the Stage.

9 Press Ctrl+Alt+S (Windows) or Command+Option+S (Mac OS) to open the Scale and Rotate panel. Scale the logo to **60%** and press OK.

Position the stick logo instance in the work area offstage above where the stick figure is standing. You may need to set the magnification of the Stage to 50% so you can see more of the work area.

Position the scaled logo offstage above the stick figure.

10 Select Frame 81 of the logo layer, and insert a keyframe. Drag the instance of the stick logo down on this frame so it looks like it's sitting on top of the stick figure.

You can use the arrow keys on your keyboard to nudge elements on the Stage into more exact positions.

11   Select the keyframe on Frame 76 of the logo layer, and choose Motion from the tween menu on the Property inspector to create a motion tween.

12   Save your work and choose Control > Test Movie to preview the animation.

Animating color

Animated color will put the finishing touch on the logo. In addition to motion, color is a great way to get someone's attention. Remember that color is one of the properties of a symbol instance (along with position, rotation, scale, and skew) that can be animated.

You're going to tween the color of the logo to make it cycle through some shades and then return to its original state.

1   Insert a keyframe on both Frame 86 and Frame 91 of the logo layer.

2   Select the keyframe on Frame 86, then select the instance of the stick logo on the Stage.

3   In the Property inspector, select Tint from the Color menu on the right. To the right of Tint, click the swatch to pick a color from the Swatches panel (the example uses red), and set the Tint amount to **50**% using the slider.

Add some color to the stick logo with a tint.

4 Because you want the color to cycle to the tint and then back to the original color, you need two tweens: one to start and one to end the process. Re-select the keyframe at Frame 86, and create a motion tween. Select the keyframe at Frame 81, and insert another motion tween.

5 Choose File > Save to save your work, and choose Control > Test Movie to preview your movie.

Animating text

In addition to adding and animating the text of the company's tagline, in this final exercise you'll extend the existing layers so that your movie lasts just a bit longer.

Don't forget to keep images onstage long enough for the audience to digest what's going on. Designers can commonly make the mistake of designing for themselves without considering the audience.

1 While holding down the Shift key, select Frame 115 on both the logo layer and the stick figure layer, and choose Insert > Timeline > Frame. This extends the duration of both layers.

Disable Onion Skin view if it's still turned on; you won't need it past this point.

2 Create a new layer by clicking the Insert Layer button (⬒) in the Timeline. Double-click the layer title to edit it, and rename the layer **text**. Drag it to the top of the layer stack.

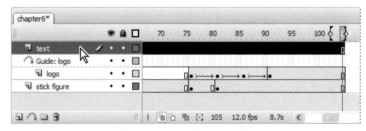

*Name the new layer **text** and drag it to the top of the layer stack.*

3 Insert a blank keyframe on Frame 91 of the Text layer.

4 Select the Text tool (T) in the Tools panel. Click on the Stage below the stick figure and logo, and type **web design and animation**. Switch to the Selection tool (▸).

5 With the new text box selected, use the Property inspector and format the new text as follows: select Arial as the font face, enable the Bold and Italic buttons, set the font size to **12**, and choose a blue shade for the color.

6 With the text box selected, choose Modify > Convert to Symbol. Name the symbol **tagline** and set the Type as Graphic. Set the registration point to center and press OK. Position the text on the Stage where you like; in the example, it's below the logo and stick figure toward the bottom-left corner of the Stage.

7   Insert a keyframe on Frame 96 of the text layer. You'll now scale the text so it starts large and shrinks to the size it is now.

8   Click on the keyframe at Frame 91 of the text layer. Select the tagline symbol on the Stage, then choose Modify > Transform > Scale and Rotate. Set the Scale value to **200%** and press OK.

9   Select Alpha from the Color drop-down menu on the Property inspector. If you don't see the Color Settings window in the Property inspector, you might need to click on the tagline symbol again to reactivate it.

10 Set the Alpha value to 0% to make the instance fully transparent.

Modify the Tagline symbol.

11 Right-click (Windows) or Ctrl+click (Mac OS) on the keyframe at Frame 91 of the text layer and choose Create Motion Tween.

12 Save your work, and choose Control > Test Movie to preview it. Choose File > Close.

Congratulations! You have finished the lesson.

Self study

One of the best ways to learn more about Flash animation is to look at other people's work. This is especially true when learning how to work with the tools and unlocking what they can do. For a good example of Flash animation, you can visit Flash-based websites by designers. One of our favorites for inspiration is hillmancurtis.com.

Video-style animation can also be incorporated into your Flash project. One way to include video but still keep your file size manageable is to make the video a JPEG Sequence and import it into Flash. Place the JPEG Sequence into a movie clip for display and you've got video without taking up a lot of space! For lessons on importing and using video directly within Flash, check out Lesson 14, "Working with Video."

Review

Questions

1   What feature in Flash allows you to view several frames of animation at once?

2   What kind of layer do you need to create a path that a motion tween can follow?

3   What setting in the Property inspector allows you to adjust the inertia of a moving object and make the animation appear more natural?

Answers

1   Onion Skin.

2   A motion guide layer.

3   Ease In/Out.

Lesson 7

What you'll learn in this lesson:

- Creating and fine-tuning shape tweens
- Masking animation layers
- Using the new Copy and Paste Motion features
- Editing multiple frames at once

Diving Deeper into Animation

In the last lesson, you used the power of tweens to build slick, lightweight animations. Now you'll learn how to add more depth to your movies by sequencing simultaneous animations across multiple layers and create unique, eye-catching morphing effects with shape tweens. You'll also harness the power of the new Copy and Paste Motion feature to apply the same animation behavior to several objects on the Stage.

Starting up

Before starting, make sure that your tools and panels are consistent by resetting your workspace. See "Resetting the Flash workspace" on page 3.

You will work with several files from the fl07lessons folder in this lesson. Make sure that you have loaded the fllessons folder onto your hard drive from the supplied DVD. See "Loading lesson files" on page 3.

See Lesson 7 in action!

Use the accompanying video to gain a better understanding of how to use some of the features shown in this lesson. Open the DynamicLearning_FlashCS3.swf file located in the Videos folder and select Lesson 7 to view the video training file for this lesson.

The project

You'll be working on an underwater scene in which many elements move and interact with each other—a perfect opportunity to try out shape tweens, masks, and animations that run across multiple layers at once. To view the finished file, choose File > Open and select the fl0701_done.fla file within the fl07lessons folder. Preview what you'll be doing in this lesson by using the shortcut Ctrl+Enter (Windows) or Command+Return (Mac OS). When you are finished, close the file or keep it open as a reference.

The finished file.

Creating shape tweens

One of the main features you will focus on in this lesson is shape tweens. Shape tweens can morph one shape into an entirely unrelated shape, such as a star into a circle, including color blends and differences in position in their morphs. Unlike motion tweens, which require two identical symbol instances, shape tweens work with raw graphics or drawing objects to make changes to the starting element's physical outline and appearance. Motion and shape tweens are similar in that both can produce motion or changes in size, which they do by reconstructing the shapes' outlines.

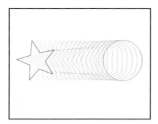

Shape tweens can manipulate outlines to create a transition between two different raw shapes.

Shape tween rules

- Shape tweens require starting and ending keyframes.
- You can use shape tweens between raw shapes or drawing objects only—no symbols!
- Starting and ending shapes can have completely different shapes, colors, and sizes.
- You can create shape tweens from the first keyframe, using the contextual menu or Property inspector.
- You can create only one shape tween on a single layer at a time.
- You can only add or remove shape hints on the first keyframe of a shape tween.

To demonstrate this theory, you'll use shape tweens to change one fish into another in an underwater struggle between good and evil.

1   Choose File > Open and navigate to the fl07lessons folder. Select the fl0701.fla file and press Open.

2   Choose File > Save As. When the Save As dialog box appears, type **fl0701_work.fla** into the Name text field. Navigate to the fl07lessons folder and press Save.

3   In the Timeline, select the Big Fish layer. If the Library panel is not open, choose Window > Library to open it.

4   From the Library panel, locate and drag an instance of the Good Fish graphic symbol to the Stage. In the Property inspector, position the symbol by entering **140** in the X field, and **280** in the Y field. You'll morph the Good Fish shape into a second shape that you'll place in step 7.

Place and position the Good Fish symbol.

5   Because shape tweens can't make use of symbols, you must first break the Good Fish symbol into raw artwork so that it can be properly tweened. Make sure the Good Fish is selected, then choose Modify > Break Apart to convert it.

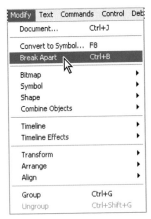

You must break apart symbols or groups before applying a shape tween.

6   Select Frame 20 on the Big Fish layer, then right-click (Windows) or Ctrl+click (Mac OS), and choose Insert Blank Keyframe from the contextual menu. Flash creates a new, empty keyframe.

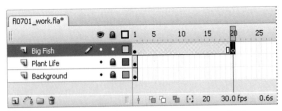

Create a second blank keyframe to contain the second shape for the tween.

7   Drag an instance of the Evil Fish symbol from the Library panel to the Stage. In the Property inspector, enter **248** for the symbol's X position and **230** for Y; this aligns it with the Good Fish graphic on the first frame.

8   Notice that the background elements are absent from Frame 20. To extend the background, hold down the Shift key and select Frame 20 on both the Background and Plant Life layers. Right-click (Windows) or Ctrl+click (Mac OS) and choose Insert Frame.

9 Select Frame 20 of the Big Fish layer, then select the Evil Fish symbol you placed on the Stage. Choose Modify > Break Apart so it can be included in the shape tween.

Break apart the Evil Fish symbol to its raw form.

10 Select Frame 1 on the Big Fish layer. From the Property inspector's Tween menu, choose Shape to apply a shape tween. The arrow and the green-shaded area between the two keyframes indicate that Flash has successfully created the tween.

Create the shape tween on Frame 1 by selecting Shape from the Tween menu on the Property inspector.

11 Press Enter (Windows) or Return (Mac OS) to play your animation. You should see the good fish transform into the evil fish, with the shape and the colors morphing from start to finish.

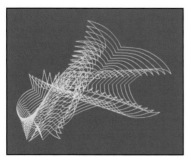

An Onion Skin Outlines view of your shape tween morph.

12 Choose File > Save to save your work.

Fine-tuning with shape hints

Depending on the shapes you choose for your tween, you may find that some transitions are effective while others could use some fine-tuning. For those that need a little help, use shape hints.

Shape hints tell Flash where it can find common points between two seemingly uncommon shapes. To use them, you place a matched set of small markers at important parts of the shapes on the start and end keyframes of a shape tween. The markers tell Flash that the indicated shapes and points are related, and should be maintained through the animation as much as possible. Say, for example, you're morphing a star into a square. You could place shape hints in the upper-right area of each shape to match those points and keep the transformation as smooth as possible. Place as many shape hints as necessary per shape tween to effectively fine-tune it.

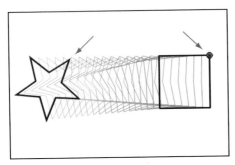

Use shape hints to match up the corners of the two shapes.

Placing shape hints

You'll use shape hints in this exercise to help Flash find common points between the good fish and evil fish for a better tween.

1   Select Frame 1 of your Big Fish layer to view the starting shape.

2   Make shape hints visible by selecting View > Show Shape Hints. To make the shape hints snap properly to corners and sides, make sure Snap to Objects is checked under View > Snapping > Snap To Objects. Shape hints do not work unless they are sitting precisely on a shape's outline.

3 Choose Modify > Shape > Add Shape Hint. A red circle marked with the letter *a* appears on the Stage.

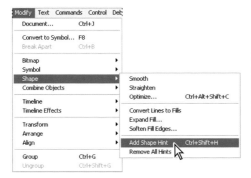

A shape hint appears as a red button marked with a letter.

4 Move the shape hint, and snap it to the bottom of the leg on the left side of the Good Fish shape.

5 Add another shape hint, this time using the keyboard shortcut Shift+Ctrl+H (Windows) or Shift+Command+H (Mac OS). A second shape hint appears, marked with the letter *b*.

6 Position the new shape hint on the bottom of the leg on the right side of the fish shape.

Position two shape hints on Frame 1.

7 Now you need to match these shape hints to their counterparts on the ending shape on Frame 20. Select Frame 20 of the Big Fish layer; two shape hints (a and b) are waiting to be positioned on the second shape.

8 Move hint *b* to the bottom right corner, then move hint *a* to the bottom left corner of the Evil Fish shape. They should snap into place and turn green, which means they're properly positioned.

Positioned properly, the shape hints turn green.

9 Select Frame 1. The shape hints are now yellow to indicate that their counterparts are properly positioned on the second keyframe.

Shape hints with successfully placed counterparts turn yellow on the starting keyframe.

10 Press Enter (Windows) or Return (Mac OS) to play the animation. Notice that the two points you matched using shape hints stay put while the rest of the shape continues to morph.

11 Choose File > Save to save your work.

Hints for successful hinting

Adding shape hints is usually straightforward, but it can get a bit tricky with complex shapes. Follow these tips to create better shape tweens with a little less confusion:

- Always enable Snap to Objects (View > Snapping > Snap To Objects). Although you can place shape hints without snapping, it's much more difficult.

- Use shape hints in sensible places; although Flash doesn't make associations on its own, it can tell when a shape hint and its counterpart are not matched in a logical way. If the second hint remains red even after you place it, Flash is alerting you to a potential problem.

- Avoid shapes that are broken into too many pieces; instead, try to tween between two whole shapes. Although Flash can tween between a single shape and a broken shape, the results are not always what you expect. If you need to tween between two multi-part shapes, consider isolating each piece and applying to each its own shape tween.

- Use Onion Skin view to assist you in placing shape hints. When you're having a hard time determining exactly what's happening in the course of a shape tween, turn on Onion Skin or Onion Skin Outlines view to follow the action and make better decisions on shape hints.

Sometimes it takes a few shape hint passes to get exactly the look you want. Try to tune and complete the fish shape tween by adding some additional hints.

1 Select Frame 1 of the Big Fish layer, and press Shift+Ctrl+H (Windows) or Shift+Command+H (Mac OS) three times to add three new shape hints; you should be up to letter *e*.

2 Position them on the first fish as shown in the image below.

Position additional shape hints on the first fish to further fine-tune the tween.

3 Select Frame 20 on the Big Fish layer. You should see the counterparts to your new shape hints waiting to be matched.

When you create multiple shape hints at once, they stack on top of each other on the second frame. Click and drag to separate them.

4 Position the new shape hints (c, d, and e) on the second shape as shown in the image below. Compare the first and second shapes; notice that the hints were matched to similar features on both shapes to help Flash find similarities.

Position the shape hints on Frame 20.

5 Press Enter/Return to play the animation. The completed tween should look much smoother now.

To remove a shape hint, right-click (Windows) or Ctrl+click (Mac OS) it and choose Remove Hint from the contextual menu. To remove all shape hints, right-click (Windows) or Ctrl+click (Mac OS) any shape hint and choose Remove All Hints.

Right-click (Windows) or Ctrl+click (Mac OS) to add, remove, or clear all shape hints.

Distributing animation across multiple layers

The more complex your movie, the more you'll need to use layers. This is especially true if you intend to have two animations occur at the same time in your movie. Only one shape or motion tween can occur on a single layer at any given time, and only one object can be tweened on one layer at a time. Even something as simple as two animations interacting with each other requires at least two layers. The advantage of using layers for animations is that you can easily isolate, reorder, hide, or move a single tween without disturbing others on the Stage.

Multiple layers for multiple fish

In your underwater movie, an unsuspecting fish is about to be eaten by the evil fish. You'll add a layer to move this new fish across the Stage until he gets snapped up.

1   In the Library panel, locate the Lil Fish graphic symbol.

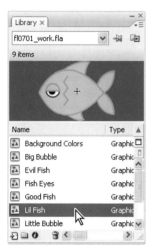

The Lil Fish graphic symbol.

2   With the Big Fish layer selected, press the Insert Layer button (⊒) at the bottom left of the Timeline to create a new layer. Double-click the new layer name to edit it, and type **Little Fish** to rename the layer.

3   Select the Little Fish layer, then drag an instance of the Lil Fish symbol from the Library panel onto the Stage. Leave the symbol selected. In the Property inspector type **580** in the X field and **80** in the Y field to position it. Next, you'll create a motion tween to move the Lil Fish from right to left across the Stage.

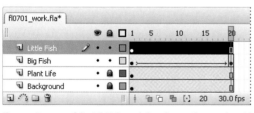 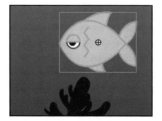

Drag an instance of the Lil Fish symbol to the new layer and position it.

4   Select Frame 20 on the Little Fish layer, and insert a new keyframe by choosing Insert > Timeline > Keyframe.

5   Click and drag the instance of the Lil Fish symbol on Frame 20 to the left of the Stage, above the evil fish. For exact positioning, use the X and Y text fields in the Property inspector to set the instance at **318** and **80**, respectively.

Position the symbol using the text-entry fields on the Property inspector.

6   Select Frame 1 of the Little Fish layer. Set a tween by choosing Motion from the Tween drop-down menu in the Property inspector.

7   Press Enter (Windows) or Return (Mac OS) to preview the animation. The little fish should move from right to left as the evil fish makes his move.

The finished animation shown in Onion Skin Outlines view.

8   Choose File > Save to save your work.

Dotting your (fish) eyes

How does that evil fish see his prey? You'll need to give the evil fish some eyes. To ensure that they move as he does, you'll create a new layer to add the eyes and a shape tween to go with them. This exercise also demonstrates how a shape tween can integrate motion, so that objects can change position along with their color or shape. Make sure the Library panel is open before you begin.

1　On the Timeline, select the Big Fish layer, then create a new layer above it using the Insert Layer button (◻). Rename the layer **Eyes**.

2　Select Frame 1 on the Eyes layer. Drag an instance of the Fish Eyes graphic symbol from the Library panel to the Stage. Position it on top of the Good Fish graphic. For this example, the eyes were positioned with X at 140 and Y at 275.

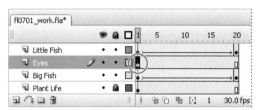 

The eyes, positioned on top of the fish on the first frame.

3　Select Frame 20 of the Eyes layer, and choose Insert > Timeline > Keyframe.

4　To make the eyes follow the motion of the fish's head, select and position the eyes on Frame 20 on top of the Evil Fish. For this example, the eyes were positioned with X set at 300 and Y set at 190.

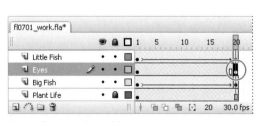 

Position the eyes on Frame 20.

5　Because you'll be applying a shape tween to make the eyes move, you'll need to break the symbols you just placed down to raw artwork. Start by selecting the instance of the eyes on Frame 20, and choose Modify > Break Apart.

6 Return to Frame 1 on the Eyes layer, and select the instance of the eyes on this frame. Choose Modify > Break Apart to break this instance down to its raw artwork as well.

Break apart the symbol instances to prepare them for a shape tween.

7 While still on Frame 1, create a shape tween by selecting Shape from the Tween drop-down menu in the Property inspector.

8 As a finishing touch, match the color of the eyes to the red color of the fish in its evil state. Select Frame 20, then use the Selection tool (k) to select both of the eyelids only.

9 Choose the Eyedropper tool (✐) from the Tools panel and click inside the body of the Evil Fish with the eyedropper tool. Flash samples the red color and applies it to the eyes.

Match the eyelid color to the body color.

10 Choose the Selection tool again and while holding the Shift key, double-click the stroke on each eyelid to select them. Select the Eyedropper tool from the Tools panel and click the stroke of the Evil Fish. This changes the stroke of the eyelids to the same color as the stroke of the body.

Match the stroke colors of the fish's body and eyelids.

11 Return to Frame 1 of the Eyes layer, and press Enter (Windows) or Return (Mac OS) to preview the animation. Choose File > Save to save your work.

The completed animation (eyes only) in Onion Skin view.

The completed eyes animation shows that shape tweens can transform color and shape, also depict motion. Although you should generally use motion tweens for more extensive movement, shape tweens are flexible enough to handle morphing, motion, and color transitions.

Reordering layers

One nice feature of layers is that you can change their stacking order, which, in turn, rearranges the relative depth of the artwork or animations that each layer holds. By default, Flash places new layers on top of the stack, putting each new layer's contents in front of other elements on the Stage. But what if the newly placed evil fish (with his eyes, of course) is supposed to be lurking behind the plants, a layer added much earlier? The answer is simple: just reposition the fish and eye layers below the plant layer. Give it a try now.

1 On the Timeline, click and drag the Big Fish layer downwards through the layer stack. Notice the dark line following your mouse pointer, which indicates where the layer will be dropped when you release the mouse button.

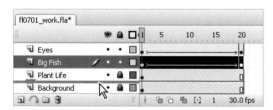

Reorder layers by clicking and dragging them within the stacking order.

2 Release the Big Fish layer below the Plant Life layer. The body of the Good/Evil fish should now peek out from behind the kelp.

3   The fish, however, still needs his eyes. Select the Eyes layer, drag it below the Plant Life layer (but above the Big Fish layer), and release it.

Position the Big Fish and Eyes layers below the Plant Life layer.

Viewing layers as outlines

When things start to get cluttered on the Stage, switching to a simpler view may help. You can view each layer as outlines only, reducing all of the layer's artwork and animations down to basic outlines. For complex compositions, Outline view can sometimes speed up animation previews on the Timeline as well.

To view a layer as outlines, click on the colored box to the right of the layer's name; the box changes to an outlined box, and the layer's contents switch to Outline mode. Click the box again to return to Normal viewing mode.

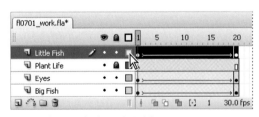

Toggle outline view for the Little Fish layer.

To toggle all layers between Outline and Normal views, click on the box in the column header area above the layer stack.

Toggle between Outline and Normal views for all layers at once.

You can change the outline colors for any layer by double-clicking the Outlines box, which launches the Layer Properties dialog box. Here you can choose a different color by pressing the color swatch next to Outline color and selecting a new color from the Swatches panel. This also affects the color of selection indicators, such as bounding boxes and paths, on this layer.

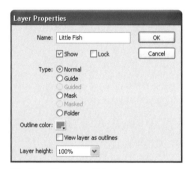

The Layer Properties dialog box.

Organizing layers using folders

When a movie expands to use many layers, consider grouping related layers together in folders. Layer folders work like the folders in your library: you can sort several layers into a single folder, then collapse (close) the folder to tidy up your view of the Timeline. This is handy, especially when you have so many layers that you need to scroll up and down in the Timeline to locate the layers you need. You can also hide or lock a folder to prevent its contents from being seen or edited. As you'll see in the following lesson, grouping related layers in your underwater scene helps keep it organized.

1   With the Little Fish layer selected, press the Insert Layer Folder button (▣) located below the Timeline to create a new layer folder. Rename the folder **Evil Fish**.

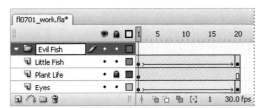

Select the Insert Layer Folder to create a new layer folder.

2   Click and drag the Evil Fish layer folder below the Plant Life layer. Use the dark line that appears as a guide, just as you did earlier when reordering layers.

3   Now add some layers to the folder: click and drag the Big Fish layer into the Evil Fish layer folder.

4   Drag the Eyes layer into the Evil Fish layer folder as well. Both layers should now appear indented below the Evil Fish folder, indicating that they are inside it. Reorder the layers, if necessary, to ensure that the Eyes layer is still above the Big Fish layer.

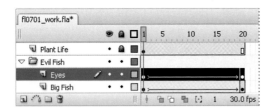

The two layers of your evil fish are now in the new layer folder.

5   To collapse the new folder, click the arrow to its left.

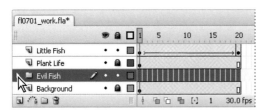

Collapse a layer folder by clicking the arrow to its left.

Layer folders behave very much like normal layers do. To reposition a layer folder, click and drag it. To lock or hide a layer folder, click the dots below the eye or padlock icons in the column header. You can also switch all layers inside of a folder to Outline view by clicking the Outline icon to the right of the layer folder.

Editing multiple frames at once

To add a bit more drama to the underwater scene, the little fish could be fortunate enough to escape the grips of the evil fish's jaws—but only for the moment. To accomplish this, you need to move the little fish so his path takes him directly into harm's way. The only snag here is that the little fish is part of a motion tween, so you have two keyframes (plus all of the frames generated in between) to worry about.

You could attempt to move and match both the starting and ending keyframes separately, but there's an easier way to grab an entire animation as one unit: Edit Multiple Frames. Edit Multiple Frames mode lets you view and select an entire sequence of frames across the Timeline and then move or transform them all at once.

This works especially well if you want to move or resize an entire tween in a single step. All of the frames in between also move or resize with them.

In this exercise, you'll use Edit Multiple Frames to grab the entire Little Fish animation and reposition it on the Stage.

1   With the Little Fish layer selected, click the Edit Multiple Frames button (▣) below the Timeline. A set of brackets appears above the Timeline; you'll use these to set the range of frames you want to edit.

Brackets allow you to determine the range of frames you want to edit.

2   Click and drag the left bracket to Frame 1 and the right bracket to Frame 20.

The fish on both the first and last keyframes of the tween appear selected on the Stage.

3   Click and drag the left little fish so that it completely overlaps the mouth of the evil fish; the second instance follows. With one move, you have repositioned the two instances, and, in turn, the entire tween.

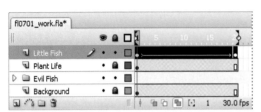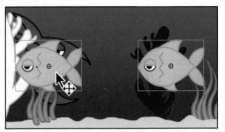

The fish instances you selected from Frames 1 and 20 move together as you reposition them.

4   You can do more than move tweens with Edit Multiple Frames mode; you can resize an entire tween as well. With the two instances still selected, choose the Free Transform tool (⊹) on the Tools panel. A single black bounding box with handles appears around both instances.

5   While holding down the Shift key, click and drag the handle at the box's top-right corner and resize the two fish down to about half their original size.

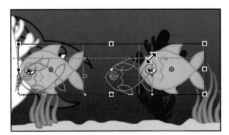

Edit Multiple Frames enables you to resize both fish at once.

6   Click the Edit Multiple Frames button (▤) again to turn off this mode; the brackets above the Timeline disappear.

7   Click and drag the Little Fish layer below the Evil Fish layer folder so the little fish appears behind the evil fish.

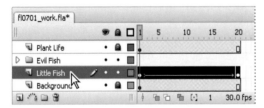

Reposition the Little Fish layer below the Evil Fish layer folder.

8 Press Enter (Windows) or Return (Mac OS) to watch your adjusted animation play.

The end of your animation (and of the little fish).

9 Choose File > Save to save your work.

Your underwater scene has come a long way, but there's still more to do. Next, you'll explore how masking and the new Copy Motion and Paste Motion features adds even more action to your movie.

Creating masks

Using masks is a fun and creative technique that spans multiple artistic mediums from the traditional to the digital. A mask is essentially a shape that hides another piece of artwork; masks cover some portions of an image and reveal others, creating a window through which you can see an isolated area of an image or graphic.

In this example, the type is partially masked.

Using Flash's mask layers, you can apply masks to reveal only selected portions of graphics or create unique effects. Mask layers don't display their contents; instead, they use their contents to determine what to reveal on the layers below them. The size and shape of the mask is completely determined by the contents of the mask layer. To better understand how this technique works, you'll use mask layers to add an underwater bubble to the Stage and magnify the background behind it.

1   In the Library panel, locate the graphic symbol named Big Bubble.

2   With the Plant Life layer selected, press the Insert Layer button (⬛) below the Timeline to create a new layer, then rename the layer **Bubble**.

3   Drag an instance of the Big Bubble symbol from the Library panel to the lower-right corner of the Stage. On the Property inspector, type **575** in the X text field, and **250** in the Y text field to reposition the new instance.

To produce the magnifying effect, you'll create a new layer with a second, slightly larger copy of your background plants. As you reveal a small portion of the larger plants, the background appears to magnify.

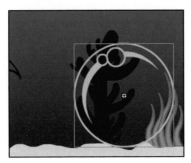

Position the Big Bubble symbol on its own layer on the Stage.

4   Select the Plant Life layer, then create a new layer using the Insert Layer button. Rename it **Bigger Plant Life**. Drag a copy of the Plants n Things symbol from the Library panel onto the new layer. Use the Property inspector to position it at X: **338**, Y: **231**; this matches its position with the original background plants on the Plant Life layer.

5   With the Plants n Things symbol instance still selected, choose Window > Transform to launch the Transform panel. With the Constrain option checked, type **120** in either the Horizontal or Vertical scaling box to slightly increase the size of the new copy. Press Enter (Windows) or Return (Mac OS) to apply the transformation. Close the Transform panel.

Scale the placed symbol to 120%.

The type-in fields on some panels require you to either Tab away from the field or press Enter/Return to apply and commit the values.

6 Because you want the new, bigger background visible only where the bubble overlaps it, you'll need a mask layer. Make sure the Bigger Plant Life layer is selected, then insert a new layer above it and rename it **Mask**.

7 Right-click (Windows) or Ctrl+click (Mac OS) the new Mask layer, and choose Mask from the menu that appears. Flash converts the Mask layer to a mask and indents the Bigger Plant Life layer below it; this indicates that the Bigger Plant Life layer is now masked by the Mask layer. Unlock the new Mask layer by clicking the padlock to the right of the layer name.

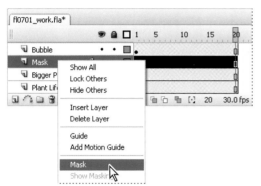

Add a new layer and convert it to a mask layer.

 Unlocking a mask layer allows you to edit its contents, but temporarily suspends the masking effect. The mask layer (and the layer being masked) must be locked for the masking to take effect.

8 To determine the size, shape, and position of the mask itself, you must place a solid shape on the Mask layer. Choose the Oval tool (○) from the Tools panel. On the Mask layer, draw an oval (make sure the oval has a fill color set, but no stroke; the color is not important). Line up the shape with the bubble. Use the Free Transform tool (✥) to adjust the size and shape to match the bubble.

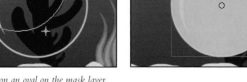

Draw and position an oval on the mask layer.

9   Click the padlock (🔒) on the Mask layer to relock it. On the Stage, the plants should appear enlarged behind the bubble, demonstrating the masking action.

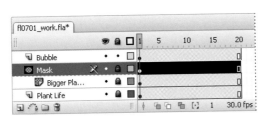

The finished mask. You can now see the larger background revealed through the bubble.

10   Choose File > Save to save your work.

Creating animated masks

You can put your masks in motion as well, animating them directly on their layers as you would any other object. The process of creating the animation is identical to what you've learned so far. Simply convert the contents of your mask layer to a symbol and create a motion tween. Try it with your magnifying bubble mask:

1   While holding down Alt (Windows) or Option (Mac OS), click the padlock on the Mask layer. This locks all other layers except the Mask layer.

2   Using the Selection tool (🔧), click on Frame 1 of the Mask layer to select the oval you created earlier.

3   Choose Modify > Convert to Symbol to launch the Convert to Symbol dialog box. Enter the name **Oval Mask** and set the Type as Graphic Symbol. Press OK. The mask is now a symbol to which you can apply a motion tween.

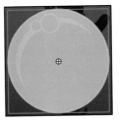

Convert the oval on the Mask layer to a symbol.

4   Select Frame 20 on the Mask layer and choose Insert > Timeline > Keyframe. An instance of the Oval Mask is created on the new keyframe.

5 Use the Selection tool to select the instance of Oval Mask on Frame 20 and reposition it on the left side of the Stage.

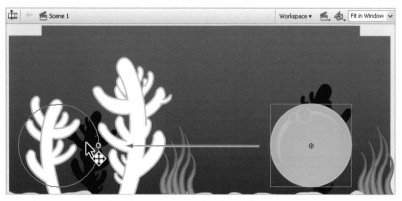

Move the instance of the oval mask on Frame 20 to the left side of the Stage to set up for the motion tween.

6 Select Frame 1, then create a motion tween by choosing Motion from the Tween menu on the Property inspector. This moves the oval from its position on Frame 1 to its new position on Frame 20. Lock the Mask layer.

Create the motion tween to move the oval mask across the Stage.

7 Press Enter/Return to play the animation; the background appears to magnify through the oval as it moves across the Stage.

8 Choose File > Save to save your work.

Copying and pasting animation

Two new and very welcome features in Flash CS3 are Copy Motion and Paste Motion, with which you can copy the tweening action from one object and paste it to another. This is an essential pair of tools if you want to precisely match animation behavior between multiple graphics. Copy Motion and Paste Motion at their most basic can capture the direction and distance of a motion tween and apply it to a stationary symbol. The Paste Motion Special feature gives you parameter-by-parameter control over the tween settings copied and reapplied between symbols.

A great way to explore these features is to copy the Oval Mask animation and paste it to the Bubble layer. The bubble then moves along with the Oval Mask, appearing to magnify the background as it glides across the Stage.

1 Unlock the Mask layer by selecting the padlock to the right of the layer name. Select the entire tween on the Mask layer by Shift+clicking Frame 1 and Frame 20.

2 Right-click (Windows) or Ctrl+click (Mac OS) on the selected area in the Timeline, and choose Copy Motion from the contextual menu that appears.

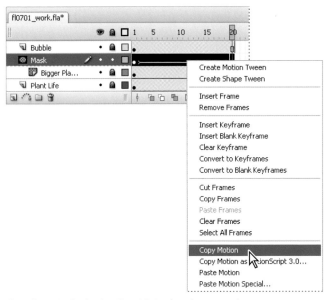

Copy the motion by choosing Copy Motion from the contextual menu.

3   Unlock the Bubble layer, and double-click on any frame on the layer to select all the frames up to Frame 20.

4   Right-click (Windows) or Ctrl+click (Mac OS) and choose Paste Motion from the contextual menu that appears. Flash applies a motion tween to the frames on the Bubble layer.

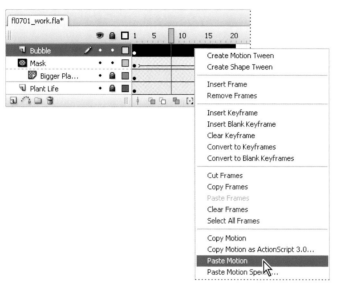

Choose Paste Motion from the contextual menu to apply the tween to the selected frames.

5   Press Enter (Windows) or Return (Mac OS) to play the animation. Because the bubble is using the same motion tween as the mask, it follows the oval exactly.

6   Choose File > Save to save your work.

With the tween applied to the bubble, the bubble's motion matches that of the oval mask.

Paste Motion Special

You can already see the usefulness of the new Copy and Paste Motion commands. Paste Motion Special gives you even more control. In the next exercise, you'll try it in your underwater scene. To get started, make sure the Library panel is visible and locate the Lil Fish symbol you used earlier in the lesson. You're going to give the unfortunate fish a little brother, who farther out of harm's way.

1   With the Bubble layer selected, press the Insert Layer button (⊒) to add a new layer. Rename the new layer Tiny Fish.

2   Select Frame 1 of the Tiny Fish layer and drag an instance of the Lil Fish symbol from the Library panel onto the Stage. In the X and Y text-entry fields on the Property inspector, type **580** and **70**, respectively, to reposition the symbol.

3   With the new Lil Fish instance still selected, make sure the padlock to the left of the W and H text fields in the Property inspector is locked. This constrains the Width and Height proportions. Enter **75** in the W text field on the Property inspector to resize it to 75 pixels wide.

The new Lil Fish instance on the Stage.

4   Now you'll copy the motion from its big brother on the Little Fish layer. While holding down the Shift key, select Frames 1 and 20 on the Little Fish layer so that the entire tween is highlighted. Right-click (Windows) or Ctrl+click (Mac OS), and choose Copy Motion from the contextual menu.

It is not necessary to unlock a layer to copy or paste motion.

5   Select the Tiny Fish layer, and double-click the gray area between Frames 1 and 20 to select all frames. Right-click (Windows) or Ctrl+click (Mac OS), and choose Paste Motion Special. This option gives you detailed control over what you paste—and what you don't—as well as the ability to match the scale, rotation, and skew from the original tween.

Use Paste Motion Special to adjust which parameters are pasted to the new layers

6   In the resulting Paste Motion Special dialog box, make sure all the options are checked, with the exception of Horizontal scale and Vertical scale. Leaving the scaling options unchecked in the Paste Motion Special dialog box ensures that no scaling from the copied tween is applied. Press OK to paste the motion.

7   Press Enter (Windows) or Return (Mac OS) to play the animation; Tiny Fish now follows the same motion behavior as its big brother.

The resulting animation is now consistent between the two fish.

8   Choose File > Save to save your work.

Moving, extending, and reversing animation

After you've created an animation, you can fine-tune it by extending, shifting, or even reversing it. You might also have some extra frames at the end that you'll want to tidy up. You can practice these techniques in the underwater movie.

Modifying keyframe length

A keyframe sometimes extends further than you want it to, leaving important elements behind.

You can easily shorten or expand how long contents of a keyframe stay on the Timeline using the square handle that appears at the end of an extended keyframe.

The square handle of a keyframe.

To move this handle, hold the Ctrl key (Windows) or Command key (Mac OS), and move your pointer over the handle until a two-way arrow appears.

You can then click and drag the handle to the left or right to shorten or lengthen the number of frames in which the keyframe content appears.

Extending tween length

Extending a motion or shape tween is as simple as repositioning the ending keyframe. For example, you can extend the motion tween on the Mask layer to Frame 40.

1   Click Frame 20 on the Mask layer to select it.

2   Click and hold the mouse button until you see a small dotted rectangle under your cursor. Drag the keyframe right to Frame 40 to extend the tween to that frame.

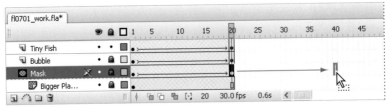

Click and drag the second keyframe of a tween to extend it.

Extending a tween can improve its overall smoothness because you're giving it more frames to accomplish the transition. Keep in mind, however, that because it takes longer to play out, it may appear to be slower.

3 Repeat steps 1 and 2 for the Tiny Fish, Bubble, and Little Fish layers.

4 Select Frame 40 and choose Insert > Timeline > Keyframe to add a keyframe for the Plant Life, Bigger Plant Life, and Background layers to extend them on the Timeline.

5 Choose File > Save to save your work.

Copying and reversing animation

Sometimes finishing up an animation is as straightforward as having it perform a complete opposite action. Whether it's a ball returning to the ground after a bounce or a plane landing after take-off, many actions require nothing more than the opposite reaction to be complete. A good example of this is the evil fish: once he gets his bait, he can return to where he came from. Rather than create a whole new tween, you can combine some new methods to copy and reverse the action to finish the movie. All of the features you need can be found in the Timeline's menu, which you can launch with a Right-click (Windows) or Ctrl+click (Mac OS).

1 Select the Big Fish layer, which is inside the Evil Fish layer folder, then unlock the layer by selecting the padlock to the right of the layer name. Hold down the Shift key and select Frames 1 through 20.

2 Right-click (Windows) or Ctrl+click (Mac OS) on the selected area to open the Timeline's contextual menu. Choose Copy Frames to copy the frames and their contents, including the tween, to the clipboard.

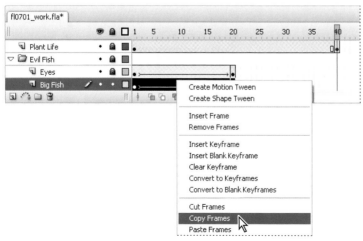

Use the contextual menu to copy the selected frames; this also copies the entire tween.

3   Select Frame 21 on the Big Fish layer, and choose Insert > Timeline > Blank Keyframe.

4   Right-click (Windows) or Ctrl+click (Mac OS) on the new frame to launch the contextual menu, then choose Paste Frames to paste the frames you copied in step 2. Press the Enter/Return key and watch the animation play twice, back-to-back.

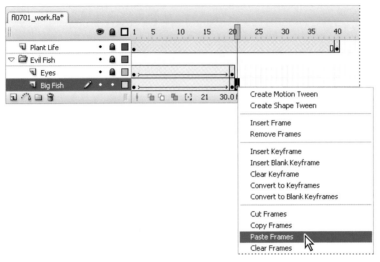

Create a new empty keyframe on Frame 21 and paste the animation you have copied.

5   While holding the Shift key, select Frames 21 to 40 so that the entire tween you pasted is selected.

6   Right-click (Windows) or Ctrl+click (Mac OS) on the selected area, and choose Reverse Frames from the contextual menu.

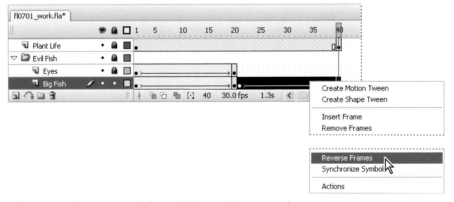

Choose Reverse Frames to reverse the frames (and the tween) that you pasted.

7 Press Enter (Windows) or Return (Mac OS) to play your movie; the evil fish animation plays and then reverses for a more complete end.

8 Repeat steps 1 through 6 for the Eyes layer so that the evil fish's eyes continue to follow the added animation.

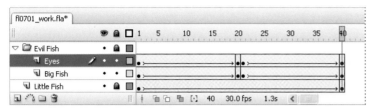

The Eyes layer now has reversed frames.

9 Choose File > Save to save your work. Congratulations, you have completed the lesson! Choose File > Close to close the file.

Wrapping up

The techniques you've learned in these lessons will help you master the Timeline and create more complex visual effects, such as masks, that you're accustomed to seeing in traditional media. In addition, new features such as Copy and Paste Motion will help speed up your workflow by minimizing repetitive work and ensuring consistency. Distributing your artwork and animations across layers helps you create more complex and interactive scenes, like the underwater scene, and you can accomplish more of the ideas that you can see in your mind's eye.

Self study

Create a lava lamp-style animation that uses shape tweens across several layers, along with a mask to isolate the viewing area on the Stage. To create that true lava lamp look, draw your shapes with the Pen tool (◊) or Pencil tool (✎) and use a variety of colors from the Swatches panel.

Review

Questions

1 What are two primary differences between Shape and Motion tweens?

2 What feature would you use to paste specific aspects of animation copied with Copy Motion?

3 True or False: To mask the animation on a layer, you need to change that layer to a Mask layer.

Answers

1 Shape tweens create morphs and color blends between two different raw (mergeable) shapes or drawing objects. Motion tweens create motion, color effects or transformation between two instances of the same symbol.

2 Paste Motion Special.

3 False: A Mask layer needs to be created separately above the layer to be masked, then set as a Mask using the layer contextual menu by right-clicking (Windows) or Ctrl+clicking (Mac OS) on the Mask layer.

What you'll learn in this lesson:

- Customizing workspace layouts

- Docking, undocking, moving, and adding panels

- Snapping elements to guides or grids

- Performing advanced alignments

Customizing Your Workflow

Those extra few seconds spent hunting for tools or aligning elements can add up. To keep moving smoothly through your project and avoid the distraction of having to locate tools, panels, and menu items, you can customize Flash's interface to your working style. Beyond streamlining its interface, Flash also provides visual aids to help you quickly and accurately place objects on the Stage.

Starting up

Before starting, make sure that your tools and panels are consistent by resetting your workspace. See "Resetting the Flash workspace" on page 3.

You will work with several files from the fl08lessons folder in this lesson. Make sure that you have loaded the fllessons folder onto your hard drive from the supplied DVD. See "Loading lesson files" on page 3.

See Lesson 8 in action!

Use the accompanying video to gain a better understanding of how to use some of the features shown in this lesson. Open the DynamicLearning_FlashCS3.swf file located in the Videos folder and select Lesson 8 to view the video training file for this lesson.

Customizing workspace layouts

Flash has many different features that enable you to customize your work environment. Although it means spending a little time organizing before you create a document, customizing saves time and headaches later when you're deep in a project. You can strategically place your tools, then save the workspace so the panels you use most often are at hand.

In this lesson, you will learn how to customize the Flash CS3 Professional workspace for a more efficient workflow. You'll also learn how visual aids and keyboard shortcuts can help you work smarter and faster.

Opening the completed file

This exercise involves assembling a small interactive .swf file for a fictional design firm. You'll place logos, text elements, and navigation buttons on the Stage with the help of guides, grids and the align panel.

Before you get started:

1   Launch Flash CS3 Professional if it is not already open.

2   Choose File> Browse to open Adobe Bridge. Use the Folders tab in the upper left of the Bridge workspace to navigate to the fl08lessons folder that you copied onto your computer. Adobe Bridge is used to navigate and open files in this lesson, but if you prefer, you can choose File > Open.

3   Once you have the fl08lessons folder open, double-click on the file named fl0801_done.fla to open it in Flash. A project file that includes a splash page for a mock design firm appears; you will reproduce this layout in the following exercises.

4   You can keep this file open for reference, or choose File > Close at this time. If asked to save changes, choose No.

5   Choose File > Browse to bring Adobe Bridge to the front. If you are not already viewing the contents of the fl08lessons folder, navigate to it now.

6   Double-click on the fl0801.fla file to open it in Flash now.

8   Choose File > Save As. When the Save As dialog box appears, type **fl0801_work.fla** into the Name text field. Navigate to the fl08lessons folder and press Save.

Working with panels

With the lesson file open, take a look at the default workspace layout. The right side of the screen contains the Color, Swatches, and Library panels; this minimal set of panels gets you started, but you will need to locate and open additional panels to complete the project at hand. For basic tasks such as aligning items on the Stage or transforming graphics, you'll need to open and place those panels before continuing your work.

*The Color, Swatches, and Library panels
are open in the default workspace.*

You can add as many panels as you need, and combine and arrange them into related groups. The process of locking and stacking panels in a vertical formation is called "docking." When panels are floating loose on the Stage, it is known as *stacking*.

Let's try to make the screen a little more designer-friendly by adding, grouping, and docking some new panels.

1 Choose Window > Align to open the Align panel, which helps you align elements along their horizontal or vertical axes.

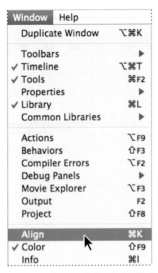

Open the Align panel through the Window menu.

The Align panel joins the Color, Swatches, and Library panels in the vertical dock on the right.

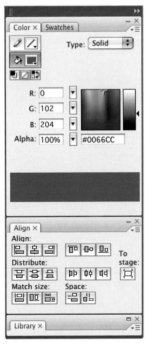

The Align panel opens in the vertical dock on the right.

2 Choose Window > Transform to open the Transform panel, which allows you to enter precise values to scale and rotate objects. Flash automatically places it to the right of the Align panel in the docking area.

3 Not all panels immediately open in the vertical dock. Choose Window > Other Panels > History to open the History panel, which tracks all the selections and menu choices made to any objects on the Stage.

Notice that it appears in the Stage area of the screen—not the most convenient location. You'll fix that in the next exercise.

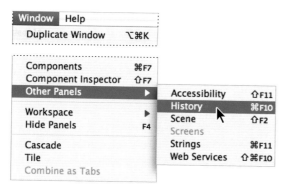

Access the History panel under Other Panels in the Window menu.

To close a panel, click the small x at the top right corner of the panel. To hide or show all panels at once without closing them, press the F4 key (Windows and Mac OS).

Stacking, shrinking, and storing panels

Sometimes you don't want to change which panels you see, but how and where they appear. The new Flash CS3 Professional interface allows you to expand panels to view more options, shrink them to icon view, or simply move a panel to a more convenient location.

1 Double-click the Library panel's tab to expand it. Double-clicking on the title tab of a closed panel expands it.

Expand the Library panel by double-clicking on its title tab.

2 To change the panels back to icon view, click the white double arrow (▸▸) in the top-right corner of the vertical dock. The double arrow is referred to as the Collapse to Icons button. When you click this button, the vertical dock collapses into icon view.

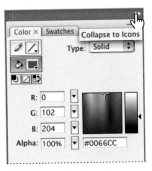

Switch the panels to icon view.

The benefit of the icon view is that it allows you to conserve space on your screen. In icon view, the Stage automatically expands slightly to the right to fill the space previously occupied by the expanded panels.

The panels in icon view.

3   Press the Align icon (▣); the Align panel expands, overlapping the Stage. Press the Align icon again to close the panel. This feature saves valuable screen space and allows you to access a panel if you need it temporarily, and then close it when you are done.

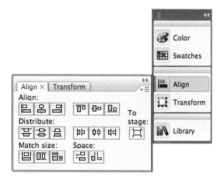

Clicking the icons expands the panels to the left.

4   To expand the dock back to its vertical size, click the Expand Dock button (the double arrows) in the upper-right corner, and the dock returns to its original size.

Switch back to full-size panels.

5   You will now dock the History panel with the Library panel. Click and hold the History panel's title tab, then drag it next to the Library panel's title tab on the right side of the screen. When the Library panel is highlighted, this indicates you are in a drop zone and can move the panel to this area. Release the History panel and it docks to the right of the Library panel.

6   Click the Collapse to Icons button (▸▸) in the upper-right corner of the vertical dock to collapse to the icon view. Note that the History panel now appears as part of the icon view. You will now rearrange the order of your panels by moving your History panel.

7   Click the History icon (▯5) and drag it into the Color and Swatches panel group. A blue highlight appears around a target panel group to indicate that it is a drop zone and that you can add the panel.

Managing workspaces

Once you arrange a layout that's ideal for your workflow, you can save it as a workspace for future use. You can save as many workspace layouts as you need, customizing them by task, project, or even for use among multiple users. Once you build up a collection of workspaces, Flash also offers controls for managing them.

Let's go ahead and set up your first custom workspace:

1   Choose Window > Workspace > Save Current.

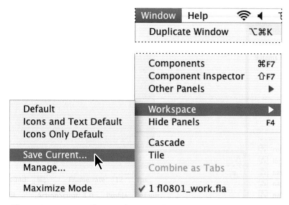

Choose Save Current from Workspace in the Window menu.

In the resulting dialog box, enter the name **Design Layout**, and press OK.

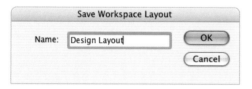

*Enter **Design Layout** in the Save Workspace Layout dialog box.*

2   Choose Window > Workspace > Default. The panels reset to the default Flash workspace layout.

3   To restore your custom workspace, choose Window > Workspace > Design Layout.

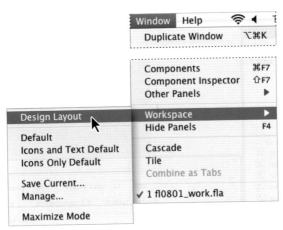

Access your saved workspace through Window > Workspace.

The panels and dock arrangement that you created in the previous exercise is now restored. Having multiple workspaces is very helpful for one person doing different types of projects or for multiple users who use the same machine. If you end up having multiple workspaces, you need a way to manage them.

4   Choose Window > Workspace > Manage.

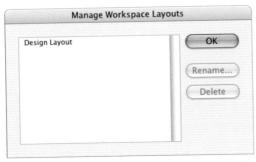

Manage your workspaces with the Manage Workspace Layouts dialog box.

The Manage Workspace Layout dialog box lists all saved workspaces, including your newly created Design Layout. Even with a single saved layout, you can edit, rename, or delete it from here.

5   Choose the Design Layout and click the Rename button. Rename it **08 Design Layout** and press OK.

6   Press OK again to exit the Manage Workspace Layouts dialog box.

You don't have to go to the menu area to switch workspaces. Click the Workspace drop-down menu (found on the right between the Timeline and the Stage) to see the same options available from Window > Workspace > Manage.

Setting preferences

Sometimes the little things can make the biggest difference in your workflow. Are you tired of seeing the welcome screen every time you launch Flash? Would you prefer having more levels of undo or a different highlight color? You can change these settings, and more, in Flash's Preferences dialog box.

1 Choose Edit > Preferences (Windows) or Flash > Preferences (Mac OS) to open the Preferences dialog box. Select General from the list of categories shown on the left.

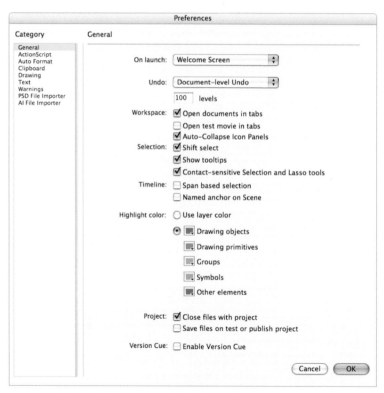

Options available in the General category of the Preferences dialog box.

2 To turn off the Welcome Screen, go to the On launch drop-down menu and choose No Document. You could also choose to have the application open a new document or even the last document saved.

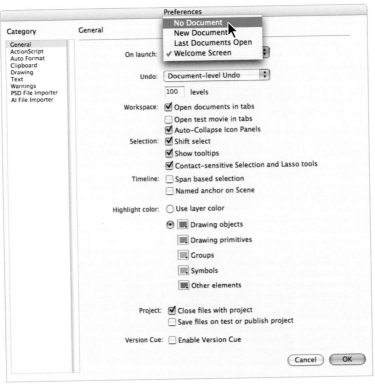

Use the On launch drop-down to turn off the Welcome Screen.

3 In the Undo section of the General preferences, the Undo levels are set to the default of 100. Type the value of 150 in this field. This increases the number of times you can Undo steps by 50. Flash supports up to 9999 undo levels, but this would likely slow down the performance of your system.

If you change your Undo preferences in the middle of a project, you will lose the history of the work you have done since you started your work session, which means you cannot go back and undo your previous actions. Object undos deal with tracking the separate steps performed on objects like the Stage, or symbols in the Library. Document undos deal with the series of linear actions you made in the current and open document like timeline changes, creating keyframes, and scaling.

4 Farther down in the General Preferences dialog box, you can set your preferred Highlight colors. You can change the default colors used for bounding boxes displayed around drawing objects, groups, or symbols. Click on the color swatch next the Drawing objects option and note that you could choose an alternate color here. Click on the main swatch color to avoid making changes at this time.

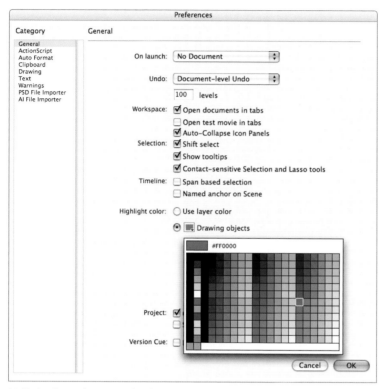

Highlight colors can be customized in the General section of the Preferences dialog box.

If you're a dedicated layer user, click the Use layer color button. This automatically sets bounding boxes to match the color assigned to each layer, so you'll know for sure to which layer a selected object belongs.

5 Press OK to commit the small changes made in this exercise.

Keyboard shortcuts

If customizing your workspace streamlines your workflow, then using keyboard shortcuts adds speed. Flash provides a window for you to view all the keyboard shortcuts in one location. You can do more than just identify shortcuts, however; you can also add, remove, and reassign shortcuts in one location, allowing you to truly customize the way Flash CS3 Professional functions.

Access the Keyboard Shortcuts dialog box from the Flash menu.

View and customize all Flash's keyboard shortcuts with the Keyboard Shortcuts dialog box.

1 Choose Edit > Keyboard Shortcuts (Windows) or Flash > Keyboard Shortcuts (Mac OS). In the Keyboard Shortcuts dialog box, choose Drawing Menu Commands from the Commands drop-down menu if it is not currently selected. Flash displays a list of all the commands specific to the Drawing menu below.

Access the Drawing Menu Commands from the Commands drop-down menu.

2 Scroll through the commands and locate Modify, then click on the triangle to the left to expand the options. Flash indicates whether or not a keyboard shortcut is assigned to any given command already. In this case, Ctrl+B (Windows) or Command+B (Mac OS) is assigned to Modify > Break Apart. You're going to change this in the coming steps.

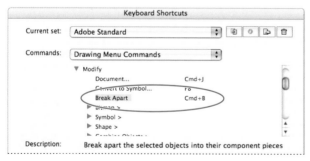

Find the keyboard shortcut assigned to Modify > Break Apart.

3 Before you can customize the shortcuts, you must first make a copy of your current set of shortcuts and save it with a new name. Immediately to the right of the Adobe Standard menu are four buttons. The first button is the Duplicate Set button (⊞). Press this now to duplicate the current keyboard shortcut set.

4 In the Duplicate dialog box, type **Mine** as the name for the duplicate set and press OK.

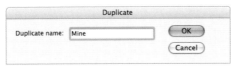

Name your new set of keyboard shortcuts.

5 Your new set, Mine, should appear selected in the Current set menu at the top, but if not, reselect it from the Current set drop-down menu.

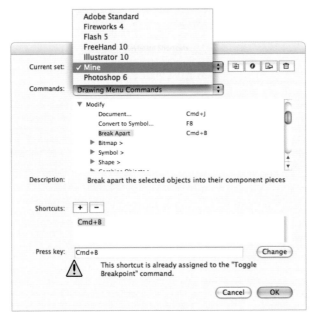

If necessary, select Mine from the Current set menu.

 To rename a set of shortcuts, click the Rename Set button (●) in the top-right corner of the Keyboard Shortcuts dialog box. To generate an HTML file listing every shortcut in the program, click the third button, Export Set as HTML, and then save the file to the desktop. You can open the file for reference at any time, or edit it with any standard text editor.

6   After saving the new shortcut set, let's edit the shortcut for Modify > Break Apart. Click on the Commands menu and choose Drawing Menu Commands. Click on the arrow to the left of Modify to expand it, and then select the Break Apart command. Click once inside the Press key field at the bottom of the window to activate the field, delete the current command, and then press Ctrl+Shift+F9 (Windows) or Command+Shift+F9 (Mac OS) on your keyboard.

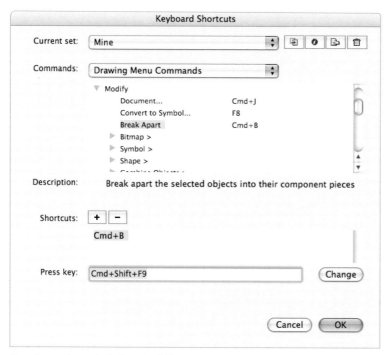

Enter the new shortcut in the Press key field.

The application can determine if the key combination you choose is available. For obvious reasons, you can only have one key combination for any given shortcut. You will now test this by trying different combinations.

7   Click inside the Press key field again and press Ctrl+M (Windows) or Command+M (Mac OS). You will receive no warning, therefore that combination is available. Now press Ctrl+K (Windows) or Command+K (Mac OS). A warning triangle appears, because that combination is the Align command's shortcut.

8   Press the Cancel button; you will not be modifying this keyboard shortcut right now.

To thoroughly customize your shortcuts, export the shortcut list as HTML, print it out, grab a pen, and circle the commands you use frequently. Choose the Shortcuts menu and try running a sequence of command keys until you find one that's usable, assign it to one of your frequently used commands, jot it down on your list, then try again for the next command.

Visual aids for alignment

Flash's visual aids streamline how you work on the Stage, whether it's drawing, placing objects, or aligning items in a layout. Rather than determining locations by eye or placing graphics through trial and error, you'll take advantage of guides, rulers, grid, guide layers, and advanced alignment tools.

Rulers and guides work together to let the user place an item on the Stage at specific locations, while guide layers change artwork into a device that can be used for alignment and reference purposes. The grid functions much like graph paper, and appears superimposed on the Stage so that you can precisely place objects on the Stage. The Align feature and Flash's various visual aids allow for very precise positioning. To put these visual aids to use and explore their benefits, you'll put together a sample home page for a design firm.

Rulers and guides

Rulers and guides work together to provide more precise placements in less time. Here's how they work.

1   Choose the View menu. If there is a checkmark to the left of the Rulers option, the rulers are currently displayed. If there is no checkmark, select the Rulers option now. When activated, rulers appear on the top and left side of your work area.

Rulers can be toggled on and off from the View menu.

By default, measurements on the rulers are displayed in pixels. You can easily change the unit of measurement in Flash CS3 Professional.

2 Choose Modify > Document. Then click on the Ruler units pull-down menu. You have the option to select inches, centimeters, millimeters, points, or pixels. Web pages and web graphics are typically designed using pixels, so select pixels if necessary and press OK.

Document Properties
Title:
Description:
Dimensions: 550 px (width) x 400 px (height)
Match: ○ Printer ○ Contents ◉ Default
Background color:
Frame rate: 12 fps
Ruler units: Pixels
Make Default / Cancel / OK

Change measurement units from the Document Properties dialog box.

3 Place your cursor on the horizontal ruler at the top of the Stage and then click and drag downwards. This pulls out a horizontal guideline from the ruler. Drag the guide to the 350-pixel mark displayed on the vertical (left-side) ruler. You will be using this guide to help you place the design firm's logo.

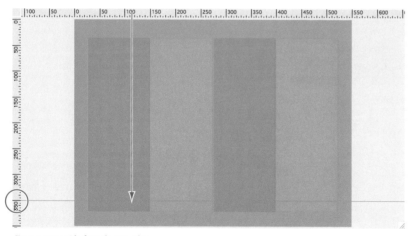

Drag a new guide from the top ruler.

4   Click on the Library tab to bring the Library panel forward, and click on the graphic symbol named logo from the list.

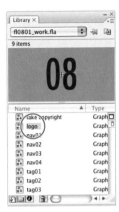

Select the logo graphic symbol.

5   Drag an instance of the logo symbol from the Library panel onto the Stage and drop it above the guide in the first orange column shown on the left. In the exact center of the logo is a small circle. This is the registration point, and you will now align it to your guide.

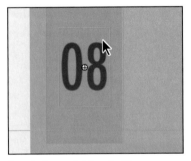

Drag the logo symbol from the Library.

6   Click the logo and drag it downwards. When the registration point approaches the guide, it snaps to it.

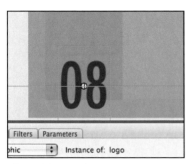

The symbol's centered registration point snaps to the guide.

So, what if you wanted the bottom of the logo to snap to the guide instead of the center? To do this, you need to edit the registration point. In order to permanently change the registration point of any library item, you need to edit the original symbol.

If you're finding that objects aren't snapping into place as you expected, check to make sure Snapping is enabled for your document. Choose View > Snapping and make sure Snap Align, Snap to Guides, and Snap to Objects are all checked.

7   Double-click on the logo graphic in the library to edit it. Once you are in the item's edit mode, select the type box with the Selection tool (▸).

In the symbol's edit mode, use the Selection tool to select the type box.

The registration mark, shown as a crosshair, appears to be centered, so you'll need to move the content relative to the registration point (the registration point itself cannot be moved).

8 If it's not already visible, choose Window > Align to open the Align panel, and click the To stage button on the right side of the panel.

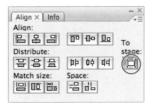

Click the To stage button on the Align panel.

The top row of buttons grouped under Align heading are all the alignment choices available to you. Place your cursor over the first button and a yellow box appears, indicating that this is the Align left edge option.

9 Place your cursor on the last button in the Align row, make sure the Align bottom edge box appears, and click once. The text box will move upwards and the registration mark is now aligned to the bottom of the text box.

By default, the alignment, sizing, and distribution options on the Align panel work by comparing two or more selected objects on the Stage. Selecting the To stage button sets the Stage itself as the ultimate point of reference, so results will be very different with this option enabled.

10 Click the Scene 1 link above the Stage to exit the symbol and return to the main Timeline. You'll see that the logo now properly sits with its lower edge resting on the guide. By default, guides always snap to the registration mark of an object.

Change the symbol's alignment so that it sits properly on the guide.

If you prefer, you can change the default snapping behavior of guides. Go to View > Snapping > Edit Snapping, and uncheck Snap to Guides to prevent objects from snapping to guides.

Guide layers

In keeping with good working practices when creating a Flash project, you will now add new layers for your text and background content. Additionally, you will learn how to make use of a new alignment tool: guide layers. Guide layers allow you to align objects on a standard layer to objects on the guide layer. The objects on guide layers act as a reference point for the objects on standard layers. Eventually, these guide layers will also help you in your animations.

Important information to consider is that objects on guide layers will not export with your final movie; objects on a guide layer are only visible within the authoring environment.

Before you work with guide layers, however, you will first add the content to your current document.

1   Click on the Insert Layer button (⊒) below the Timeline. Double-click the new layer name to rename it and type **Text**.

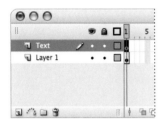

Create a new layer and name it **Text**.

2   Double-click on the existing layer 1 name, and rename this layer **Background**. You will now move the logo you added in the previous exercise to the Text layer

Rename the bottom layer **Background**.

3 Click on the logo "08" to select it, then choose Edit > Cut.

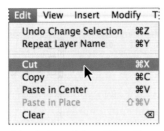

Select the logo and choose Edit > Cut.

4 Click on the Text layer to select it and then choose Edit > Paste in Place.

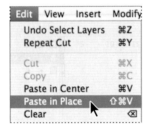

Move the logo to the Text layer.

The logo is placed on the new layer in the exact location it occupied on its original layer.

You are now going to convert the orange Background layer to a guide layer. This will allow you to use the structure of the columns to align the text you will be adding shortly.

5 Click the dot below the padlock column on the Background layer. This locks the orange columns so they can't be moved accidently. You will now remove the guide you added in the previous exercise. Part of the benefit of guide layers is that they remove the need to add multiple guides to your document. Instead of aligning to a guide, you align to an object.

6 Click the guide at the bottom of your document and drag it back to the ruler on the top. It is removed from the page.

7   Right-click (Windows) or Ctrl+click (Mac OS) on the Background layer in the Timeline, and choose Guide.

Choose Guide from the Background layer's contextual menu.

The standard layer icon converts to a T-square icon (✎), indicating that this is now a guide layer.

8   On the Text layer, select and drag the logo down to the bottom of the first orange column until the registration point snaps to the bottom of the column.

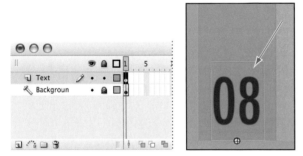

Drag the logo down to the bottom of the orange column.

Sensitivity

You can adjust how close a graphic needs to be to a guide before it snaps by choosing View > Snapping > Edit Snapping.

In the resulting dialog box, you can use the checkboxes at the top to set the type of snapping behavior you'd like to use.

A number of options are available for snapping behavior.

To change the pixel distance, or tolerance, click the Advanced button to access the Advanced options. Stage Border is how close the graphic needs to be before it snaps; increase or decrease that number according to your feel for moving elements around the Stage.

The good thing is that you can set it and forget it by clicking Save Default just under the Cancel button on the top-right side of the dialog box. Your new settings become the standard setting for the entire program, not just the current document.

9 Now you'll continue using the guide layer to position more graphics on the Stage.

Select the Text layer so it's active. Select the nav01 graphic symbol in the Library panel and drag an instance of it onto the Stage within the first orange column on the left. Do the same to place nav02, nav03, and nav04 in the second, third, and fourth columns, respectively.

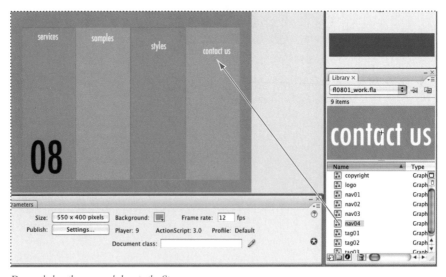

Drag and place the nav symbols onto the Stage.

10 To align the graphics, click and drag each one until its bounding box baseline is on top of its respective column, as shown below.

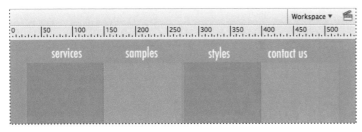

Place the nav symbols above their orange columns.

You will now convert the Background layer back into a standard layer.

11 Right-click (Windows) or Ctrl+Click (Mac OS) on the Background layer and deselect the Guide option. This converts this layer back to a standard layer.

12 Choose File > Save to save your work.

Advanced alignment

Because all four navigation elements are at the top of the columns, you will now properly align them, not just across the columns but also in spatial relation to each other.

1 Double-click the Align pane to open it and click the To stage button to turn it off.

2 Select the instance of nav01 (services) on the Stage and make sure it's centered above the column.

You can cycle through and select symbols on the Stage by using the Tab key.

3 Click on the padlock icon (🔒) to the right of the Background layer to unlock it. You will be aligning the navigation elements to the column and you need to be able to select the column.

4   Shift+click to select the orange column underneath the nav01 symbol instance you already have selected, so that both the symbol instance and the column are selected. Click on the Align panel, then click Align horizontal center to center the nav01 symbol above the column.

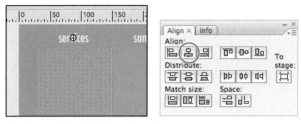

Align the symbols with their respective columns.

5   Click on the last navigation element (contact us) and then Shift+click on the column beneath it. Click on the Align horizontal center button in the Align panel to center it.

Now that the first and last navigation elements are aligned with their respective columns, you will work with the Distribute feature. Distribute is designed to evenly distribute the space between objects and doesn't necessarily have anything to do with alignment.

6   Shift+click the four navigation elements to select them all at once, then click the Distribute horizontal center button. The first and last objects are fixed and the second and third objects are now evenly distributed between them. Each element should be centered over its assigned column.

Select and distribute all four nav symbols.

Distribute looks at the registration point, not the bounding boxes, of each graphic. So, when you look at the four graphics, the centered registration marks are evenly distributed.

7 With all four items still selected, click the Space evenly horizontally button ( ). Notice how nav02 and nav03 shift a bit. It's the space between the bounding boxes, and not the center points, that becomes even. Distribute distributes the center points of graphics, while Space distributes the spacing between the bounding boxes of graphics.

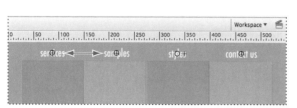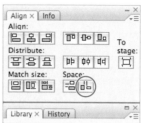

Choose settings that even the spaces between the symbols' bounding boxes.

8 The last few items you need to place on the Stage are the tag graphics. Drag the tag01 symbol from the Library panel to the Stage and position it in the top third of the third column.

9 Click and drag the tag02 text and place it in the third column beneath the tag01 text you just added. Drag tag03 and place it in the middle of the fourth column. You will now be using the Align panel to center these.

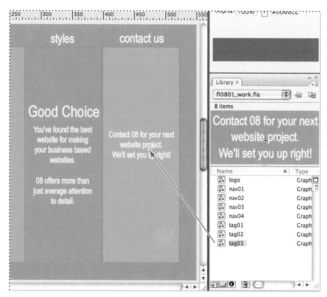

Drag instances of tag01, tag02, and tag03 into the second and third columns.

10   Shift+click tag01 and tag02 to select both graphics, double-click the Align panel if necessary, and then click the Align horizontal center button in the Align panel to center the two graphics. You will now group these two graphics so you can align all of the text inside the last column.

11   Choose Modify > Group to group tag01 and tag02 together. Grouping two objects together allows you to align the entire unit within the column.

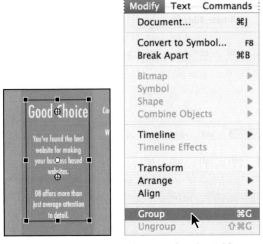

After centering tag01 and tag02, select Group from the Modify menu.

12   Shift+click the third orange column to select both it and the grouped text, then click Align vertical center and Align horizontal center.

13   Click on tag03 in the fourth column and then Shift+click the fourth column to select it as well. Click the Align vertical center button and the Align horizontal center button. Aligning your text in this fashion is much more precise than doing it by hand.

Refining your aligned objects

The devil is always in the details. Although you have been able to align tag03 within its own column, what if you wanted to align the top of the paragraph in column four with the top of the paragraph in column three? You could use a guide, but there is a more efficient method using the align techniques you have been learning.

1 Select the group that contains tag01 and tag02, and choose Modify > Ungroup to ungroup the two graphics. You must now ungroup these so you can align the two text boxes.

Ungroup tag01 and tag02.

2 Shift+click tag02 and tag03 to select both graphics. Choose Align top edge in the Align panel; tag03 jumps upward to align itself with tag02.

 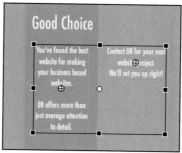

Select tag02 and tag03 and click the Align top edge button in the Align panel.

3 Congratulations! You have have finished this lesson. Choose File > Save to save your work.

Grids

If you find that rulers and guides become too time-consuming for you, consider setting up a grid system to assist in placing graphics on the Stage. To turn on the grid behind the Stage, choose View > Grid > Show Grid.

To edit the grid details, such as color or increments, choose View > Grid > Edit Grid.

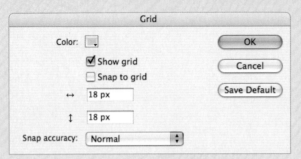

Grid options can be accessed by choosing View > Grid > Edit Grid.

In the Edit Grid dialog box, you can choose to show or hide the grid, change the grid line color, and adjust snapping accuracy. It can be very frustrating to move a graphic onstage and see it randomly jump to a guide or grid line. Change snapping accuracy to suit your working style, and you'll have fewer surprises during layout.

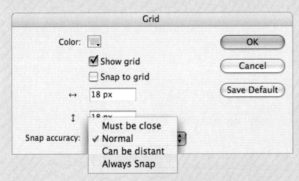

The Snap accuracy drop-down menu adjusts tolerance levels for snapping.

Self study

To do more with the interactive .swf file you just made for the fictional design firm, read about how to turn nav01, nav02, nav03, and nav04 into clickable buttons in Lesson 11, "Creating Button Symbols." In Lesson 11, you'll learn how to assign and cue different visual and audio effects that will occur when a user clicks or rolls over a button.

To make the logo graphic a little jazzier, it could be created as a movie clip that could slowly strobe between different color states or alpha states. Lesson 13, "Introducing Movie Clips," covers how movie clips are created and how animation is contained within them.

To make the best use of all these new additions, it's essential to get yourself organized and establish a good workflow. Write down how many buttons, graphics, and movie clips you'll need to place on the Stage before starting your project. Sketch out a flowchart that illustrates how many screens are needed as links for each one of your navigation buttons. A little pencil and paper time will save hours on the creation of your designs.

Review

Questions

1 How do you add or modify keyboard shortcuts to work more efficiently?

2 How can you increase the sensitivity of snapping to guides on the Stage?

3 How do you determine whether Flash tracks object- or document-level changes for the Edit > Undo command?

Answers

1 Go to Flash > Preferences or Edit > Preferences and choose an element to make a shortcut from the Commands drop-down menu.

2 You can set the tolerance to be higher or lower from this menu: View > Snapping > Edit Snapping. If you need to change the pixel distance or tolerance, click on the Advanced button.

3 From the Preferences menu, go to the General tab. Change the Undo drop-down menu to either Object or Document.

What you'll learn in this lesson:

- Importing images from other applications

- Using layered Photoshop and Illustrator files

- Modifying artwork used in Flash

Working with Imported Files

Even once you've learned to create vector artwork and text directly in Flash, you may still need a little help from the outside. Fortunately, Flash can import a wide variety of file formats into Flash documents. With this capability, you can create raster and vector images, audio files, and even video in other applications, and then import them for use in Flash.

Starting up

Before starting, make sure that your tools and panels are consistent by resetting your workspace. See "Resetting the Flash workspace" on page 3.

You will work with several files from the fl09lessons folder in this lesson. Make sure that you have loaded the fllessons folder onto your hard drive from the supplied DVD. See "Loading lesson files" on page 3.

See Lesson 9 in action!

Use the accompanying video to gain a better understanding of how to use some of the features shown in this lesson. Open the DynamicLearning_FlashCS3.swf file located in the Videos folder and select Lesson 9 to view the video training file for this lesson.

The project

In this lesson, you will work with a series of bitmap and vector images to practice importing and manipulating external files. First, you'll import a flat bitmap image and learn the techniques for modifying and updating it. Then, you'll move on to artwork in Adobe Photoshop and Illustrator native formats (.psd and .ai, respectively) to take advantage of Flash CS3's new import features for these files.

In addition to still images, Flash can import both audio and video files, making it a very flexible multimedia authoring environment. Although the process of bringing both these types of media into Flash is similar to the way in which you import images, each media constitutes its own unique situation. This lesson concentrates on still images only. Working with audio files is covered in Lesson 12, "Adding Sound to your Movies," and working with video is covered in Lesson 14, "Working with Video."

Import formats

One of the strengths of Flash is its ability to import a wide variety of file formats. Flash can read and import these file types:

- Adobe Illustrator (.ai)
- AutoCAD (.dxf)
- Bitmap (.bmp)
- Enhanced Windows Metafile (.emf)
- FreeHand (.fh, .ft)
- GIF and animated GIF (.gif)
- JPEG (.jpg)
- PNG (.png)
- Flash Player (.swf)
- Windows Metafile (.wmf)

If you add the QuickTime Player plug-in, a free download for both Windows and Mac OS users, from *Apple.com*, you can import six additional formats:

- Mac Paint (.pntg)
- PICT (.pct)
- QuickTime Image (.qtif)
- Silicon Graphics Image (.sgi)
- TARGA (.tga)
- TIFF (.tif)

Import options

Flash offers four separate commands that enable you to import a variety of external media and control how it's treated once it is in Flash. Import to Stage, Import to Library, Open External Library, and Import Video all perform slightly different, but equally important, operations:

Import to Stage: Automatically places an instance of the imported file on the Flash Stage at the time of import.

Import to Library: Places the imported file in your library and allows you to manually place it onto the Flash Stage.

Open External Library: Allows you to open the library of any Flash file (.fla) and use its assets.

Import Video: Opens the Import Video wizard to walk you through the steps needed to bring your video files into Flash.

If you select a video file while in the Import dialog box for Import to Stage or Import to Library, Flash automatically opens the Import Video wizard. The option you choose depends on how you want to work with Flash. Some people prefer to import everything into the Library at once and then pull the content from there, while others prefer to import assets onto the Stage as they are needed.

Importing still images

Still images, such as photographs, scanned artwork, and graphics created in Photoshop, are some of the most common types of files that users want to bring into Flash. You can choose how to import images and how you work with them once they are in Flash. Imported bitmap images can even be directly edited in an external application such as Fireworks or Photoshop. The images are then updated automatically without having to be reimported. In the following exercises, you'll explore some of those choices.

Viewing the completed lesson file

1 If you don't already have Flash CS3 Professional open, launch it now.

2 Choose File > Open and locate the file named fl0901_done.fla within the fl09lessons folder that you copied to your desktop. Click Open.

3 The fl0901_done.fla file is the completed file that you will make in this lesson. Keep it open for reference, or close it by choosing File > Close.

The finished file.

Import a bitmap image

One of the easiest ways to import a bitmap image is with the Import to Stage command.

1 Create a new Flash file by choosing File > New, or pressing Ctrl+N (Windows) or Command+N (Mac OS). When the New Document dialog box appears, choose Flash File (ActionScript 3.0). Click OK.

2 Select File > Save As. In the Save As dialog box, navigate to the fl09lessons folder, then type **fl0901_work.fla** into the Name text field. Press Save.

3   Choose File > Import > Import to Stage to open the Import dialog box.

Import to Stage can be found under Import in the File menu.

The keyboard shortcut for Import to Stage is Ctrl+R (Windows) or Command+R (Mac OS).

4   In the Import dialog box, select the fl0901.jpg file from the fl09lessons folder. This is a scanned pencil drawing for you to use as stand-in artwork for an electronic greeting card. Press Open (Windows) or Import (Mac OS).

5   Flash detects that the file you are trying to import may be a part of a sequence of images, and pops up a dialog box asking if you want to import them all. Press No to import the selected image only.

Flash detects a sequence of images in the folder containing fl0901.jpg.

When using Import to Stage, you can import individual still images or image sequences that have been manually created or exported from video editing and animation programs. If Flash sees that a sequence exists, it gives you the option to import the entire series of images. Flash can then place these images sequentially in consecutive frames in the Timeline.

The imported item appears in your Library panel, and Flash places an instance of it on the Stage.

The library stores .jpg files as well as symbols.

The library doesn't store just symbols. All imported items, whether bitmap graphics, sound files, or video clips, appear in the Library panel.

6   Now that you have your stand-in image in Flash, you can begin to build the e-card around it. The graphic and the Stage are very different sizes, so the first order of business is to change the Stage to match the size of your image. Click in the background of the Stage to deselect the image. This changes the display of the Property inspector to show the document's properties.

The Property inspector is dynamic, showing you the properties of the document when no object is selected.

7 In the Property inspector, press the Size button. In the Document Properties dialog box that appears, type **286** in the (width) text field and **500** in the (height) text field. Press OK.

Change the dimensions of your document in the Document Properties dialog box.

8 Your image may not be centered on the Stage. To fix this, select the image with the Selection tool. Choose Window > Align or press the keyboard shortcut Ctrl+K (Windows) or Command+K (Mac OS) to open the Align panel.

9 Make sure the To stage button is selected and select the Align horizontal center and Align vertical center buttons to center the image on the Stage.

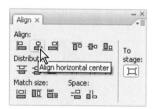

The Align panel allows you to align and distribute artwork on the Stage.

10 Choose File > Save to save your work.

Adding text

1   In the Timeline, double-click on Layer 1 to rename it **background**. It is always a good idea to change the default layer names to more descriptive names that help you identify content at a glance.

2   With the background layer selected, press the Insert Layer button (⬛) below the Timeline to add a new layer. Double-click on Layer 2 and rename it **text**. This layer is where you will insert and animate the words *Happy Halloween* for your e-card.

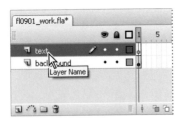

Layers can be renamed by double-clicking them.

3   In the Timeline, select Frame 1 of the text layer, then select the Text tool (T) from the Tools panel. In the Property inspector, select Times New Roman (Windows) or Times (Mac OS), then type **55** in the Font size text field or move the slider to about 55. Press the Text (fill) color button and choose black from the Swatches panel.

4   Click anywhere on the Stage and type **Happy Halloween** in the text box that appears. Press Enter (Windows) or Return (Mac OS) after you type the word *Happy* to place *Halloween* on a separate line.

The Property inspector allows you to set the behavior of tools and objects you create in Flash CS3 Professional.

5   Choose the Selection tool (▶) from the Tools panel and select the text box. In the Property inspector, enter **–264** in the X text field and **367** in the Y text field to position the text to the left of the Stage.

6   You now have a keyframe on your text layer, but to animate the text, you need two keyframes. Right-click (Windows) or Ctrl+click (Mac OS) on Frame 40 of the text layer and select Insert Keyframe. The new keyframe copies the contents of the keyframe before it.

7   With the Selection tool, select the *Happy Halloween* text in the gray work area. Type **7** in the X text field in the Property inspector and then press the Tab key to apply the change. This places the text onstage. Next, you will bring the image to Frame 40 so both the stand-in and the text are visible.

By changing only the X position of the text, the image now moves from left to right.

8   Select Frame 40 in the background layer. Right-click (Windows) or Ctrl+click (Mac OS) and select Insert Frame from the contextual menu. Now both the image and the text are visible in this frame.

Layers are only visible when they have frames or keyframes in the Timeline.

9   Click on Frame 1 of the text layer in the Timeline and select Motion from the Tween drop-down menu in the Property inspector. Press the Enter (Windows) or Return (Mac OS) key to preview the animation. The text should move from left to right on the screen.

10   Select File > Save to save your work. Keep this file open, as you need it for the next exercise.

Swapping out an imported file

The Library panel has the ability to replace one imported image with another. This is a very helpful feature when, for example, you want to use a stand-in image as a placeholder while the final artwork is still being developed.

Now you will swap out the basic image you imported from Photoshop with the image you will use in your final e-card.

1   Select the fl0901.jpg file in your Library panel and click the Properties button (**o**) at the bottom of the panel.

2   In the Bitmap Properties dialog box that appears, choose Import.

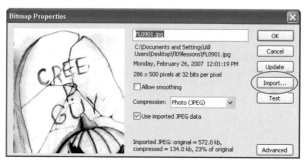

Use the Import button to swap the selected target file for another image.

3   In the Import Bitmap dialog box, select fl0902.jpg from the fl09lessons folder and press Open.

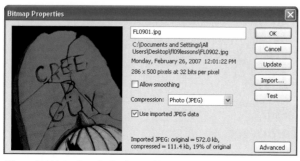

Choose fl0902.jpg from the fl09lessons folder to import.

4   In the Bitmap Properties dialog box, press OK. The new image replaces the original fl0901.jpg wherever it occurs in your project.

5   Choose File > Save to save your work.

A full-color image replaces the line drawing on the Stage.

Modifying imported artwork

One of the advantages of working in Flash is that you can easily modify imported artwork using an external editor, and have the changes take effect in Flash. When you want to modify imported artwork, Flash gives you the option of opening the external editor directly from the Library panel. In this exercise you will use Adobe Photoshop CS3. If you do not currently have Photoshop CS3 installed, you can download a trial version from *Adobe.com.* or you can skip this step and jump ahead to the next exercise in this lesson.

1   If necessary, open your Library panel by choosing Window > Library. Right-click (Windows) or Ctrl+click (Mac OS) on the fl0901.jpg file shown in the Library panel.

2   From the contextual menu that appears, choose Edit with.

Right-click or Ctrl+click to use Edit with.

If Flash recognizes that you have Adobe Photoshop installed, then Edit with Photoshop appears above the Edit with option. You can use Adobe Photoshop to edit any standard bitmap image.

3 From the Select External Editor dialog box that appears, navigate to the Photoshop CS3 application and press Open.

Photoshop CS3 allows users to create and manipulate artwork.

 Except when using Photoshop as mentioned previously, Adobe Flash CS3 Professional requires that you browse for your image editing application each time you want to edit a file.

4 In Photoshop, select Image > Adjustments > Curves to open the Curves dialog box. In Photoshop, curves are used to adjust the shadows, mid-tones, and highlights of an image. You will use curves here to darken the image to make it a little spookier.

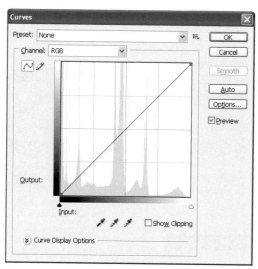

The Photoshop CS3 Curves dialog box.

5 Place your cursor at the middle point of the diagonal line, then click and drag down to create an arc. As you drag the curve deeper, the image becomes darker. Adjust the curve to your liking, remembering that you want it to look spooky but not so dark that you can no longer make out the image's details. Press OK.

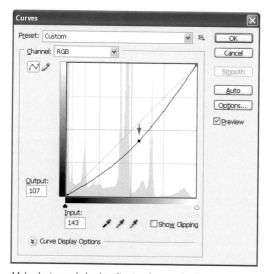

Make the image darker by adjusting the curve level.

6   Select File > Save. If the JPEG Options dialog box appears, click OK to accept the default settings and choose File > Close to close the image. Choose File > Exit to close Photoshop. Return to Flash. Your image has been updated automatically.

7   In Flash, select File > Save. Do not close this file.

Updating imported files

What if you forget to use Edit with, and you simply open Photoshop (or another external editor) and modify previously imported images? You may want to update those files in the Flash library without the time and trouble of re-importing them. Flash offers an easy solution.

1   Select the fl0901.jpg file in the Library panel.

2   Press the Properties button (●) at the bottom of the Library panel to open the Bitmap Properties dialog box.

3   In the Bitmap Properties dialog box, press Update. Changes you made to the imported image outside of Flash should now be visible.

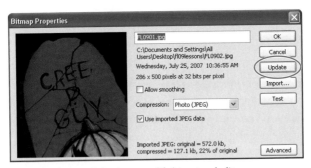

The Update button refreshes images modified in external editors.

4   Press OK to exit the Bitmap Properties dialog box. Keep this file open for the next part of this lesson.

Importing Photoshop files

In addition to importing standard bitmap image formats, Flash now offers enhanced native import of Photoshop .psd files. Now you can import layered Photoshop files (including full support for Layer Comps) and choose which layers to import and how to treat each one as it's placed in Flash.

Importing a layered Photoshop file

To see how these settings work, import a layered .psd file:

1   With fl0901_work.fla still open, choose File > Import > Import to Library.

2   In the Import to Library dialog box, select fl0903.psd from the fl09lessons folder and press Open (Windows) or Import to Library (Mac OS). The PSD Import dialog box opens.

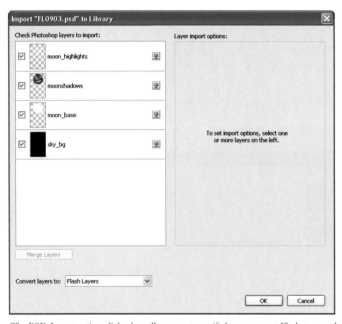

The PSD Import options dialog box allows you to specify how you want Flash to treat the layered Photoshop file.

Photoshop import options

When you import a .psd file, Flash automatically opens the new Photoshop Import dialog box, which is divided into two main areas: On the left, you choose which layers to bring into Flash from your Photoshop document (by default, all layers are selected for import). When you highlight a layer on the left, its options appear on the right.

The layer options are:

Import this image layer as: Specifies whether to import the layer as a flat bitmap image or with layer styles as editable sections of the image.

Create movie clip for this layer: Creates a movie clip symbol from the imported bitmap layer at import and adds it to your library.

Publish settings: Defines the compression setting with which each bitmap image is published. Flash uses two types of compression: the Lossy setting, which applies JPEG compression, and Lossless, which applies PNG compression. By default, the compression setting is the same setting as in your Flash file's Publish Settings.

3 In the PSD Import dialog box, uncheck the checkbox next to the layer named sky_bg. Since you are importing this PSD into a Flash movie, you do not need the background layer.

4 Shift+click on the three remaining layers: moon_highlights, moonshadows, and moon_base.

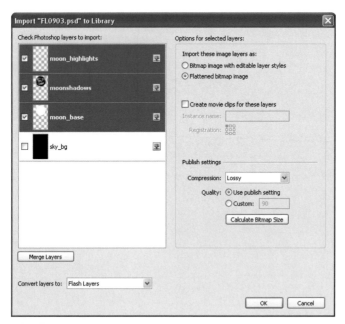

Select all three layers.

5 Click the Merge Layers button at the bottom of the list of layers. This allows Flash to treat all three layers as if they were one. You will use this to create a new movie clip directly from the PSD Import dialog box.

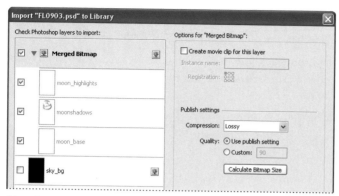

Merge the top three layers.

Selecting multiple layers is a great way to apply the same operation to all layers at once, or to merge layers into one object within the Flash environment.

6 Double-click on the name of the new Merged Bitmap layer and rename it **Moon**.

7 With the Moon layer selected, select the checkbox next to Create movie clip for this layer. Center the movie clip's registration point. Leave all other settings as you find them and press OK.

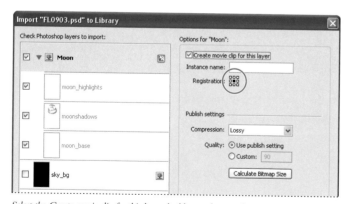

Select the Create movie clip for this layer checkbox and center the registration point.

8 You now have two new items in the library: a graphic symbol named fl0903.psd and a folder named fl0903.psd Assests. The graphic symbol contains all the objects that were in the Photoshop file in their original positions and their relation to each other, while the folder contains the individual imported bitmap layers (located in the Assets sub-folder) and the movie clips created during import.

In the Library panel, double-click on the fl0903.psd Assets folder to open it.

9 Click on the Insert Layer button (⊒) below the Timeline to create a new layer. Double-click on the layer name and rename it **moon**. Select the first frame of the new moon layer.

10 Drag the Moon movie clip symbol from the fl0903.psd Assets folder within the Library panel to the Stage. Do not worry about where you place it; you will deal with that in a few moments.

Working with the Moon

Once a PSD has been placed into Flash, it can be edited like any natively created content. In addition, Flash has a variety of built-in filters that can be used to add style to your artwork.

1 With the Selection tool (▸), select the moon image on the Stage and go to Window > Transform to open the Transform panel.

2 Click on the constrain checkbox if it is not currently selected and change either value to **50**. Press Enter (Windows) or Return (Mac OS). The moon is reduced in size by half.

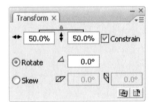

Reduce the moon to 50% of its original size.

3 In the Property Inspector, change the X position of the moon to **258** and the Y position to **40**. This positions it in the upper-right corner of the Stage.

4   With the moon still selected, select the Filters panel, located behind the Property inspector, to make it active. Press the Add filter button (⊕) and select Glow from the list of filters. Set Blur X and Blur Y to **36**. Set Strength to **50** and Quality to Medium. Select white for the color. This creates a nice, subtle glow around the moon.

Setting up the glow for the moon graphic in the Filters panel.

5   The glow from the previous step is nice, but this project would be much more interesting if the glow were animated. Click on frame 40 in the moon layer. Right-click (Windows) or Ctrl+click (Mac OS) and choose Insert Keyframe from the menu that appears.

6   On the Stage, select the moon with the Selection tool and in the Filters panel change the Blur X and Blur Y to **70**. Change the Strength to **85** and leave the Quality at Medium.

Change the Filter setting to animate the moon's glow.

7   Select Frame 1 in the moon layer. In the Property Inspector, choose Motion from the Tween pull-down menu.

You are now going to duplicate the blur animation on the moon image and extend the Timeline to 80 frames.

8   In the Timeline, right-click/Ctrl+click on Frame 1 of the moon layer. Select Copy Frames from the menu. Select Frame 80 and right-click/Ctrl+click and choose Paste Frames from the contextual menu.

9   Select frame 40 of the moon layer. In the Property Inspector, choose Motion from the Tween pull-down menu.

10 Shift+click to select Frame 80 of both the text and background layers. Right-click/ Ctrl+click and select Insert Frame from the menu. This extends the layers so that they are visible for the duration of the animation.

11 Choose Control > Test Movie to preview your Flash animation and choose File > Save. Keep the file open for the next part of this lesson.

Importing Illustrator artwork

As with .psd files, importing and using native Illustrator .ai files in Flash is now enhanced with a variety of features to make integration with Illustrator more seamless than ever.

Enhanced import options available in the new AI Import dialog box give you the flexibility to build your layered projects in Illustrator, and then determine how the artwork on individual layers should be handled on import.

Let's import an Illustrator file to see these features in action:

1 With fl0901_work.fla still open, Select Insert > New Symbol. In the Create New Symbol dialog box, rename the symbol **bat_mc**, and choose Movie clip for Type. Press OK.

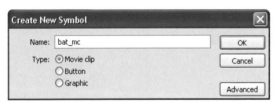

Create a new symbol named **bat_mc.**

2 In your new movie clip's timeline, double-click the layer named Layer 1 and rename it **bat**.

3 Choose File > Import > Import to Stage.

4 In the Import to Stage dialog box, select fl0904.ai from the fl09lessons folder and press Open (Windows) or Import (Mac OS).

The AI Import dialog box opens with each layer and sub-layer of your Illustrator document represented. The AI Import dialog box is divided into two main areas. On the left you select the layers or sub-layers you want to import, and on the right you specify the options for how Flash treats each layer.

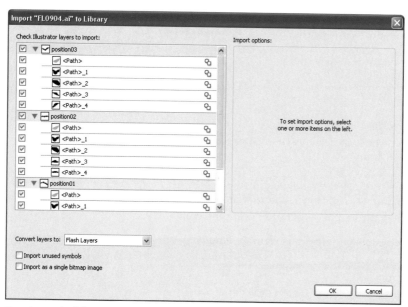

Every layer and sub-layer in your Illustrator file is visible in the Import dialog.

5 To make viewing more manageable, collapse all of the sub-layers by clicking the triangle icon to the left of the following three layer names: position03, position02, and position01.

To easily collapse or expand all layers at once, right-click/Ctrl+click inside the layer view on the left side of the dialog box and choose Collapse All/Expand All from the contextual menu that appears.

6   Select the Illustrator layer named position01. On the right, click the checkbox next to Create movie clip. Enter **position01** in the Instance name field and choose a centered registration point.

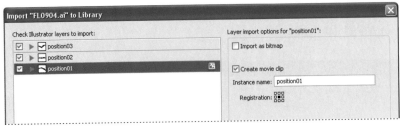

The AI Import dialog box streamlines the process of importing Adobe Illustrator files.

Setting the registration point of a movie clip is very important. The registration point determines how a movie clip is scaled, rotated, or otherwise transformed.

7   Repeat the previous step for the layers named position02 and position03. Remember to change the name of each movie clip to match the name of the Illustrator layer and also be sure to click the center registration point for each.

What's in an instance name?

When you import the contents of a layer as a movie clip, you have the option to specify an instance name. Instance names are used by ActionScript (Flash's built-in scripting language) to programmatically manipulate and animate movie clip instances on the Stage. This name serves as a unique identifier that ActionScript can use to target a specific movie clip instance on the Stage. Instance names for a movie clip instance can be set at any time from the Property inspector.

8   Click on the Convert layers to menu and choose Keyframes. This imports each individual Illustrator layer as a separate keyframe. Since you used the Import to Stage command here, each keyframe is positioned on your movie clip's timeline, providing you with a ready-made animation straight from Illustrator.

More Illustrator Import Options

The AI Import dialog box offers three additional options:

Import as bitmap: Converts vector artwork from Illustrator into a bitmap image on import.

Import as a single bitmap image: Converts all vector Illustrator layers into a single bitmap image on import.

Import unused symbols: Imports any unused objects from the Illustrator symbols panel into Flash.

9 Press OK to import the Illustrator file. The Illustrator layers should now occupy the first three frames of the bat_mc timeline.

The Timeline now shows three keyframes for each layer added to the Stage.

10 Select the Scene 1 link above the Stage to return to the main timeline. Click on the moon layer, and press the Insert Layer button (⬒) on the Timeline to insert a new layer. Double-click the new layer name and rename it **bat**.

11 Drag an instance of the bat_mc movie clip onto the Stage from the Library panel. Don't worry about the position of the movie clip just yet.

12 Choose File > Save to save your work.

Animating the Bat

Movie clips can be animated using basic motion tweens, just as the Happy Halloween text was animated.

1 With the Selection tool (⬉), select the instance of the bat_mc movie clip that is on the Stage.

2 If it is not already open, select Window > Transform to open the Transform panel. Confirm that the Constrain checkbox is checked and type **10** in either the Height or Width fields. Press the Tab key to apply the changes. This scales the bat movie clip down to ten percent of its original size.

3 In the Property inspector, set the movie clip's X coordinate to **332** and the Y coordinate to **–35**. This positions it off the Stage, to the right of the moon.

4 Select Frame 40 of the bat layer. Right-click (Windows) or Ctrl+click (Mac OS) and choose Insert Keyframe from the contextual menu. Use the Selection tool to select the bat.

5 In the Property inspector, change the movie clip's X coordinate to **115** and the Y coordinate to **95**.

6   In the Transform panel, change the movie clip's width or height value to **30**. Press Tab to apply the changes. This gives the impression that the bat is flying toward the viewer.

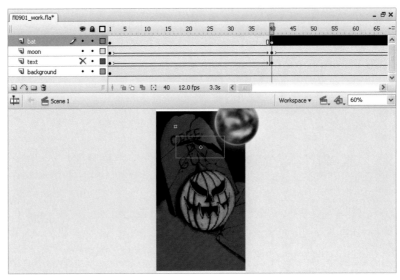

Using the Timeline to animate the bat.

7   Select Frame 80 of the bat layer. Right-click/Ctrl + click and choose Insert Keyframe from the contextual menu. Click on the bat to select it. In the Property Inspector, change the movie clip's X coordinate to –217 and the Y coordinate to 46. In the Transform panel, change the movie clip's width or height value to 50. Press Tab to apply the change.

8   Select Frame 1 in the bat layer and in the Property Inspector chose Motion from the Tween drop-down menu. Repeat this for Frame 40.

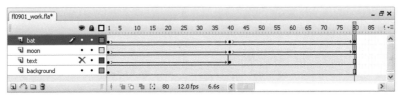

Finishing the bat animation.

9   Choose Control > Test Movie to preview your Flash animation. The bat will fly from the upper-righthand corner to the lower-left and slowly scale larger. Choose File > Save to save your work.

Congratulations! You have finished the lesson. Choose File > Close.

Self study

Import a variety of bitmap images into your Flash file and then practice replacing and updating them.

Import a Photoshop or Illustrator file into Flash, and practice combining the layers together to create different parts of the image that are editable in different fashions. Experiment with Import to Stage to see how the layer contents can be distributed among Flash layers and keyframes.

Review

Questions

1 What is the advantage of importing layered Photoshop and Illustrator files?

2 What is the advantage of being able to update an imported bitmap image?

3 What are the four options in the Import sub-menu, and what do they do?

Answers

1 Each individual layer of a layered file can be imported as a separate object in Flash. In addition, you can pick and choose which layers you want to import.

2 Updating an imported image allows you to make changes or corrections to the original image without having to re-import it into Flash. When you update an image, all occurrences of that image in your Flash movie are also be updated.

3 Import to Stage automatically places an instance of the imported file on the Flash Stage at the time of import. Import to Library places the imported file in your library and allows you to manually place it onto the Flash Stage. Open External Library allows you to open the library of any Flash file (.fla) and use its assets. Import Video opens the Import Video wizard to walk you through the steps needed to bring your video files into Flash.

What you'll learn in this lesson:

- Understanding ActionScript basics
- Using the Actions panel
- Comparing ActionScript 3.0 and ActionScript 2.0
- Placing actions on the Timeline
- Controlling playback
- Using frame labels

Introducing ActionScript

When it's time to do more with your movies, Flash's built-in scripting language, ActionScript, puts you in the driver's seat. In addition to controlling timelines and enabling buttons for navigation and user controls, ActionScript can handle dynamically generated animation, database connectivity, and real-time loading and control of images, sound, and video.

Starting up

Before starting, make sure that your tools and panels are consistent by resetting your workspace. See "Resetting the Flash workspace" on page 3.

You will work with several files from the fl10lessons folder in this lesson. Make sure that you have loaded the fllessons folder onto your hard drive from the supplied DVD. See "Loading lesson files" on page 3.

See Lesson 10 in action!

Use the accompanying video to gain a better understanding of how to use some of the features shown in this lesson. Open the DynamicLearning_FlashCS3.swf file located in the Videos folder and select Lesson 10 to view the video training file for this lesson.

The project

You will learn how to stop, play, and loop an animation, using ActionScript to control the timeline. To view the finished file, Choose File > Open and select either the fl1002_done.fla or fl1003_done.fla file from within the fl10lessons folder. There are two done files for this lesson because you will be learning how to create the same animation using ActionScript 2.0 and ActionSctipt 3.0. Close the file when you are finished, or keep it open as a reference.

The finished file.

Exploring the lesson file

The lesson file features animation of a basketball being thrown through a hoop, hitting the ground, and bouncing back up again. It is composed of several tweens and a motion guide, which steers the basketball through the initial toss into the basket. To keep the timeline manageable, all layers related to the animation have been grouped into a single layer folder named Basketball.

1   Choose File > Open, and navigate to the fl10lessons folder.

2   Select the file named fl1001.fla and press Open.

3   Before you get started, choose File > Save As, type **fl1001_work.fla** in the File name text field, then navigate to the fl10lessons folder and press Save.

4   Leave the file open, as you'll be using it in the next exercise.

What is ActionScript?

ActionScript is Flash's built-in scripting language and your way of sending instructions to the Flash Player and exerting more control over your movie. Using Flash's Actions panel, you can create and place lines of ActionScript code (often referred to as actions), in keyframes on the timeline, in external files, or directly on buttons and movie clips (ActionScript 2.0 only). These actions are then interpreted and carried out by the Flash Player during playback. If the idea of typing code seems a little overwhelming, don't worry; the Actions panel features Script Assist mode, which helps you create and place actions with minimal effort.

At its most basic level, ActionScript can control the playhead to fine-tune the behavior of animations or enable user controls for navigation of the Timeline (such as stop and play buttons). Beyond this, ActionScript is a powerful language that can manage virtually any object, visible or not, throughout your movie. It can even retrieve and display information from databases, files, and web services.

ActionScript 2.0 or 3.0: which should you use?

The first step when working with ActionScript is deciding which version to use. Flash comes with both ActionScript 3.0, the latest version, and 2.0, the previous version. The Flash Player continues to run ActionScript 2.0 and 3.0 side-by-side via two virtual machines (VM1 and VM2), one dedicated to each version. At this writing, ActionScript 2.0 is still in use for most Flash movies and continues to be supported in both Flash CS3 and Flash Player 9. Version 3.0, however, adds many features and improvements in speed and performance in conjunction with the new Flash Player 9.

ActionScript 3.0 is built upon object-oriented programming (OOP) concepts that make it more modular and performance-oriented, essential for building large-scale Flash applications.

That said, users who do not have a scripting background or who are unfamiliar with the principles of object-oriented programming languages may find the learning curve for ActionScript 3.0 to be a bit steep. In addition, you can no longer place actions directly on buttons or movie clip instances, which may throw users with previous ActionScript 2.0 experience a bit of a curve.

This chapter will demonstrate concepts in both versions to ensure that you are equipped to work with existing Flash content as well as the new generation of movies that will benefit from the power of ActionScript 3.0.

An important note about Publish Settings

You must adjust the ActionScript version in your Publish Settings to match your preferred version of ActionScript.

1 Make sure that no objects on the stage are selected, and choose File > Publish Settings or select the Publish Settings button in the Property inspector.

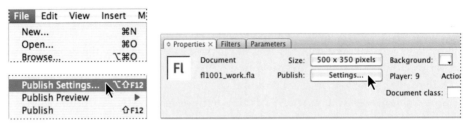

Access your Publish Settings through the File menu or Property inspector.

2 In the Flash section of the resulting dialog box, select the appropriate version from the ActionScript Version menu, then press OK. You might want to switch versions so you can see how to use both with the exercises in this lesson.

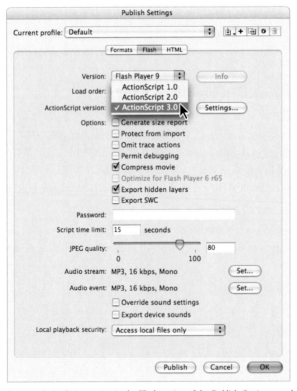

Set your ActionScript version in the Flash section of the Publish Settings panel.

The Actions panel at work

The Actions panel is a script wizard, a text editor, and a code-checker, all in one. To open the Actions panel, choose Window > Actions, press F9 (Windows) or Option+F9 (Mac OS).

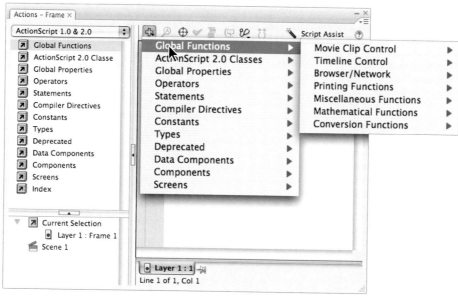

Open the Actions panel by choosing Window > Actions.

Here you build scripts (groups of actions) and place them in your movie. To place actions directly on an object, select a frame, button, or movie clip instance on the stage and launch the Actions panel. You can type scripts directly into the panel, choose scripts from drop-down menus, or use the Actions toolbox, which is a categorized menu of actions on the left side of the panel. To use the toolbox, double-click the script or click and drag it to the window on the right. You can use actions from the toolbox and drop-down menu in either standard or Script Assist mode.

Standard (default) script editing mode

By default, the Actions panel opens up in a standard editing mode that lets you type freely in the Script window on the right. In this mode, you can still insert scripts from the Actions toolbox on the left, or by using the Add a new item to the script button (⊕) at the top. This mode is generally recommended for users who are more experienced with ActionScript or comfortable with typing code in general.

Using Script Assist

For the novice user, the thought of dealing with a new scripting language can be overwhelming. Because ActionScript is very sensitive to both case and spelling, trying to type code freely before you're comfortable with the language can result in errors. To spend more time working and less time troubleshooting, try the drop-down menus or the Actions toolbox in Script Assist mode, which function together like a wizard that lets you pick, modify, and apply scripts without the need to type directly into the script window. After choosing your ready-made actions, you can tweak them with a series of form and menu controls at the top of the Actions panel.

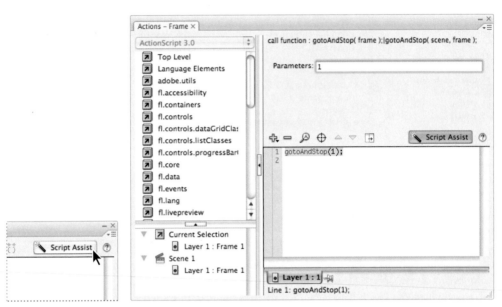

Script Assist mode lets you modify scripts with form and style controls.

Adding & removing actions

In Script Assist mode, click the Add a new item to the script button (✥) at the top of the script window to add actions and click the Delete the selected action(s) button (⊜) to remove them. If you need to reorder scripts, use the Move the selected action(s) up (▲) and Move the selected action(s) down (▼) buttons.

As you highlight lines of code in the script window, menus will appear at the top of the Actions panel that let you adjust and set options for the selected action.

Adding actions to frames

With a firm grasp of ActionScript fundamentals, you're ready to do some real work on the project. In this exercise you'll use ActionScript to prevent the animation from looping, which is the default behavior of the Flash Player.

Using *stop( )*

To stop a timeline at a specific point or prevent an animation from looping when it reaches the end, you use the *stop( )* action. A *stop( )* action halts playback at the frame upon which you place it. When you test, preview, or publish a movie, the default behavior of the Flash Player is to loop playback; *stop( )* actions override that behavior to ensure that the movie doesn't loop unnecessarily.

Steps for both ActionScript 3.0 and 2.0 are included in this lesson. Try this exercise in ActionScript 2.0, then switch Publish Settings and follow the steps for ActionScript 3.0. (For instructions on switching ActionScript versions, refer back to the section "An important note about Publish Settings.")

1 If it's not already open, choose File > Open and open the file named fl1001_work.fla, which you saved earlier.

Although you aren't required to place actions on their own layer, it's a good practice to help avoid accidentally selecting a script versus an object on the stage (and vice versa).

2 Test the movie using Control > Test Movie. Notice that the animation continues to loop back to the beginning. Let's change that.

3 Like any object on the stage, actions can be placed on keyframes only. Select Frame 41 on the new Actions layer, and create a new keyframe by pressing the F6 shortcut key.

You'll place an action to stop playback on the new keyframe on Frame 41.

4 Select the new keyframe, and choose Window > Actions to launch the Actions panel. Press the Script Assist button in the upper-right corner of the Actions panel to enable Script Assist mode.

5 **ActionScript 2.0:** Press the Add a new item to the script button (⊕) at the top of the Actions panel, and choose Global Functions > Timeline Control > stop to place a stop action in the script window.

ActionScript 3.0: Press the Add a new item to the script button and choose flash.display > MovieClip > Methods > stop. In the Object text field at the top of the Actions panel, type **this**. Because ActionScript 3.0 requires you to tell it which object needs to be stopped, you use the special *this* keyword to refer the main timeline to itself, which is the equivalent of a person saying *me* or *I* to refer to himself.

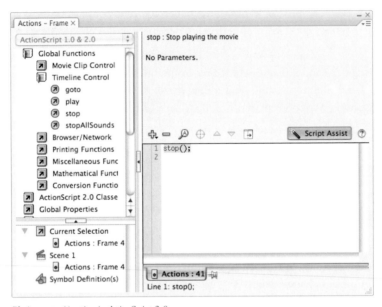

Placing a stop( ) action in ActionScript 2.0.

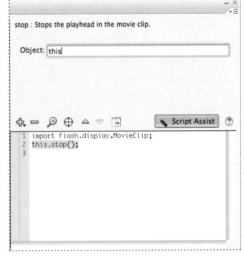

Placing a stop( ) action in ActionScript 3.0.

6 Close the Actions panel and look at the frame. The icon that looks like a lowercase *a* indicates that the frame contains actions that will run when the playhead passes it during playback.

The lowercase a icon indicates that actions exist on Frame 41.

7 Test your movie by choosing Control > Test Movie. The animation should play and stop abruptly at Frame 41, exactly where you placed the action. The basketball should stop halfway through the hoop.

8 Choose File > Save to save your work.

Using the *goto* action to navigate the Timeline

To make the playhead jump forward or backward to a specific frame, turn to the *goto* actions. The two variations—*gotoAndStop( )* and *gotoAndPlay( )*—jump to a specific frame, then stop playback and resume playback from that point, respectively. In this exercise, you'll add actions to keep the ball bouncing on the ground after it goes through the net.

1 Select Frame 41 on your Actions layer, and launch the Actions panel (Window > Actions). You must first remove the *stop( )* action so the movie can play through until the end.

2 Select the line that contains your *stop( )* action—in ActionScript 2.0 this will simply read *stop( )*; in ActionScript 3.0 this will read *this.stop( )*. Press the Delete the selected action(s) button (⊖) at the top of the script window to remove the entire line of code. Note that in ActionScript 3.0, an import statement (*import flash.display.MovieClip*) is added at the top of the Script window—this gives your movie access to methods such as *stop( )*. It's not necessary to delete this, even if the *stop( )* actions are removed.

Remove the stop( ) action on Frame 41.

3 Keep the Actions panel open, then select Frame 100 on the Actions layer and place a new keyframe there by pressing F6. Next, you'll add *goto* actions to instruct the movie to jump back to the first frame and stop or play. The specific steps will depend on your version of ActionScript.

ActionScript 3.0 has some key differences with ActionScript 2.0 in the way it references objects on the stage (including the main timeline itself).

If you would like to further your knowledge of the key differences and new features in ActionScript 3.0, check out the articles and tutorials on Adobe's Developer Network site at http://www.adobe.com/devnet/ or take a look at Essential ActionScript 3.0, published by O'Reilly Media, ISBN 978-0-59652-694-8.

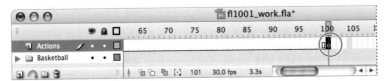

Add a keyframe to Frame 100.

In ActionScript 2.0:

a. Click the Add a new item to the script button (✛) and choose Global Functions > Timeline Control > goto. The script window will read *gotoAndPlay(1)*. You want to go to Frame 1, but you want to stop when you get there.

b. At the top of the panel, click the radio button next to *Go to and stop* to switch the action in the script window.

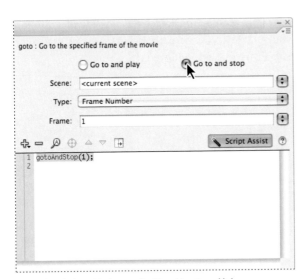

Your script window with the gotoAndStop( ) action added.

c. Choose Control > Test Movie to preview your movie. The movie should play to the end, jump back to the first frame, and stop. Now you're ready to use *gotoAndPlay( )* to do something more useful.

d. Return to the Actions panel, and click the *Go to and play* radio button. Instead of accepting the default frame number, replace 1 with **61** so the action reads *gotoAndPlay(61)*. This forces the playhead to jump back and resume playback from Frame 61, creating a loop.

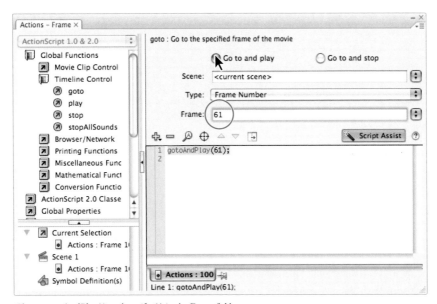

Choose gotoAndPlay( ) *and specify* **61** *in the Frame field.*

e. Choose Control > Test Movie. The ball now falls through the hoop, hits the ground, and continues to bounce. Because you created a loop between frames 61 and 100 using *gotoAndPlay( )*, the animation between those frames continues to play.

In ActionScript 3.0:

a. Press the Add a new item to the script button and choose flash.display > MovieClip > Methods > gotoAndStop. You'll be able to specify three values: Object, Frame, and Scene.

b. In the Object text field, type **this**. The *this* keyword always makes a movie clip (in this case, a movie clip timeline) refer to itself. In the Frame text field, type **1**, and delete the text in the Scene text field completely.

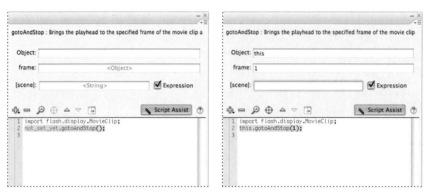

Modify the entry fields for the gotoAndStop() action to instruct the playhead to jump to Frame 1 and stop.

c. Choose Control > Test Movie to preview your movie. The movie should play to the end, jump back to the first frame, and stop. Next, you'll use *gotoAndPlay( )* to send the playhead to a specific frame.

d. Return to the Actions panel, and press the Add a new item to the script button (✛) to choose flash.display > MovieClip > Methods > gotoAndPlay. This adds the *gotoAndPlay( )* action underneath your existing code, so you must remove the old *gotoAndStop( )* action. Select the *gotoAndStop( )* line in the script window, then press the Delete the selected action(s) button (➖).

Add the action at flash.display > MovieClip > Methods > gotoAndPlay.

e. In the Object text field, type **this**. In the Frame text field, type **61**; remove any text from the Scene text field.

The finished script.

f. Choose Control > Test Movie. The ball should fly through the hoop, hit the ground, and continue to bounce. To keep the animation running, you created a loop between frames 61 and 100 using *gotoAndPlay( )*.

Definition: Parameters

You may see the word *Parameters* a lot in the Actions panel. Parameters are additional pieces of information you feed to ActionScript functions to make them work. For instance, *gotoAndPlay( )* requires you to specify a frame number, a parameter it uses to complete its task. Many functions in ActionScript take parameters, some of which are required and some which are optional.

You enter parameters for selected actions using the menus and type-in fields that appear at the top of the Actions panel in Script Assist mode.

4   Choose File > Save to save your work, and keep the document open.

Navigating to frame labels

As an alternative to frame numbers, which can get unwieldy in a complex movie, frame labels are an intuitive and friendlier way to name and refer to any keyframe on the timeline. As opposed to telling ActionScript, *go to frame 1*, you can just as easily say, *go to the frame labeled start*. In the Property inspector you can assign frame labels for any selected keyframe.

Because ActionScript uses frame labels as locators, certain naming restrictions apply:

- Frame names cannot contain dead spaces (start frame), but can include underscores to connect several words together (start_frame).

- Frame names can contain numbers (frame3), but not as the first character (3rdframe).

- Frame labels cannot contain punctuation of any type.

- You can use both uppercase and lowercase letters, but make sure you reference the frame using the exact case you used originally; ActionScript treats myCoolFrame and mycoolframe, for example, as completely different frames.

Examples:

INVALID	VALID
my frame	my_frame
3rdframe	frame3
**mycoolframe!	Mycoolframe

Frame labels versus frame numbers

In the previous exercise, you used frame numbers to tell ActionScript to jump to a specific frame on the timeline. There is one drawback to this approach: if significant events within your animation (for instance, when the ball starts bouncing) are moved, you must then adjust their frame numbers in any script that references them.

To avoid this and create a more intuitive way to navigate the timeline, you can assign labels to any keyframe. Labels are friendly names that you can assign to a keyframe that can be referred to in ActionScript, just as you would refer a frame number. However, frames and their labels move together, meaning scripts referring to the frame label can still find the frame, even when its actual location on the timeline has changed.

Now you'll try using *gotoAndPlay( )* again, but this time you'll specify frame labels instead of numbers. Because the basic concept of labels works the same in both ActionScript 2.0 and 3.0, this exercise will detail the steps for ActionScript 2.0 only.

1 With the Actions layer selected, create a new layer by pressing the Insert Layer button (⊐) below the Timeline. Rename the new layer **Labels**.

 You can place labels on layers that already have content or ActionScript. For the sake of keeping items organized, however, a better practice is to place labels on their own layer.

Create a new layer and name it Labels.

2 Select Frame 1 of the Labels layer and launch the Property inspector, if it isn't already open (Window > Properties > Properties).

3 In the Frame field that reads <Frame Label>, enter **my_label** to name your frame. A small flag (▸) and the label name will appear on the Timeline at the frame you labeled. You can now modify your ActionScript to jump to this frame, simply by referencing its name.

A flag and the label name will appear on the Timeline at the frame you labeled.

4 Select Frame 100 on the Actions layer, and launch the Actions panel (Window > Actions). The script window should read *gotoAndPlay(61)*. You should still be in Script Assist mode, able to see the form and selection controls at the top of the panel. Locate the Type menu there, and select Frame Label. Now the Actions panel is expecting a label name. Whatever you enter in the Frame field will now be treated as a frame label, rather than a number.

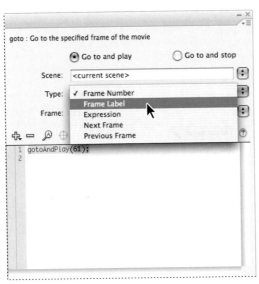

Switch the Type menu to Frame Label in the Actions panel.

5 Change the number 61 to **my_label**, the name you assigned to the first frame in step 3. The script window now reads *gotoAndPlay("my_label")*.

*Type in the name of your label, **my_label**, into the Frame field.*

6   Choose Control > Test Movie. The animation should play through the end and begin looping again from the very first frame, or, more specifically, from the my_label frame.

7   Now, move the first frame and its label to a different point in the Timeline: click and drag the first frame of the Labels layer all the way to Frame 61. Line it up with the beginning of the ball's bounce.

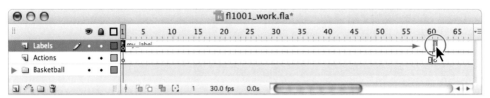

Move the my_label frame to Frame 61 so it sits where the ball begins bouncing.

8   Choose Control > Test Movie. The animation should now loop from the beginning of the bounce sequence. Because you used a frame label, you didn't need to adjust your code when you moved the frame. Actions continue to jump to a specified frame label, regardless of where it sits on the Timeline.

9   Choose File > Save to save your work, and choose File > Close to close the document.

Congratulations! You have finished the lesson.

Wrapping up

ActionScript offers a world of possibilities. Lesson 11, "Creating Button Symbols," demonstrates how you can apply ActionScript to buttons to create controls and navigation. There you'll learn the power of another ActionScript staple: event handlers, which are specific directions that tell a button what mouse or keyboard event should trigger the action assigned to it. Because a button can be clicked, rolled over, released, or pressed and held down, event handlers help the button sort out when to perform which action, whether it's jumping to a frame on the timeline, stopping playback, or launching a website in a browser window. Unlike frame-based actions, button-based actions can occur at any time, or not at all, based on what the user chooses to do.

Self study

Create a new, blank Flash file by choosing File > New > Flash File (ActionScript 3.0). Create a basic motion tween on the Timeline using a graphic of your choice. Add actions on the last frame to stop, loop, and play your movie from different locations on the Timeline. Create at least two different keyframes along the Timeline and assign the Frame labels. Modify your ActionScript on the last frame to jump to and play from these points using *gotoAndPlay( )*.

Review

Questions

1 On what items can actions be placed in ActionScript?

2 Which action is used to jump to a specific frame and stop playback?

3 What menu command should you use to preview actions applied to your movie?

Answers

1 In ActionScript 3.0, scripts can be placed on keyframes on the Timeline or in external files. In ActionScript 2.0, scripts can also be placed on Button and Movie clip instances.

2 *gotoAndStop( )*.

3 Control > Test Movie.

What you'll learn in this lesson:

- Creating buttons that change during user interaction

- Using buttons to navigate between frames

- Using buttons to control the movie playback

- Linking to an external website

Creating Button Symbols

Flash is great for creating highly interactive navigation controls for websites, DVDs, and CD-ROMs. Buttons give you more flexibility while designing in Flash, and give your users more control when viewing your movies or web pages. In this lesson, you'll learn how to utilize the power of button symbols.

Starting up

Before starting, make sure that your tools and panels are consistent by resetting your preferences. See "Resetting the Flash workspace" on page 3.

You will work with several files from the fl11lessons folder in this lesson. Make sure that you have loaded the fllessons folder onto your hard drive from the supplied DVD. See "Loading lesson files" on page 3.

See Lesson 11 in action!

Use the accompanying video to gain a better understanding of how to use some of the features shown in this lesson. Open the DynamicLearning_FlashCS3.swf file located in the Videos folder and select Lesson 11 to view the video training file for this lesson.

The project

In this lesson, you'll be designing the interface for an informational CD-ROM about Fred Smith and his freelance photography studio. You'll build a few buttons, then link them to key points within the Flash movie and a sample website. For a preview of the final result, open the fl1101_done.fla file in the fl11lessons folder. Close the file when you are finished, or keep it open as a reference.

Working with button symbols

Buttons are one of three symbol types in Flash and, like all symbols, they live in the library and are managed from the Library panel. Buttons are designed specifically to react to the user's mouse and keyboard actions. Like graphic symbol instances, each button instance can have its own transformation and color characteristics.

A button symbol has a unique timeline featuring four main frames in each layer—Up, Over, Down, and Hit. Each represents a button's appearance in different states of use.

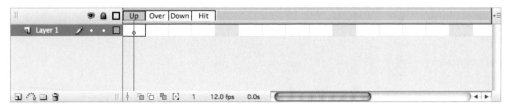

The timeline of a button symbol.

The Up state is the button's default appearance when it's just sitting on the Stage without any user interaction. When a mouse pointer moves over it, the button changes to its Over state, indicating to the user that the button is a point on the interface that reacts when clicked. You can characterize the Over state with anything from a simple color or text change to an animation or sound.

When the user clicks down on the mouse button, the button symbol changes to its Down state. It remains in its Down state until the user releases the button. Because the Down state is visible only briefly during a mouse click, customizing a button's Down state with a long animation or sound is not the best idea.

The Hit area defines the *hot spot* where the button will become active when the user moves over it. This state is never visible, and content placed on the Hit frame only defines the active area. This is especially crucial for buttons that are based on text with no underlying shape. Because the Hit area defines the active area of the button and is not visible, the size and shape of the content on the Hit frame matters most—color choice, for instance, will have no effect on the button's operation.

What makes a good Hit state? The best Hit states are solid shapes that are generally as big as, or slightly bigger than, the visible states of the button. If your button changes shape from state to state, consider choosing a shape for the Hit state that is fairly neutral and encompasses as much of the visible area of the button as possible.

Building buttons

With a solid introduction to button symbol theory, you're ready to begin work on the project. The first step is to create a new button symbol and design its Up, Over, and Down states.

To build your first button:

1   Choose File > Open and navigate to the fl11lessons folder. Select the fl1101.fla file and choose Open.

2   Choose File > Save As. When the Save As dialog box appears, type **fl1101_work.fla** into the Name text field. Navigate to the fl11lessons folder and press Save.

3   Choose Insert > New Symbol. When the Create New Symbol dialog box appears, enter **about_btn** for the symbol's name, set the Type to Button, and press OK to create a new button.

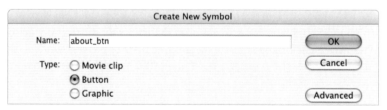

Create a new symbol named about_btn.

4 You are now in the edit mode for the new button symbol. In edit mode, you see the button's timeline with the 4 states up, over, down and hit above the Stage.

Select the Rectangle tool (▢) from the Tools panel. Using the Fill and Stroke color swatches at the bottom of the Tools panel, set the Stroke color to black and set the Fill color to light gray. The black and gray combination will help distinguish the button more clearly from other objects on the Stage. Click and drag on the Stage to create a small rectangle.

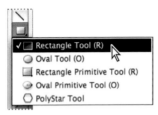

Select the Rectangle tool from the Tools panel.

5 Choose the Selection tool (►) in the Tools panel and double-click the fill inside the rectangle to select both its fill and stroke.

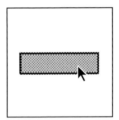

Double-click on the new rectangle to select both fill and stroke.

6 In the Property inspector, enter **121** in the Width text field and **30** in the Height text field. This resizes the button so that it fits in the area on the left of the vertical divider on the main menu. If necessary, click the padlock icon (🔒) to the left of the text fields so that changing one value does not affect the other. Press Enter (Windows) or Return (Mac OS).

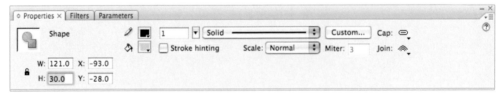

You can use the Property inspector to enter precise sizes for objects on the Stage.

7 Choose Window > Align to open the Align panel. You'll need to set up the button's registration point, from which changes in size and rotation will originate.

8   In the Align panel, click the To stage button to make sure it is selected. Click on the Align horizontal center button (⬓) and the Align vertical center button (⬗) to center the button with the crosshair registration point on the Stage.

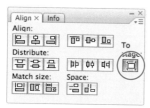

Make sure the To stage button is selected.

9   The next step of the design process is to establish different colors for the Over and Down states so that the button changes its appearance with mouse interaction. Select the Over frame on the button timeline, then choose Insert > Timeline > Keyframe to insert a new keyframe.

10 Select the copy of the rectangle on the new keyframe, and use the Fill color swatch at the bottom of the Tools panel to change the rectangle's fill color to light blue (#66FFFF).

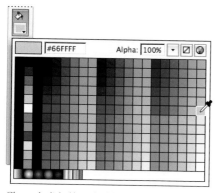

Choose the light blue color labeled #66FFFF.

11 Select the Down frame, insert a new keyframe, and change the rectangle's fill color to pale orange (#FFCC66).

If nothing is placed on the Hit frame, the button will use the content on the Down frame (if any) to determine the Hit area.

Button design tips

When designing buttons, keep your users in mind and follow these guidelines:

- Aim for an interesting design that makes the navigation process easy for users to understand. An interesting-looking button may entice users to click on it.

- Make a button's purpose clear. Although you already know what all your buttons do and where they'll lead, users aren't as familiar as you are with what's going on.

- Make buttons easy to find. If the buttons are hard to pick out on the interface, or if their functions are unclear, using your interactive project is a frustrating experience for the user.

Also, let the content drive the need for buttons. Know the sections you want to include in your project before you start to design the buttons. Developing content as you design your buttons can slow you down. A flowchart is a simple way to plan basic layout and navigation, and gives you a blueprint to work from when setting up your movie in Flash.

Adding text to a button

Like other symbols, and like the main timeline itself, buttons can have multiple layers. Using layers helps you to create more complex designs and add more information while keeping everything carefully organized. In this exercise, you'll add a new layer to incorporate text into your button.

1   Click the Insert Layer button (⊒) below the button timeline to add a new layer to the button.

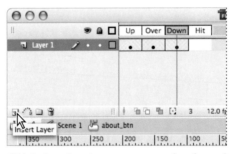

Click the Insert Layer button to create a new layer for your button symbol.

2   Double-click the layer name of the new layer to edit it, and rename it **Text**.

3   Double-click Layer 1's layer name to edit it, and rename it **Shape**.

Keep your layers organized with descriptive names. Otherwise, you will spend a lot of time trying to figure out what's on each layer.

4 Select the Up keyframe on the Text layer, and select the Text tool (T) from the Tools panel. Click on the Stage and type the phrase **About Fred**.

5 Click and drag inside the text frame to select the entire phrase, and go to the Property inspector and choose Verdana. Set the Font size to 10, Style to bold, Alignment to Center, and Text color to black. The centered text alignment is important, because it will make the button easier to modify for other uses later.

6 You now need to line up the text with the rectangle on the Shape layer. Choose the Selection tool (**k**) in the Tools panel and select the text frame. Open the Align panel by choosing Window > Align, if it isn't already open, and make sure the To stage button is selected.

7 Click the Align horizontal center (⊕) and the Align vertical center (⊕) buttons to center the new text with the crosshair registration point on the Stage.

Use Align horizontal center and Align vertical center to position the text.

8 Choose File > Save.

That's one button down. The next button will be much faster and easier to create because you can build on what you've already done.

Duplicating and modifying buttons

Why build a completely new button when you can copy and modify an existing one? Using the Library panel's Duplicate command is faster, and it ensures that new buttons are consistent with those you've already created.

1   In the Library panel, select the about_btn symbol. If necessary, choose Windows > Library to open the Library panel.

2   Choose Duplicate from the Library panel's menu, and, when the Duplicate Symbol dialog box appears, enter the name **services_btn**. Leave the Type set as Button and press OK. A new copy of your original button, named services_btn, now appears in the Library panel.

A symbol can be duplicated using the Duplicate option found in the Library panel's menu.

3   Double-click the services_btn symbol in the Library panel to edit it. Check below the Timeline to see that it now reads services_btn next to Scene 1, indicating that you're editing the correct button.

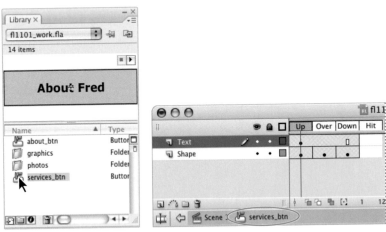

The symbol currently being edited is indicated below the Timeline, next to Scene 1.

4 Choose the Text tool (T), select the text *About Fred* to activate it, then type **Services** in its place. Because you chose center alignment for the original button text, you won't need to reposition the new button text here.

5 Choose File > Save to save your work.

Aligning buttons on the Stage

Now it's time to organize what you have created. In this exercise, you'll add the existing buttons to the Stage, organize them into layers, and align them using the Align panel.

1 Click the Scene 1 button below the Timeline to return to your movie's main timeline.

2 Select the graphics layer in the Timeline, and press the Insert Layer button (⊒) twice to add two new layers to the top of the layer stack. Double-click each new layer name and rename the layers **about button** and **services button**.

Add two new layers above the graphics layer.

3 Select Frame 1 of the about button layer. Drag the about_btn symbol from the library and place it on the Stage on the left side of the divider toward the top of the Stage. Don't worry about precise placement just yet.

4 Select Frame 1 of the services button layer. Drag the services_btn symbol from the library to the Stage below the about_btn symbol.

5 Using the Selection tool (↖), hold the Shift key and click both buttons on the Stage so that they are selected. The Align panel will help you line up these buttons evenly on the Stage.

6 In the Align panel, make sure that the To stage button is turned on. Select the Align left edge button to line up the buttons flush along their left edges.

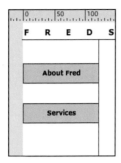

The buttons now appear properly lined up.

7 Deselect the two buttons by clicking in the gray work area. Select the about_btn symbol on the Stage. Go to the Property inspector and, just below the Button drop-down menu, click in the text field that says <Instance Name> and rename the button instance **about_btn**. Do the same for the services button, naming it **services_btn**.

8 Choose File > Save to save your work.

Testing buttons on the Stage

A good way to avoid design issues and bugs in your Flash movie is to test along the way and address problems immediately. Once you've added buttons to the Stage, you can test their behaviors and appearances directly within the authoring environment using the Enable Simple Buttons command. Enable Simple Buttons lets you quickly test button behavior without launching the Flash Player, and prevents you from selecting, moving, or editing buttons on the Stage.

At this point, you can test your buttons to ensure that the color changes and Hit area are working. You won't be able to test functionality just yet, since your buttons haven't been linked to anything.

1 Choose Control > Enable Simple Buttons.

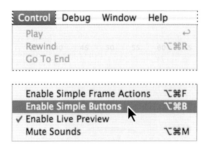

The Enable Simple Buttons command lets you preview button behavior directly on the Flash Stage.

2   Move the mouse over each button to see its Over state.

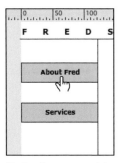

Preview the states on each button.

3   Click and hold down on each button briefly to check the Down state. When you release the mouse button, the button you're interacting with will revert back to its Over state (as long as your mouse pointer is still over the button).

4   When finished, choose Control > Enable Simple Buttons to toggle it back off.

Creating text-based buttons

Text-based buttons work differently because they are formed only from text, with no solid area or shape that defines them. A problem with text buttons is that if the mouse pointer is not precisely on a type character, the button remains inactive, appearing not to work. This is where the Hit area comes into play. By defining a hot spot in the Hit frame of your button, you create a solid and easy target for users to click.

Let's see how it works:

1   Choose Insert > New Symbol.

2   When the Create New Symbol dialog box appears, name the symbol **istock_btn**, and set the symbol Type as Button. Press OK.

3   Choose the Text tool (T) from the Tools panel, then click on the Stage and type **www.istockphoto.com**.

4 Highlight the text and choose Verdana, 10pt, set Letter spacing to 5, and the color to black, and finally choose center alignment. Choose the Selection tool in the Tools panel and select the www.istockphoto.com text. Click the Align horizontal center (⬓) and Align vertical center (⬓) buttons in the Align panel.

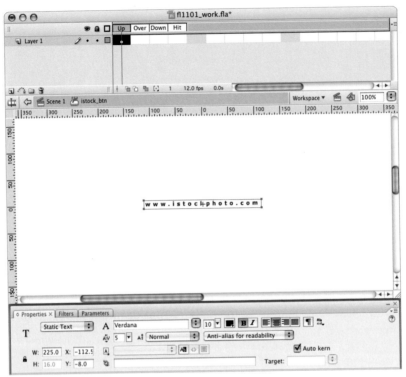

After formatting the text, be sure to center it on the Stage.

5 Insert a new keyframe in the Over frame. Using the Text tool, select the text and use the color swatch on the Property inspector to set the color to light blue (#66FFFF). This is the same color you used for the Over states of the buttons you built earlier.

Keeping colors consistent is important in interactive design. Using different colors for each button can confuse users. Part of the interactive experience is making the process intuitive as well as interesting. If colors keep changing, a user can start to wonder why, and be distracted from the information you're trying to share. If the colors are consistent, there's no distraction to users, and they'll know that when a certain color comes up, it indicates a link or active button.

6 Insert a keyframe in the Down frame. Select the text, and use the color swatch in the Property inspector to set its color to the same pale orange (#FFCC66) used earlier in the graphic buttons' Down states.

7 Insert a keyframe in the Hit frame. Select the Rectangle tool (□) from the Tools panel, and choose red for Fill color to contrast the text color. Set Stroke to No Color (⊘).

Remember that the Hit area delineates a zone in the button that becomes active. Just a plain shape of any color will do because it will be invisible. The Hit area is also helpful if you want to use a picture as a button and make an isolated area of the picture interactive.

8 Draw a rectangle that stretches out around the entire length and height of the text. If the box covers the text rather than sitting beneath it, you are in object drawing mode, but remember that the hit state is invisible and therefore the visibility of the box is not relevant

In the Hit frame, draw a red rectangle around the text.

9 Click the Scene 1 link below the Timeline to return to the main timeline. You now need to place the new text button on the Stage and test it.

10 Select the about button layer in the Timeline and click the Insert Layer button (⊐) to add a new layer at the top of the stack.

11 Double-click the layer name of the new layer to edit it, and type in **istock button**. Select Frame 1 on the new layer and drag an instance of the istock_btn symbol from the Library panel to the Stage below the FS logo, positioning the text button where you think it looks best.

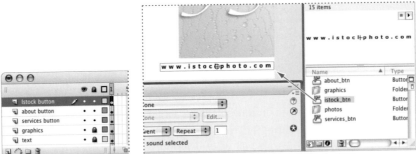

*Name the new layer **istock button** and drag an instance of the istock_btn symbol onto the Stage.*

12 Select the istock_btn symbol on the Stage. In the Property inspector, just below the Button drop-down menu, click in the text field that says <Instance Name>. Rename the button instance **istock_btn**.

13 Choose Control > Enable Simple Buttons, and move your mouse over the new button to test it. Thanks to the Hit area you established, the button should become active when the mouse gets near it. Notice that you don't have to be right on top of the text, just in the territory of the Hit area.

14 Choose Control > Enable Simple Buttons to toggle it off.

15 Choose File > Save to save your work.

Navigating in Flash

One of the main functions of a button is navigation, enabling users to get from one point to another and back again. A simple approach is to organize content across multiple frames or scenes within your movie, and allow users to jump from one frame to another in the Timeline when a button is clicked.

Planning it all out

It is important to consider how you're going to present the navigation tools to users. Will the navigation buttons be available in every section, or will there be one main menu to which users must return? In this design, the main menu will only be available in the first section. You'll need to build a button to allow users to access this menu from the About Fred and Services sections.

1 Select the about_btn symbol in the Library panel.

2 Choose Duplicate from the Library panel menu. When the Duplicate Symbol dialog box appears, type **main_btn** in the Name field. Make sure Button is selected as Type, and press OK.

3   Double-click the main_btn symbol in the Library panel to edit it. You should see main_btn displayed to the right of the Scene 1 link below the Timeline.

4   Click on the About Fred text with the Text tool (T) to activate it. Highlight the text and type **Main Menu**. You won't need to worry about centering it because the text was initially set up with center alignment.

5   To keep the Library panel organized, click the New Folder button (▣) at the bottom of the panel. Type **buttons** in the name field next to the new folder that appears. Press Enter/ Return to commit the change.

Create a new folder in the Library.

6   Select and drag all your button symbols into the new buttons folder.

7   Click on the Scene 1 link below the Timeline to return to the main movie timeline, then choose File > Save to save your work.

Building destination points

Before you can use ActionScript to make your buttons jump somewhere, you'll need to give them somewhere to jump to. Let's start by creating frame-to-frame navigation for the About Fred and Services sections.

1   On the Timeline, insert keyframes at Frame 5 of both the graphics layer and the text layer.

2   Select the istock button layer in the Timeline, and click the Insert Layer button (⊟) to add a new layer. Double-click the layer name to edit it, and enter **main button**.

3   Insert a keyframe at Frame 5 of the main button layer.

To create keyframes, you can also select a frame on the Timeline and press the F6 shortcut key, which works on both Windows and Mac OS systems.

4 Select the keyframe on Frame 5 of the main button layer, then drag an instance of the main_btn symbol from the Library panel onto the Stage. Place it somewhere in the left navigation area where the other buttons were positioned.

5 To have the main_btn symbol's position coincide with the position of the other buttons, use the about_btn symbol's position as a reference. Select Frame 1 on the Timeline and select the about_btn symbol on the Stage. Take note of the X and Y values shown in the Property inspector.

6 Select Frame 5, and then select the main_btn instance on the Stage. Enter the numbers you noted above. This is an easy way to match the positions of two items that exist at different points along the Timeline.

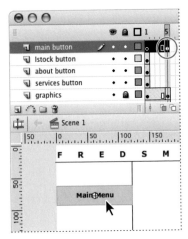 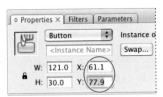

Screen position of the selected image.

7 Using the Selection tool (k), select the main_btn symbol on the Stage. In the Property inspector, just below the Button drop-down menu, click in the text field that says <Instance Name> and rename the button instance **main_btn**.

Organizing the Timeline

As you can see, the Timeline is starting to fill up with layers. You'll add a new folder to the layer area of the Timeline to cut down on some of the space taken up here.

1 Below the Timeline, click the Insert Layer Folder button (). This adds a new folder to the layer stack.

Add a new folder to the Timeline.

2 Double-click the folder's layer name and rename it **buttons**.

3 Drag each button layer in the Timeline into the buttons folder you just created.

 An easy way to select all the button layers at once is to click the top button layer, hold down Shift on your keyboard, and select the bottom button layer. You can then click and drag the whole group into the new folder in one action.

Setting up for new content

The button layers now appear indented below the new layer folder. You can collapse the buttons folder to save some space in the Timeline when you're not working on your buttons.

Now you'll add more content to the About Fred section that you're building.

1 Click the arrow to the left of the buttons folder to collapse and hide the button layers.

2 Select the graphics layer in the Timeline and click the Insert Layer button to add a new layer just above it.

3 Double-click the layer name and name it **content**.

4 Click the Insert Layer button again to create another new layer. Rename it **headers**.

Be careful—if a layer folder is selected, any new layers will be automatically added to that folder. If the folder is collapsed, you won't see the new layers as they are added.

5 Insert a keyframe in Frame 5 of both the content and headers layers you just created.

6 Choose File > Save to save your work.

The Timeline should look something like this when you're finished:

The reorganized Timeline.

You'll need to add the content to these new layers now.

7 Click on the keyframe on Frame 5 of the headers layer and select the Text tool (T) in the Tools panel.

8 Click on the Stage and type **About Fred** on the Stage.

9 Select the About Fred text and choose Verdana sized at 18pt, with black as its color. Enable the Bold and Italic buttons in the Property inspector.

10 Using the Selection tool (⬉), drag the text on the Stage toward the upper-right corner.

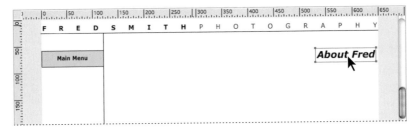

Drag the About Fred text toward the upper-right corner.

Adding content to your frames

The text content for the information about Fred has been included for you, and you can open up simple text files from directly within Flash. You'll select, copy, paste, and reformat the text.

1   Choose File > Open.

2   In the Open dialog box, navigate to the fl11lessons folder. Click on the Files of type menu (Windows) or the Enable menu (Mac OS), and select All Files so that the dialog box allows you to choose additional file types.

Choose All Files from the Files of type/Enable drop-down menu.

3   Select and open the fredbio.txt file. You'll see the text file open as a new panel on top of the Stage.

4   Click and drag through all the text to select it. Choose Edit > Copy to copy the selected text.

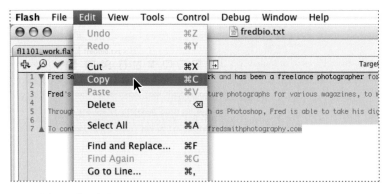

Copy all the text from fredbio.txt.

5   Click the fl1101_work.fla tab above the Timeline to return to your main movie document.

6 Select the keyframe on Frame 5 of the content layer, then choose the Text tool (T) from the Tools panel.

7 Go to the Property inspector and select Verdana as the font. Select 10pt for the size, then select the left alignment button and deselect the bold and italic buttons. Select Frame 5 on the content layer and choose Edit > Paste in Center. When you paste it, your text will assume the type properties you've just set.

8 With the Selection tool (⬏), grab any of the text frame's corners to resize the frame so it maximizes the space on the right side of the Stage. If necessary, add line breaks to the text to distribute it properly. Position the text on the right side of the divider, below the About Fred header.

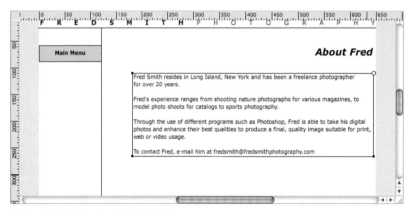

Position the text below the About Fred header.

9 Choose File > Save to save your work.

Building the Services section

Now that the About Fred section is done, it's time to build the Services section. You'll be able to repeat, reuse, and update some of the existing information to speed up the process.

1 Insert keyframes at Frame 10 of the following layers: headers, content, graphics, and text. This will copy the content from the previous keyframe (5). You'll deal with the main menu button a little later when you start to assign ActionScript.

2 Choose the Text tool (T) in the Tools panel and click Frame 10 of the headers layer, select the About Fred text. Type **Services** in its place.

3 Highlight the text in the content layer at Frame 10. Change it to read the following:

Digital Photography

Photo Restoration and Touchup

Location Shooting

Black and White Photography

Live Event Photography

Multiple Formats Available

4 Format the type as you wish. This example uses Verdana, 15pt, black, and bold type, with left alignment. In the Edit format options of the Property inspector, the Line spacing was set to 15pt.

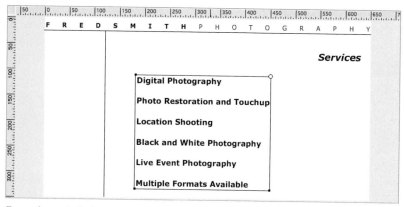

Format the text in the Services section.

Now you'll move into coding some of the buttons so you can navigate through the project.

Creating frame labels for ActionScript

To instruct your button symbols to respond to user interaction and accomplish frame-to-frame navigation, you'll need to add some basic ActionScript. You should be familiar with some of the following concepts from Lesson 10, "Introducing ActionScript."

Introduced with Flash Player 9.0 and Flash CS3 Professional, ActionScript 3.0 has a new syntax for actions and quite different methods for creating button scripts. For more details on ActionScript 3.0, including the syntax for stop( ) *and* goto( ) *actions, see Lesson 10, "Introducing ActionScript."*

If you skipped Lesson 10, we recommend that you go back and run through the exercises before proceeding any further.

To link the button symbols to their destination screens, you'll first add labels to help mark and navigate to important locations along the Timeline. Once you label important frames, ActionScript uses these labels to direct the playhead.

You can also use labels to add comments or notes for yourself directly on a layer in the Timeline.

1 Start by selecting the headers layer in the Timeline. Click the Insert Layer button (◲) twice to add two new layers above it. Rename the new layers **actions** and **labels**, and drag them above the buttons folder in the layer stack.

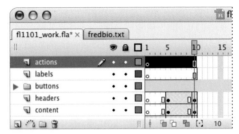

Rename the two new layers and drag them above the buttons layer folder.

2 Insert keyframes at Frames 5 and 10 on both the actions and labels layers. Before you assign ActionScript, you'll apply labels to these new keyframes.

3 Click on Frame 1 of the labels layer.

4 On the left side of the Property inspector, enter **main menu** in the Frame field to set a frame label for this frame. Press Enter/Return. You should see a red flag icon (▸) appear inside the keyframe.

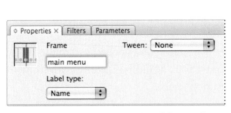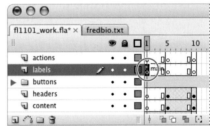

After naming the frame label, notice the red flag icon that appears in the Timeline.

In the drop-down menu below the Frame field, you can specify the type of label. For example, choose Comment if you want to use labels for notes and not as navigational tools.

5 Repeat steps 3 and 4 to add the label **About** at Frame 5 and the label **Services** at Frame 10 of the labels layer.

If you're having a hard time reading the labels on the Timeline, magnify frames by using the Frame View pop-up menu in the upper-right corner of the Timeline.

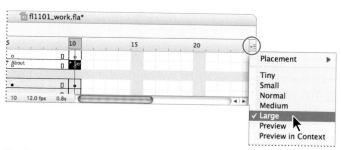

The Frame View menu lets you set the width, style, and height of frames for easier viewing.

Adding ActionScript: event handlers and functions

With everything labeled and organized, you're ready to code your buttons.

Adding ActionScript to buttons

You've already explored basic ActionScript in Chapter 10, "Introducing ActionScript," and learned to navigate the Timeline using frame-based actions. While working with buttons is similar, there are some new concepts you'll need to familiarize yourself with to get your buttons up and running. The process of scripting buttons hinges on two important items: events and event listener functions.

Understanding events

Simply put, an event is an occurrence that triggers something else to happen. In the case of ActionScript, events (such as a mouse click) occur, and scripts run in response to those events.

If you are an employee at a company, you respond to events each day. When you receive phone calls, e-mails, or direct requests from managers and other staff, you respond to those events by carrying out certain tasks. Very often, those tasks are outlined ahead of time (*file an expense report* or *design a logo*) so you're ready to respond when the time is right.

In ActionScript, event listeners are added to buttons so those buttons know what to do when a specific event occurs. An event listener is written as a function—a named set of scripts that is defined ahead of time and ready to run when the appropriate event occurs.

To connect a specific button instance with an event handler function, you'll use the *addEventListener( )* method. The method is attached to a specific button instance, and is told what event to respond to, such as a mouse click or rollover, and what event handler function will need to be called to complete the task. Sample code may look something like this:

```
mybutton_btn.addEventListener(MouseEvent.CLICK, myEventFunction);
```

To use the employee metaphor from earlier, you could think of your work flow represented in pseudo-code like this:

```
employee.addEventListener(Boss.CALL, runExpenseReport);
```

To code your buttons in the next exercise, you'll create an event listener function, and then attach that function to your button instances using the *addEventListener( )* method.

Adding a *stop( )* action

You will now begin to add interactivity to your buttons through ActionScript. You are creating a simple navigation in which users click on a button, for example the *About Fred* section and then are sent to that location in the movie. Because the different sections of the site are all on the same timeline, you will add a *stop( )* action on frames 1, 5 and 10 of the timeline. Frame 1 is the introductory screen, Frame 5 is the About Fred section and Frame 10 is the Services section.

After you add the *stop( )* actions to these frames you will then add ActionScript to each button. Each button, when clicked on by a user, will send the user to the designated section of the timeline.

1   Choose Window > Actions to open the Actions panel, and make sure the panel's Script Assist button (located in the top-right corner) is selected. If it is not selected, click on it and the panel expands, moving the code section to the bottom.

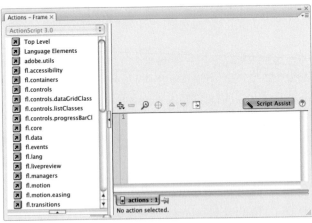

Open the Actions panel and make sure the Script Assist button is selected.

If the Actions panel is in your way, and floating in the middle of the screen, you can dock it to the Property inspector. Click on the Action panel's name tab (upper-left corner) and drag it on top of the Property inspector. When the Property inspector becomes active, drop the Actions panel to dock it. Now the panels will move together as a group.

2   In the actions layer, click on Frame 1, which is the first frame you'll want the playhead to stop at in the Timeline. This will also be where your scripts are added to control buttons on the Stage. It's best to keep timeline-based scripts on the first frame in their own layer on the Timeline.

3   Press the Add a new item to the script button (⊕) above the Script window, and select flash.display > MovieClip > Methods > stop.

4   In the Object field above the Script window, type **this**. This will instruct the script to stop the current timeline.

The special this *keyword is used in ActionScript to have a script refer to the current timeline, or have an object refer to itself. It's the equivalent of a person saying me or I to refer to themselves in conversation.*

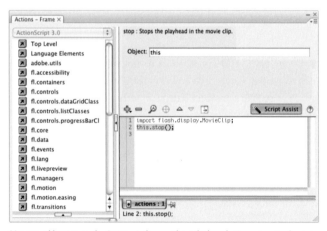

You can add scripts to the Script window on the right by selecting categorized scripts from the Actions toolbox on the left.

5   Repeat steps 2 through 4 to add *stop( )* actions in Frames 5 and 10 of the actions layer.

6   Choose File > Save to save your work.

Linking buttons to specific frames

Now that you have added the stop actions to each frame, you will link each button to a specific frame label on the timeline. Each frame label corresponds to a specific section of the site. The end result is that when the About Fred button is clicked, users are sent to that section, when the Services button is clicked, users are sent to that section and when the Main Menu button is clicked, users are sent back to the Main Menu.

1 Click on Frame 1 of the actions layer in the Timeline. Open the Actions panel, if it is not already open.

One way to tell what you have selected is to look at the bottom of the Script window in the Actions panel. The tab just below the code window will reflect what you currently have selected, and, in turn, to which frame you are applying ActionScript.

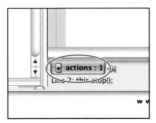

The tab below the Script window confirms that you have the actions layer selected.

2 At the top of the Script window, click the Add a new item to the script button (⊕) and choose Language Elements > Statements, Keywords & Directives > definition keyword > function. You will now build your first event handler function, which will later be associated with a specific button instance on the Stage.

3 In the Name field up top, type **gotoAbout** to name the function. In the Parameters field, type **event:Event**. This lets the function know to expect some type of event—an event listener always takes some type of event as its sole parameter. For type, select void from the drop-down menu. This means that the function doesn't return any value—it simply performs an action.

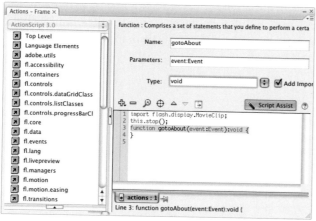

Compiling ActionScript 3.0 using the Actions panel.

4 Select the top line of the function that you just added (line 3). You'll now tell the function what to do when it is called. From the Add a new item to the script button, choose flash.display > MovieClip > Methods > gotoAndPlay.

In the Object field that appears above the script window, type **this**. In the frame text field, type **"About"** (include the quotes). This tells the current timeline (in this case, the main timeline) to go to the frame labeled About.

Be absolutely sure that you pay attention to your capitalization when working with ActionScript. Since you should have labeled your frames About and Services, make sure that the "About" and "Services" entries in the Frame text field are similarly capitalized.

5 Now you'll connect the listener with the button instance, so it knows what function to call when it's clicked.

Select the last curly brace at the bottom of your function. From the Add a new item to the script button (✛) at the top of the panel, select flash.events > Event Dispatcher > Methods > addEventListener.

6 In the Object field, type **about_btn** (the instance name of the button). In the type field, enter **MouseEvent.CLICK**, and in the listener field, type the name of your function, **gotoAbout**. This attaches an event listener to the about button, and tells it to call the gotoAbout function, which advances to the about frame when it's clicked.

We have created two text files that contain the necessary ActionScript that will link the services button and the main menu button to their respective frame labels in the timeline. You will now open these files and copy and paste the code into the Actions panel on keyframe 1 for the services button and keyframe 5 for the main menu button.

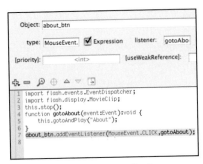

Setting up the addEventListener function.

7 Choose File > Open and click on the Files of Type (Windows) or Enable (Mac OS) drop-down menu, and choose the All Files option. Locate the services_btn.txt and main_btn.txt files included in the fl11lessons folder. Shift+click to select both files, then press Open.

8 Click on the services_btn.txt tab to view the code. Click and drag to select all the code. Right-click (Windows) or Ctrl+click (Mac OS) on the Stage and choose Copy from the contextual menu.

9 Click on the fl1101_work.fla tab to return to your document. Click on Frame 1 of the actions layer. Open the Actions panel, if it is currently closed, and select the last line of text to highlight it. Right-click/Ctrl+click in the Script window, then choose Paste.

10 Click on the main_btn.txt tab to view the code. Click and drag to select all the code. Right-click (Windows) or Ctrl+click (Mac OS) on the Stage and choose Copy from the contextual menu.

11 Click on the fl1101_work.fla tab to return to your document. Click on frame 5 of the actions layer. Open the Actions panel, if it is currently closed, and select the last line of text to highlight it. Right-click/Ctrl+click in the Script window, then choose Paste.

12 Click on Frame 10 of the main button layer and insert a keyframe by pressing F6. This button instance already has its ActionScript assigned.

13 To make sure the main_btn symbol works, you'll have to copy and paste some of your code onto the frames where the main_btn symbol resides. Select frame 5 of the actions layer and open the Actions panel. In the code, select the line that says: *main_btn.addEventListener(MouseEvent.CLICK, gotoMain);* and right-click/Ctrl+click and choose Copy.

Click in frame 10 of the actions layer. In the Actions panel, right-click/Ctrl+click in the Script window and choose Paste to place the code below the *stop( )* action code that you placed there earlier.

14 Choose File > Save to save your work, and choose Control > Test Movie to preview your movie and try out each of your buttons.

The main menu buttons, the about button, and the services button should all be navigating to their corresponding frames. If not, double-check each button's code, the labels, and the event listener function to make sure the buttons are navigating to the appropriate frame and that an event listener has been assigned to each button using its *addEventListener* method.

For those of you who have worked with ActionScript 2.0 (and even those who haven't), you may find the process of setting up a button in ActionScript 3.0 a bit confusing. It takes time, but eventually the process will make sense. The important thing to remember is that each button needs to be assigned to an existing event listener function. In the *addEventListener* method, you tell it what event the button should look for to call its assigned event listener function.

Linking buttons to a web site

In addition to linking buttons to specific frames, you can instruct them to jump to a local web page, external website address, or file download. In this exercise, you'll code the text button on the main menu using the same methods you used in the last exercise, and adding the new *navigateToURL* method to have your event listener function browse to an outside URL. When users click the button, they'll be linked to one of Fred Smith's clients' websites.

1 Select Frame 1 of the actions layer and, if necessary, choose Window > Actions to open the Actions panel. When the panel opens, make sure Script Assist mode is enabled. Select the last line of the scripts currently on Frame 1 to ensure that any new scripts are added below it.

2 From the Add a new item to the script button (⊕) above the Script window, choose Language Elements > Statements, Keywords & Directives > definition keyword > function.

3 A new blank function definition is placed here, which you'll convert to a new event listener for the istock photo button on the Stage.

In the Name field, type **istockBtn** to name the function. In the Parameters field, enter **event:Event**, and from the Type drop-down menu, choose void. This lets the function know that it is receiving an event and returning no information.

When entering full website addresses for the URLRequest( ) *object, be sure to include the* http:// *prefix in the URL field. If you don't, it will mistake the address for a local file name and the link won't work properly.*

4   With the first line of the new function selected, choose flash.net > Methods > navigateToURL from the Add a new item to the script button (⊕).

In the request field, type **new URLRequest("http://www.istockphoto.com")**. This creates a new *URLRequest( )* object that contains the website address you want to send users to. In the [window] field, type **_blank** and uncheck the Expression checkbox to the right of the window to have the link opened in a new browser window.

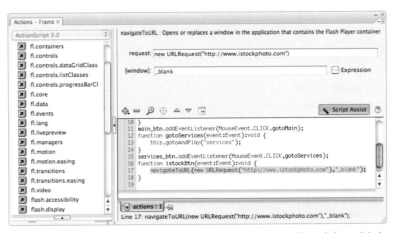

The code being generated here will launch a URL in a browser window when the istock_btn is clicked.

Now you'll connect the listener with the button instance, so it knows what function to call when it's clicked.

5   Select the last curly brace at the bottom of your function. From the Add a new item to the script button (⊕) at the top of the panel, select flash.events > Event Dispatcher > Methods > addEventListener.

6   In the Object field, type **istock_btn** (the name of the button). In the type field, type **MouseEvent.CLICK**, and in the listener field, type the name of your function, **istockBtn**.

This attaches an event listener to the istock button, and tells it to call the istockBtn function, which launches a web browser and navigates to the istockphoto.com website.

7   Choose File > Save to save your work, and choose Control > Test Movie to preview your movie and try out the button.

If you're online, the istockphoto.com site will open in a new browser window. Even if you're not connected to the Web, clicking the text button (www.istockphoto.com) opens a web browser with the istockphoto URL displayed in the address window.

In ActionScript 3.0, methods that navigate to or download from external web addresses expect to be passed a URLRequest ( ) *object to work with. A* URLRequest ( ) *object can be defined at any time, and contains a single local or absolute URL. In ActionScript 2.0, most methods took the URL itself as a parameter, but in ActionScript 3.0 URLs must be wrapped inside of a* URLRequest ( ) *object to be interpreted.*

Self study

As you can see, interactive projects can become very involved, but one way to experiment and save yourself time on future projects is to build an interactive template. Create a project similar to the one you just created for this lesson, and use File > Save as Template to save the project as a reusable template. Later on, you can create a new file based on this template in the New Document panel, and then update the content as needed.

Organization is a big part of the process; creating a template will cut down on your setup time quite a bit.

Review

Questions

1 What are the three button states that can be used to change the appearance of the button during user interactivity? Which state controls the clickable area of a button?

2 What ActionScript item is used to carry out a task in response to an event?

3 What is the significance of instance names?

Answers

1 Up, Over, and Down. The Hit state controls the clickable area of a button. Since this state is not visible, however, it has no effect on the actual appearance of a button.

2   An event listener function.

3 Instance names can give a symbol instance a unique name by which ActionScript can identify (and control) it.

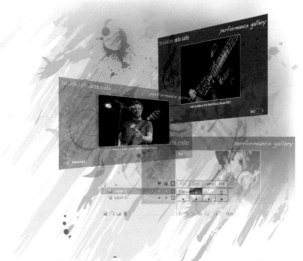

What you'll learn in this lesson:

- Preparing and importing sound files
- Placing sounds on the Timeline
- Editing sounds and creating effects
- Controlling sound behavior and performance

Adding Sound to Your Movies

You've honed your animation skills; now you'll hear how professional your movies can be. With the ability to import, manipulate, and place sound files, Flash CS3 Professional offers many creative and practical possibilities for adding sound effects, narrations, background music, and an extra level of accessibility for users with visual impairment.

Starting up

Before starting, make sure that your tools and panels are consistent by resetting your preferences. See "Resetting the Flash workspace" on page 3.

You will work with several files from the fl12lessons folder in this lesson. Make sure that you have loaded the fllessons folder onto your hard drive from the supplied DVD. See "Loading lesson files" on page 3.

See Lesson 12 in action!

Use the accompanying video to gain a better understanding of how to use some of the features shown in this lesson. Open the DynamicLearning_FlashCS3.swf file located in the Videos folder and select Lesson 12 to view the video training file for this lesson.

The project

In this lesson, you will build an interactive slideshow with background music to keep the listener engaged, narration to walk the user through the various slides, and sound effects to make the navigation feel more interactive and tactile. You will complete the slideshow by importing and placing sounds included with the lesson files. You will also explore how Flash lets you optimize the use of long- and short-form audio for great performance, without sacrificing quality or presentation. To view the finished file, choose File > Open and select the fl1201_done.fla file within the fl12lessons folder. Close the file when you are finished, or keep it open to reference the exercises you complete in this lesson.

You'll use your Flash tools to enhance the performance gallery for the Brooklyn Arts Cafe.

Preparing sound files for Flash

Before bringing your audio files into Flash, you need to understand some of the characteristics and settings for digital audio files. The more pre-production work you do on files before importing them into Flash, the more likely it is that you'll get the results you want the first time around. In the next few sections, you'll explore the key properties of digital audio files along with some recommendations for preparing your files for import and use in your Flash movies.

Sample rate and bit depth

Digital audio is sound that has been converted from analog sound waves into a series of bits and bytes. The conversion takes place through the use of an A/D (analog-to-digital) converter. Your computer microphone jack contains a very basic converter; audio professionals use high-end units capable of reproducing sound at a much higher level of quality and accuracy. The quality of digital audio is determined by two important factors: sample rate and bit depth.

The sample rate refers to the number of samples of an audio waveform that the converter digitizes in one second, and it is analogous to the resolution of a digital photo. The more samples (or pictures) captured in each second, the more accurately the waveform is represented. Although the sample rate is specified when the sound file is recorded or converted, you can adjust it down or up later. As with digital images, however, if the detail wasn't in the original file, increasing the sample rate (or resolution) will not improve it.

Always capture audio at a higher sample rate than you think you'll need. If necessary, you can downsample later to a lower sample rate, which reduces audio file size.

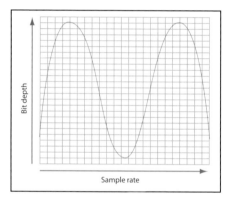

An audio waveform representation of sample rate and bit depth.

Bit depth determines the amount of information that each sample contains; think of it as similar to a digital photo's color depth setting. The higher the color depth of a photo, the wider the range of shades available to reproduce the original colors. In the audio world, bit depth is responsible for reproducing the amplitude (loudness) and dynamic range of an audio waveform. Low bit-depth settings, such as 8 bits or less, produce poor recordings of limited quality, akin to a telephone answering machine. In contrast, a bit depth of 16 bits is sufficient for reproducing the wide range of instruments and vocals found in professionally recorded music.

For reference, audio on a commercial compact disc has a sample rate of 44.1kHz (or 44,100 samples per second) and a bit depth of 16.

If you plan to record your own audio, pay attention to the sample rate and bit depth settings in your software and consider what they'll mean to the quality of the original sound. Mid- to professional-level audio applications, such as Digidesign Pro Tools, Steinberg's Cubase or Nuendo, Apple Logic and Adobe Soundbooth CS3, provide a range of options and tools for recording, importing, editing, and exporting digital audio into a variety of formats. If you'd prefer to let someone else do the recording, you can find many royalty-free sound effects and loops online in a variety of formats and quality settings.

Editing your audio

Although you can perform basic editing and trimming in Flash, to conserve space you should edit your sound files to some degree before importing them. Large audio files sitting in your library can bloat your Flash document (.fla file) unnecessarily. Why import unwanted, extra audio that you know will never be used in your movie?

If you need a basic sound editing application, your choices range from low-cost shareware to full-featured professional programs. If you are creating original audio for your movie, consider an application that at least lets you trim, cut, copy, and paste, as well as export a variety of popular file formats. (You'll learn about Flash's built-in editing controls later in the lesson.)

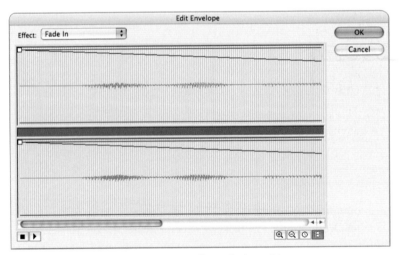

Flash's Edit window provides basic trimming, pan effects, and volume editing.

Mono or stereo

The nature of your source audio will determine whether you should stick with mono or stereo channels for your final output. Single-channel mono audio is a suitable choice for a solo recording of narration or voice. If you are working with prerecorded music or sound effects that pan from left to right, stereo is the best choice; with mono recording, you may lose a great deal of the perspective and placement (this is especially true with music). Keep in mind that stereo files include two channels (left and right), and will often take up twice as much storage space as a mono sound file of the same recording. Whether you record in mono or stereo, Flash has a series of built-in effects, such as fades and stereo effects, that you can set up for any sound you import.

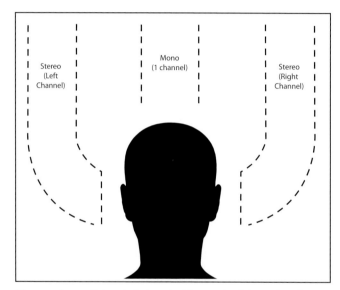

Mono reproduces audio in a single channel, while stereo does it in two channels.

Audio file formats

Flash imports three common file formats: Windows .wav, Mac OS .aiff, and .mp3. If you have QuickTime installed, you can also import System 7 sounds, Sun audio, Audio-only QuickTime files, and Digidesign's Sound Designer II format. The .mp3 format differs slightly from the others because it compresses audio to facilitate file exchange and streaming over the Web. In addition, .mp3 files use a system of Kbps (kilobits per second) to determine overall quality. The average is 128kbps, but you can encode at a much higher level if your software supports it. For the highest quality. keep your source .mp3 files in the 128 to 192kbps range.

Which file format is the right one? The answer largely depends on your operating system, as well as the software you use to create and export audio. No matter which you start with, Flash performs its own compression on audio included in your movies and converts all of the audio in your final .swf file to .mp3 format. You can set specific quality parameters in the Publish Settings for your movie.

Importing sounds

To use a sound in Flash, you first must import it using the Import menu's Import To Library command. You'll import this lesson's sound files, so you can begin to explore and place them on the Timeline.

1   Choose File > Open and navigate to the fl12lessons folder. Select the file fl1201.fla and press Open.

2   Choose File > Save As. When the Save As dialog box appears, type **fl1201_work.fla** into the File name text field. Navigate to the fl12lessons folder and press Save.

3   Choose File > Import > Import To Library. The Import dialog box opens and prompts you to locate the desired files.

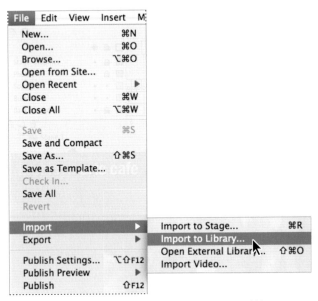

Use Import to Library to import all of the sounds from the lesson folder.

4   Open the Sounds folder inside the fl12lessons folder. Hold down the Shift key, select the folder's nine .mp3 sound files, and choose Open (Windows) or Import to Library (Mac OS) to import the files directly to your Library panel.

For more details on importing, see Lesson 9, "Working with Imported Files."

5 If it's not already open, launch the Library panel by choosing Window > Library. The nine sound files appear as assets marked with a speaker icon.

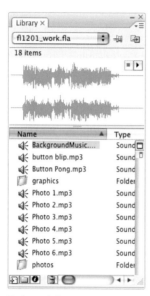

Each sound file appears in the Library panel with a speaker icon.

6 In the Library panel, select the button blip.mp3 sound file. Notice that the Preview window at the top of the panel now shows the sound as a waveform and also features small Play and Stop buttons in the upper-right corner.

A waveform is a visual representation of a piece of audio. The peaks in a waveform represent the amplitude (loudness) of the audio, with the valleys representing lowest parts of the audio, or silence.

7 Click the Play button to listen to the sound. Try this with the other sounds to get an idea of what each file contains.

8 Choose File > Save to save your work.

Import to Library is best for sound files for two reasons: only one sound file can be placed on a frame on a single layer at any given time, and sound files have no physical properties. You can't sort them out on the Stage if you import them in bulk. If you choose Import to Stage, Flash places the sound files in your library, not on selected frames on the Timeline.

Placing sounds on the Timeline

To play a sound at a specific point in your movie, you place the sound on the Timeline. When the playhead reaches the frame where you placed the sound, you'll hear it. To place a sound, you'll select a keyframe and use the Sound menu found on the right side of the Property inspector.

You'll see in the following lessons how additional options in the Sound menu can loop sounds or create effects such as fades and pans. There are a few simple rules: sounds must be placed on keyframes, and you can place only one sound per keyframe.

Adding sound to your slideshow project

The lesson file contains a photo slideshow with six photos and captions arranged across the Timeline. Two buttons underneath the photo let the user move forward or backward through the photos. You'll enhance this photo slideshow by adding background music, a vocal narration for each photo, and subtle sound effects for the Next and Previous navigation buttons.

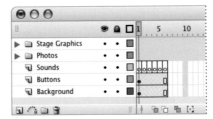

The slideshow already contains layers and keyframes for sounds and background music.

To begin, make sure your Property inspector is visible by choosing Window > Properties > Properties.

1 Locate the empty layer titled Sounds. Select the keyframe on Frame 1.

2 With the keyframe selected, find the Sound menu on the right side of the Property inspector. This menu lists all of the sounds available in the library; you should see the sound files that you imported earlier.

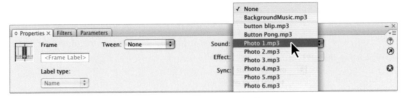

Use the Sound menu to place a sound from your library on the keyframe.

3 Select the sound named Photo 1 from the Sound menu to place that sound on the selected frame.

4 From the Sync drop-down menu, make sure Event is selected. For an explanation of Sync options, see the sidebar "Sync options and sound types."

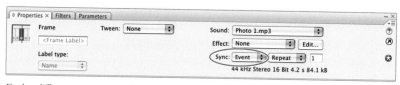

Explore different sync options in the Property inspector.

 By default, each new sound added to the Timeline has the Repeat option selected and set to 1. You will learn how to change this later on.

5 Press Ctrl+Enter (Windows) or Command+Return (Mac OS) to preview the movie in the Flash Player. You should hear the Photo 1 sound play when the movie appears. Close the Flash Player and return to the main stage.

6 Choose File > Save to save your work.

Adding a sound on the Timeline is that easy. There's more to explore, however. You'll take a look at some of the sound options that help you control sounds on the Timeline.

Adding the remaining narration

You'll now add the remaining pieces of narration to their respective photos on the Timeline. Remember that these sounds should occur right when the playhead moves and the new photo is shown, so you'll need to set each one as an Event sound. The steps should be familiar to you.

1 Locate the Sounds layer and select Frame 2. Use the Sound menu on the Property inspector to select the sound from the list named Photo 2.

2 Make sure Event is selected in the Sync drop-down menu. By default, Flash uses the last Sync settings chosen, so it's often unnecessary to reselect this option.

3 Repeat steps 1 and 2 for the remaining four photos, setting the sound Photo 3 on Frame 3, Photo 4 on Frame 4, and so on, until you finish Photo 6.

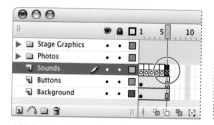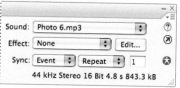

Add the last of the six pieces of narration to the photo on Frame 6.

4   Preview your movie by pressing Ctrl+Enter (Windows) or Command+Return (Mac OS). Use the buttons to move among the photos. You may notice that if you move too quickly, the pieces of the narration blend into each other. You'll fix this with a little ActionScript later in the chapter. Close the Flash Player.

Sync options and sound types

From the Sync menu, you can tell Flash how to handle a sound. Sync options can be used to control sound overlap, stop sounds, and control how sounds work along with content on the Timeline.

Event sounds must fully load before they play back, and they respond to events (such as the playhead reaching a certain frame, as in the previous exercise) or actions (such as a button click, as in the *Adding sound effects to buttons* section). Because you want the slideshow narrations to occur in tandem with the user clicking the Next and Previous buttons, be sure to set them to Event sounds, as you did in the previous exercise.

Stream sounds work best for long-form animation, as the audio is matched to the playback like a soundtrack. Flash does everything it can to keep the sound in sync with the animation, including dropping frames if necessary. A continuous sound (i.e., a soundtrack or one continuous piece of dialog) that needs to sync with the Timeline from start to finish would be ideally set as a Stream sound.

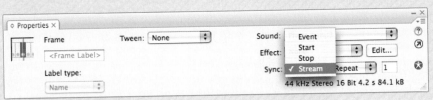

You can set Sync options for each sound in your movie, and control how the sound is handled.

Start plays a sound so that no other instance of that same sound file can be playing at the same time. This makes Start sounds a great choice if you want to prevent unwanted overlap. A start sound will play all the way through the end, and can only be stopped by an instance of the same sound whose Sync is set to Stop.

Stop sounds don't play a sound, but rather stop a specific sound. When choosing Stop for a selected sound, you will stop any instance of that sound that's already playing. Stop sounds can only stop instances of the same sound whose Sync is set to Start.

Adding sound effects to buttons

Sounds are a great way to enhance navigation, and they can make interacting with buttons feel more "real." You learned about button symbols in Lesson 11, "Creating Button Symbols." You know that buttons contain four frames, three of which correspond to the buttons' different visual states. The Over and Down frames of the slideshow navigation buttons are the perfect locations to place Event sounds that will trigger on a rollover (the Over state) and click of the mouse (the Down state), respectively.

Placing Event sounds on button frames

Event sounds work independently of the Timeline and must be fully loaded before they can play back. The best example of this is a short sound placed on a button frame. Your user can click a button at any time, so an Event sound will be ready to respond to that click without any relation to other content on the Timeline. In this exercise, you'll place some Event sounds from your library on your Next and Previous buttons for both rollover and click actions. Both the Next and Previous buttons are instances of the Arrow button symbol in the library, so you'll only need to edit one to add sounds to both instances.

Edit in Place through the Previous button.

1   Double-click the Previous button to edit it directly on the Stage. In the button's Edit mode, you should see its four frames: Up, Over, Down, and Hit. You'll be placing sounds on the Over and Down keyframes. These sounds will go off when a user rolls over or clicks on the buttons.

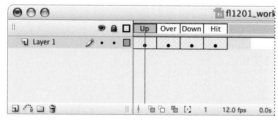

The button symbol has four keyframes.

2   Press Insert Layer icon (⌐) below the Timeline to add a new layer to your button. You'll place the sounds on this layer.

3   In the new layer, create a blank keyframe on the Over frame by using the F7 shortcut key. Select the keyframe and make sure the Property inspector is open.

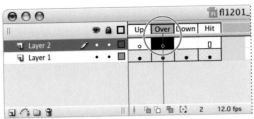

Create a blank keyframe on the new layer you created at the Over state.

4   Using the Sound menu on the right side of the Property inspector, choose the button blip.mp3 sound. In the Sync drop-down menu, make sure Event is selected.

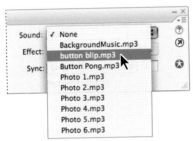

Use the Sound menu to add the button blip sound to the Over state.

5   Create a new blank keyframe on the Down frame by pressing F7. Select the new keyframe, choose the Button Pong.mp3 sound for this frame, and select Event from the Sync menu.

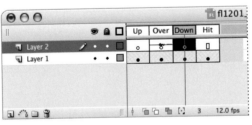

Add the Button Pong.mp3 sound to the Down state using the Sound menu.

6   Exit the button by clicking the Scene 1 link above the Stage, and return to the main timeline. Since both buttons are instances of the Arrow button symbol, it's not necessary to edit the Next button.

7   Press Ctrl+Enter (Windows) or Command+Return (Mac OS) to preview your movie. Rolling over the buttons should trigger a different sound than clicking them.

8   Close the Flash Player, and choose File > Save to save your work.

Controlling sounds

Once you've placed some sounds, you'll want to make sure you take the extra step to control the behavior of those sounds. Flash doesn't know when one sound should start and another should stop—it plays what you ask it to until the sound is done. This can result in a cacophony of sounds playing all at once if you don't set things up right. Sound control should be an essential part of adding sound, not an afterthought. One example is the narration that plays as you shuffle through photos in your slideshow. If a user jumps to the next (or previous) photo before the current narration is done, the two overlap. The best solution here is to use a bit of ActionScript to stop any other sounds before playing the next one.

Introducing *stopAllSounds( )*

The sole purpose of ActionScript's *stopAllSounds( )* command is to stop the playback of any and all sounds currently playing in your movie. Although this may seem a little broad, it's a good solution for the slideshow's narration overlap. In this exercise, you'll attach *stopAllSounds( )* to your Next and Previous buttons to ensure that sound is stopped before the next photo is displayed and the new narration begins.

1   Select the Previous button on the stage and open the Actions panel by choosing F9 (Windows), Option+F9 (Mac OS), or Window > Actions.

2   You will see the existing ActionScript on the button. It contains an event handler and the *prevFrame( )* function, which moves the playhead back one frame. Make sure Script Assist mode is selected (top right), then select the first line of code, which begins with *on(release)* {.

The Actions panel shows the script currently attached to the Previous button.

3 Using the Add a new item to the script button (⊕) at the top of the panel, choose Global Functions > Timeline Control > stopAllSounds. This will add *stopAllSounds( )* above the *prevFrame( )* action. The command's location is important because you want to stop sounds before the playhead moves to the new frame, not stop the new narration before it begins. If *stopAllSounds( )* is not above the *prevFrame( )* action, adjust it using the up or down arrow at the top of the panel. The code should now read:

```
on(release) {

stopAllSounds( );

prevFrame( );

}
```

4 Leave the ActionScript panel open and select the Next button. You should see the code for this button, including the *nextFrame( )* command move the playhead forward one frame.

5 Select the first line of code, which reads, *on(release) {*.

6 Press the Add new item to the script button and choose Global Functions > Timeline Control > stopAllSounds to add *stopAllSounds( )* above the *nextFrame( )* action.

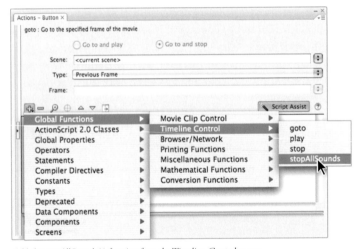

Add the stopAllSounds( ) function from the Timeline Control menu.

Again, if *stopAllSounds( )* is not above the *nextFrame( )* action, reposition it using the up or down arrow at the top of the panel. The code should now read:

```
on(release) {
stopAllSounds ( );
nextFrame ( );
}
```

7   Close your Actions panel and preview your movie by pressing Ctrl+Enter (Windows) or Command+Return (Mac OS). The narrations should now properly stop and start without bleeding together when you move back and forth between photos.

It's all about the order

Ordering the ActionScript commands correctly on the mouse buttons is essential, because ActionScript executes sequentially from top to bottom. The sounds for each slideshow photo are triggered when the playhead reaches their respective frames, so the current sound must stop before Flash advances to the next one. Had you reversed the command order in the exercise, the button would have moved you to the next photo, played the new sound but immediately stopped it, because the *stopAllSounds( )* function was called after the new sound began. Remember, although it seems that several ActionScripts run almost simultaneously, they are actually executed in order.

Editing sounds

If you find you need to adjust imported sounds, Flash offers some very useful tools for basic editing, effects, and sound manipulation. You'll explore these tools' options while adding the background music loop to your photo slideshow.

Little audio dynamite: the Edit Envelope panel

When your sounds still need a little something, Flash's Edit Envelope panel offers you many ways to trim, fade, and pan your audio for the best possible soundtrack. The Edit Envelope panel is opened using the Edit button that appears on the Property inspector when a sound on the Timeline is selected.

The Edit Envelope panel displays your sound as a waveform, or visual representation, of the length and volume of the sound. Each channel of a sound displays its own waveform in the panel; a line above the waveform indicates the sound's current volume. You can edit volume by adding handles to the volume envelope to move the line up or down. By default, the line is all the way up (full volume).

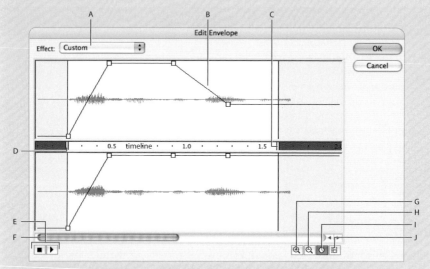

*A. Volume/Pan Presets. **B**. Volume envelope and handles. **C**. Right trim handle. **D**. Left trim handle.*
*E. Stop and Play buttons. **F**. Scroll bar. **G**. Zoom In. **H**. Zoom Out. **I**. Seconds. **J**. Frames.*

The lower-left corner features simple Play and Stop buttons so you can preview your sound as you edit it. Scrollbars let you move through the waveform and two magnifying glasses at the bottom-right corner let you zoom in or out to see more or less of the waveform in the window at one time.

The clock and filmstrip icons in the right corner let you toggle the Timeline between your waveforms to display seconds or frames. Use the sliders on your Timeline (there are two) to trim the beginning and end of the sound to eliminate unwanted dead space or set specific in and out points for longer pieces of audio.

In the upper-left corner, a drop-down menu lets you choose from preset envelope and pan settings such as Fade In and Fade Out, Pan Left or Right, or Sweeping Left To Right (and vice versa). Any custom volume (envelope) edits automatically display as Custom in the Preset menu.

Trimming sound

Sometimes a sound contains a certain amount of silence or "dead air" before or after the material you need. Usually you want to minimize or eliminate this dead space to make playback as seamless as possible, especially if a sound needs to loop. Flash lets you trim sounds by adjusting their starting and ending points. This type of trimming can also be useful for selecting a small portion of a longer sound file for use. To edit a sound's starting or ending point, you'll first need to place it on the Timeline.

1   With the Sounds layer selected, create a new layer on the Timeline using the Insert Layer button (⫿). Rename the layer **Background Music**.

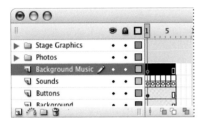

Insert a new layer to contain background music you'll add later on.

2   Select Frame 1 of the new layer, and make sure the Property inspector is open.

3   From the Sound menu on the Property inspector, choose the sound called BackgroundMusic.mp3.

4   Click the Edit button underneath the Sound menu to open the Edit Envelope dialog box. Press the Zoom out button (𝒬) until it becomes visible. Listen to the sound by clicking the Play button in the lower-left corner of the dialog box.

5 Click and drag the marker in the Edit Envelope dialog's middle ruler toward the right. The farther you drag it, the more you trim the beginning of the sound. Drag it as shown below, so that the sound starts when the waveform truly begins, eliminating the dead space at the beginning.

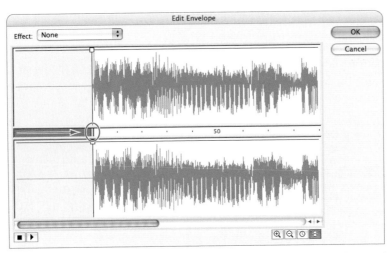

Use the sliders in the middle of the waveform to trim the empty space out of the beginning of the sound.

6 Use the scrollbar or arrows at the bottom of the Edit Envelope dialog box to move forward to the end of the sound, where you'll find another marker. Click and drag this marker left to trim the end of the sound and adjust its length. Click and drag it so that the sound ends just before the waveform stops, at about 23 seconds.

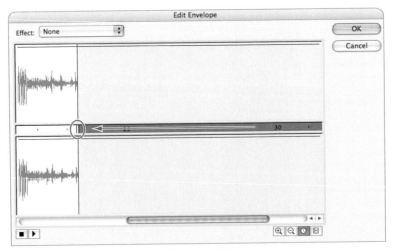

Use the right slider to trim the empty space from the end of the sound.

7 Click the Play button to preview the sound. The sound plays between the adjusted start and end points. Press OK to close the Edit Envelope dialog box.

Now preview your entire movie. Press Ctrl+Enter (Windows) or Command+Return (Mac OS) to see how the music plays out. Don't use the buttons to navigate; just sit back and listen. The sound should play once without repeating.

8 Choose File > Save to save the file.

Repeating and looping sounds

When you want a sound to repeat more than once, you can use either the Repeat or Loop options under the Sound portion of the Property inspector. Experiment with both options with your newly placed background music:

1 Select Frame 1 of the Background Music layer. Locate the Sound menu on the Property inspector.

2 Below the Sound menu, you will see the Repeat drop-down menu and text field. This option allows you to specify the number of times you want your sound to play before it stops. By default, all sounds are set to repeat at least once.

3 Change the number of Repeats to **3**.

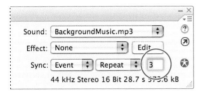

Set the number of times you want your sound to repeat.

4 Preview your movie by choosing Ctrl+Enter (Windows) or Command+Return (Mac OS). The background loop should play three times and stop. Close the Flash Player.

Looping sounds

The Repeat option can be useful in situations where the sound needs to repeat in tandem with events on the Stage, or if you want to put a limit on the number of times a piece of music can repeat. If you are certain you want a piece of music or a sound to repeat continuously, you should choose the Loop option, which plays the sound repeatedly until the movie is closed down. This is a good choice for your background music loop, because you don't want the music to stop while the visitor is enjoying the slideshow. Try Loop instead of the Repeat to hear the difference.

1   Select Frame 1 of the Background Music layer and locate the Sound menu on the Property inspector.

2   Select Loop from the Repeat drop-down menu. The Repeat text field disappears, as a loop is infinite and has no set number of repeats.

Try repeating and looping your sound to hear the difference.

3   Preview your movie by choosing Ctrl+Enter (Windows) or Command+Return (Mac OS). The background loop should play continuously as long as the movie is open. Close the Flash Player.

If you're hearing the background music being shut off by your buttons, don't worry—you'll learn how to fix this in the following exercises.

4   Choose File > Save to save the file.

More sync menu controls: stop and start

You may notice that using the Previous and Next buttons stop your background music from playing. This is because both buttons contain a *stopAllSounds( )* command, which is designed to stop any sound playing in a Flash movie at once. In the following lessons you'll learn how to selectively stop the narration without affecting the background music.

Beyond Event and Stream the Sync menu offers two more behavior options for sounds: stop and start. These options allow very fine control over the playback of specific sounds in your movie. You will use them now to fine-tune and complete your slideshow.

Start sounds

Because sounds placed on a frame are triggered when the playhead reaches that frame, you run the risk that a sound may overlap itself at some point. Consider your background music: you want to ensure that a user returning to the first frame to view the photo doesn't re-trigger the background loop and cause it to overlap. To avoid this, set the Sync option for the sound to Start. Start sounds play only one instance of themselves at a time, preventing overlap. A Start sound also plays until the end and can only be stopped by a matching Stop sound (more on this in a minute). By setting the background loop as a Start sound, you can make sure it will not be re-triggered unintentionally if it's already playing.

1 Select Frame 1 of your Background Music layer.

2 Choose Start in the Sync menu in the Property inspector, if it is not selected. Leave the Loop options as they are.

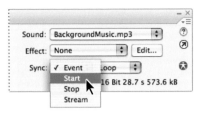

Switch the background music's Sync setting from Event to Start to avoid overlap.

3 Preview your movie by pressing Ctrl+Enter (Windows) or Command+Return (Mac OS)and return to the first photo using the Previous button. The background music should play properly without overlap. Close the Flash Player to return to the Timeline.

Stop sounds

Because it is built to stop all sounds, sometimes *stopAllSounds( )* is more stopping power than you need. For example, it not only stops each narration before another begins, it also prematurely stops your background music when a new photo is called. To remedy this, you need a more targeted stop method. The Sync menu's Stop option works with a single sound you specify via the Sound menu, stopping only that sound, if it is playing. Stop is a great way to terminate any piece of audio narration without affecting the background music at all. Put it into practice for the slideshow:

1 With the Background Music layer selected, create a new layer using the Insert Layer button (⊒). Rename the layer **Stop Sounds**. Select Frame 2 on the new layer and press F7 to insert a blank keyframe.

*Add a new layer called **Stop Sounds**.*

2 Using the Sound menu on the Property inspector, choose Photo 1. Although you are on Photo 2, the goal is to stop the Photo 1 narration when switching to this frame so that the Photo 2 sound can play.

3   With Photo 1 selected, choose Stop from the Sync menu. Rather than play the Photo 1 sound at this frame, it will stop any instances of only this sound, leaving other sounds unaffected.

Set the sound to the Stop option.

4   Select the Next button on the stage, and open your Actions panel by choosing Window > Actions or pressing F9 (Windows) or Option+F9 (Mac OS). To ensure that your background music is not shut off prematurely, you must remove the button's *stopAllSounds( )* action.

5   Turn Script Assist on by pressing the Script Assist button and select *stopAllSounds( )* in the Script window. Press the Delete the selected action(s) button (⊖) at the top of the panel to remove it. You no longer need it because a Stop sound is set for the Photo 1 narration.

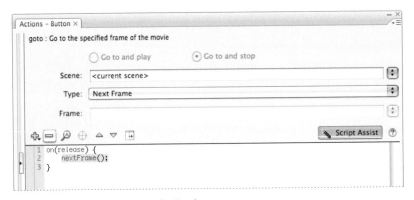

Remove the stopAllSounds( ) action on the Next button.

6   Close the Actions panel and preview your movie. Move quickly from the first photo to the second. The Photo 1 narration should stop and the Photo 2 narration should begin, without interrupting other sounds in your movie.

7   Use the same methods outlined in steps 1–3 to place a Stop sound on each remaining keyframe in the Stop Sounds layer for Photo 1.mp3 through Photo 5.mp3. These will stop any animation from the previous photo from running as you move ahead.

8   Choose File > Save to save the file, then choose File > Close.

Congratulations. You have completed the lesson.

Sound publishing options

When you publish your movie for final delivery to the Web, CD-ROM, or other destination, you can adjust how Flash exports the audio and packages it with your movie. By default, Flash compresses sounds in your movie into the .mp3 format regardless of the original file format. However, you can set the sound quality for both Stream and Event sounds in the Publish Settings > Flash panel. In the Flash panel of the Publish Settings dialog box, you can set export quality for both Audio Stream and Audio Event sounds in your movie. You'll learn more about this, as well as other techniques related to publishing your final Flash movie in Lesson 15, "Delivering Your Final Movie."

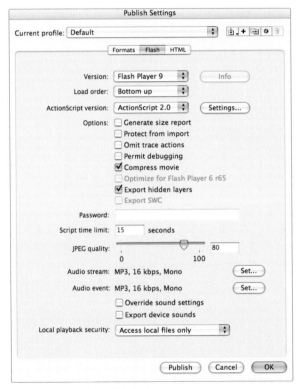

Determine your movie's Publish Settings.

Remember that just like quality settings for bitmap images, sound quality settings have a direct effect on the final file size. Before making a final decision, experiment with different quality settings for Audio Stream and Audio Event until you reach an acceptable quality level.

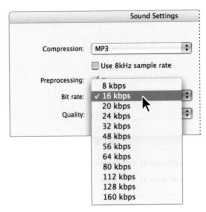

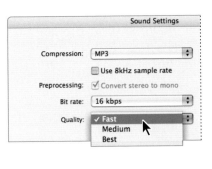

Bit rate determines the quality of the exported audio.   *Three presets fine-tune the quality by changing the sample rate.*

Wrapping up

Sounds are a great way to enhance your movie, and, paired with ActionScript, the applications and ideas are limitless. Always take great care and planning when working with sounds, as a certain level of preproduction on your original files will help guarantee the best possible results in Flash. Where possible, always make sure the user has an option to discontinue or temporarily mute sounds.

Self study

Use the techniques you've learned here to import and place a song from your mp3 library to one of your own Flash movies. Experiment with different sync and loop options to see which works best for your new soundtrack. Design and add a mute button which uses the *stopAllSounds( )* action. Make sure to preview your movie to see how the sound will perform for your users.

Review

Questions

1 What three sound formats can Flash import by default (not including additional QuickTime-enabled formats)?

2 What Sync option is best for shorter sounds that respond to button events?

3 True or False: Several sounds can be added to your movie on a single keyframe.

Answers

1 Windows WAV, AIFF and MP3.

2 Event sounds.

3 False—while your movie can play back several sounds at once, each needs to be placed on its own keyframe and its own layer.

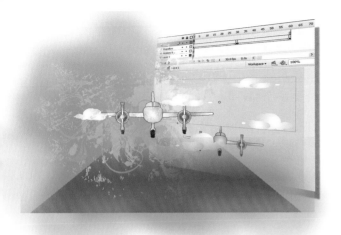

What you'll learn in this lesson:

- Using movie clips
- Creating, editing, and reusing
- Understanding instance names
- Nesting movie clips
- Viewing movie clip animation

Introducing Movie Clips

As your animations become richer and more elaborate, you may find that they can't be easily managed on a single timeline. Movie clip symbols enable you to break complex animations into smaller pieces that can be manipulated individually.

Starting up

Before starting, make sure that your tools and panels are consistent by resetting your preferences. See "Resetting the Flash workspace" on page 3.

You will work with several files from the fl13lessons folder in this lesson. Make sure that you have loaded the fllessons folder onto your hard drive from the supplied DVD. See "Loading lesson files" on page 3.

See Lesson 13 in action!

Use the accompanying video to gain a better understanding of how to use some of the features shown in this lesson. Open the DynamicLearning_FlashCS3.swf file located in the Videos folder and select Lesson 13 to view the video training file for this lesson.

The project

In this lesson, you will create an animation of a common, complex machine in motion: an airplane taking off. Using the power of movie clips, you'll break the airplane's various moving parts into individual animations. The graphics for the propellers and landing gear are provided; you'll simply put them all together while learning how to create complex yet manageable animations beyond the main timeline.

About movie clips

Movie clip symbols have the same advantages as other symbol types: all instances of a movie clip remain attached to their master in the library, and you create new instances by dragging them to the Stage from the Library panel. Each movie clip instance can be modified with transformations and color effects, just like a graphic. The real power that sets movie clips apart is that each movie clip contains its own timeline, independent of the main timeline. Movie clip animation, therefore, neither depends on nor needs to synchronize with anything happening on the main timeline. Each movie clip can contain its own animation, which you can place on the main timeline whenever and wherever you need it.

The lesson's airplane is a good analogy: it's a complex machine made of lots of separate parts and smaller machines. Although the starter, alternator, and windshield wipers make up the whole machine, each component has a different motion, rate, and function. Trying to build a plane out of one component would be impossible. Similarly, some complex animations can't be built on one timeline alone; they require the flexibility of separate parts. Each part needs to move at its own pace along its own timeline. Movie clips allow you to break animations into separate manageable and reusable pieces.

Think about the airplane again: some smaller machines (like the engine) are built from lots of smaller moving parts, but still need to be treated as one whole piece. Movie clips can contain other movie clips, so you can build a single movie clip from several others. They can also contain any number of graphic or button symbols.

Creating movie clips

As with graphic and button symbols, you can create movie clips by choosing Insert > New Symbol or by converting existing graphics or animations on the Stage with Modify > Convert to Symbol. You'll get plenty of practice with this in the next exercise.

Laying the foundation: your first movie clip

To begin your airplane animation, you'll build a propeller to power your plane.

1   Choose File > Open and navigate to the fl13lessons folder. Select the file fl1301.fla and press Open.

2   Choose File > Save As. When the Save As dialog box appears, type **fl1301_work.fla** into the File name text field. Navigate to the fl13lessons folder and press Save.

3   Open the Library panel by choosing Window > Library, if it is not already open. Locate the Propeller graphic symbol. This propeller blade is the foundation for an entire propeller assembly that you'll save as a movie clip symbol.

The Propeller graphic in your Library panel is the starting point for your first movie clip.

4   Choose Insert > New Symbol to open the New Symbol dialog box.

5   Name the new symbol Propeller Animation, and select Movie clip for Type. Press OK. The blank Stage and new timeline you now see indicate that you're in Edit mode for the new symbol.

Create a new empty movie clip.

6   Locate the Propeller graphic in the Library panel and drag an instance to the Stage. Choose Window > Align to bring up the Align panel. In the Align panel, make sure the To stage button is turned on, then press Align vertical center (⬌) and Align horizontal center (⬍) to center the Propeller graphic on the Stage.

7   To prepare for a motion tween, create a new keyframe at Frame 20 by pressing F6 or by right-clicking (Windows) or Ctrl+clicking (Mac OS) on the frame and selecting Insert keyframe; Flash will create an instance of the propeller there as well.

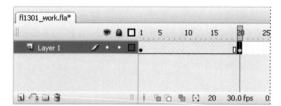

Set up for a motion tween by creating a new keyframe on Frame 20.

8   Select Frame 1 on the Timeline, and choose Tween > Motion from the Property inspector to create a new motion tween between Frames 1 and 20.

9 While still on Frame 1, choose CW from the Rotate drop-down menu in the Property inspector and enter **1** in the text-entry field that appears to its right. The Rotate drop-down menu enables you to automatically apply rotation to the symbols in your tween; here you have applied one clockwise revolution.

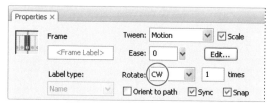

Set the direction and number of rotations for your propeller.

10 Press Return to play your animation. The propeller should now rotate clockwise once.

Watch the propeller spin clockwise once.

11 Select the Scene 1 link below the Timeline to exit the movie clip.

12 Choose File > Save to save the file.

Previewing movie clip animation from the main timeline

Because movie clips each operate on their own timeline, it's not as easy as pressing the Return key to see them working on the main timeline or along with other movie clips. You can view your movie using Publish Preview to see the clips play. Now you'll try placing some instances of your new movie clip on the Stage, and view them all in action.

1 Locate the new Propeller Animation movie clip in the Library panel and drag an instance to the Stage.

2 Press the Enter (Windows) or Return (Mac OS) key. Nothing happens, but that's okay; nothing is supposed to happen. You must view the movie in Publish Preview to see the movie clip play.

3   Choose File > Publish Preview > Flash, or go to Control > Test Movie, to export and launch your movie in the Flash Player. You should see your propeller moving now.

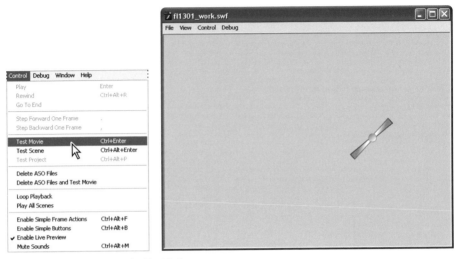

Preview your movie using Control > Test Movie.

4   Close the Preview window and return to the Timeline. Drag another instance of the Propeller Animation movie clip to the Stage.

5   Choose File > Publish Preview > Flash. Now you should see two propellers spinning at once. With movie clips, reusing an animation is as easy as drag and drop.

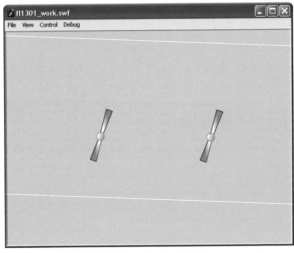

Two instances of the propeller turning simultaneously in Preview mode.

Creating the landing gear

You've seen two instances of the same movie clip combined. What about multiple instances of different movie clips? Assembling the airplane's retractable landing gear will give you plenty of practice. Before you begin, make sure the Library panel is open, and locate the Wheels graphic symbol.

1   Choose Insert > New Symbol to open the New Symbol dialog box.

Create a new movie clip symbol.

2   Assign the name **Landing Gear** to your new symbol, and specify Movie clip for its type. Press OK.

3   Now you're in Edit mode for the new symbol. Drag a copy of the Wheels graphic from the Library panel onto the Stage and position it so the top of it lines up with the crosshair in the middle of the Stage.

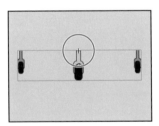

Position the Wheels graphic underneath the center of the crosshair.

4   Create a new keyframe on Frame 30 by pressing F6 or right-click/Ctrl+click the frame and select Insert keyframe; this creates another instance of the wheels on this frame. Select Frame 30 and, while holding the Shift key, drag the graphic symbol upward until the bottoms of the wheels are just above the crosshair in the center of the Stage.

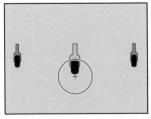

Animate your landing gear.

5   Return to Frame 1 and create a motion tween by choosing Tween > Motion in the Property inspector.

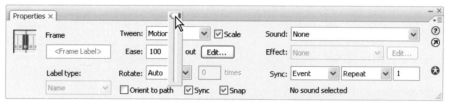

Add a motion tween on Frame 1 to set the wheels in motion.

6   With Frame 1 still selected, locate the Ease slider and set the ease to 100.

7   Select the Scene 1 link below the Timeline to return to the main timeline.

8   Locate and drag a copy of the new Landing Gear movie clip onto the Stage from the Library panel. Choose File > Publish Preview > Flash to view your movie in the Flash Player and set both propellers and the landing gear in motion.

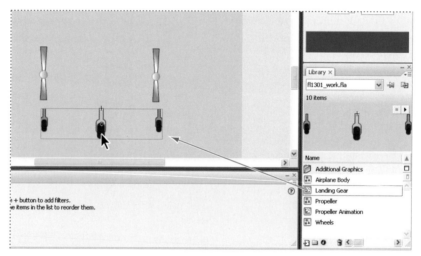

An instance of your Landing Gear movie clip on the Stage.

Combining movie clips and main timeline animation

With some key parts in working order, you're ready to match the body of your airplane to them. Locate the Airplane Body graphic symbol in the library; you'll be placing this on the Stage in the next steps.

1   With Layer 1 selected, create a new layer on the main timeline, using the Insert Layer button (◻). Double-click the layer name and change it to **Airplane Body**.

*Add a new layer and name it **Airplane Body**.*

2   Drag an instance of the Airplane Body graphic symbol from the Library panel onto the Stage. Use the Property inspector to position it at X: 260, Y: 100.

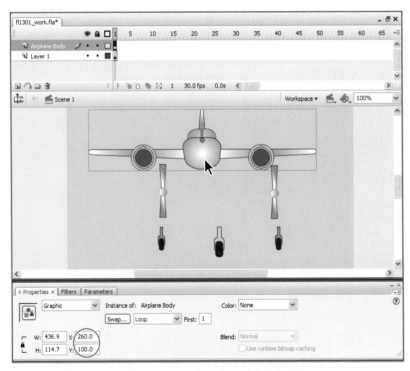

Drag and position an instance of the Airplane Body graphic symbol on the Stage.

3 Select the landing gear on Layer 1 and position it at exactly X: 260, Y: 150, using the Property inspector. It should now be in its proper place at the bottom of the airplane body.

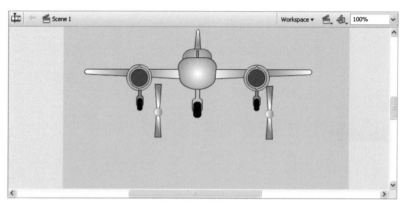

The landing gear now in place at the bottom of the airplane.

4 Holding down the Shift key, select both instances of the animated propeller movie clip. You need to move these onto a new layer above the plane body because they should appear in front of it. Choose Edit > Cut to remove the instances from the Stage.

5 With the Airplane Body layer selected, press the Insert Layer button to insert a new layer and rename it **Propellers**. Choose Edit > Paste to place the propeller movie clips back on the Stage on the new layer. Using the Property inspector, position one on the left wing at X: 147, Y: 132 and one on the right wing at X: 373 Y: 132.

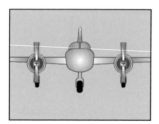

Move the propellers to your new layer.

6 Preview your movie in the Flash Player by selecting File > Publish Preview > Flash, or use the keyboard shortcut Ctrl+Enter (Windows) or Command+Return (Mac OS). The airplane should now be in full force with all parts moving.

7 Choose File > Save to save your work.

Nesting movie clips

When creating complex animations, you can simplify your main timeline by leveraging a movie clip's ability to nest, or to include movie clips inside other movie clips. In other words, you can create one single movie clip from several others. (Remember the engine analogy?) This gives you amazing flexibility and the ability to drag and drop very complex animations to the Timeline as effortlessly as simpler graphic or button symbols. Of course, you can modify and maintain movie clips as easily as other symbols by updating multiple instances of a complex movie clip from its master symbol in the library.

In this exercise, you'll convert the airplane and all its moving parts into a single movie clip symbol that you can tween, modify, or duplicate just as easily as any other symbol in your library. Movie clips can be created from existing movie clips, animations, or graphics on the Stage, using Modify > Convert to Symbol.

1 On the Timeline, select the Airplane Body, Propellers, and Landing Gear movie clips by choosing Edit > Select All. Choose Modify > Convert to Symbol to open the Convert to Symbol dialog box.

Wrap all the selected movie clips into one new movie clip.

2 To convert the whole group into a single movie clip symbol, assign the name **Full Airplane** and set the Type as Movie Clip. Use the registration grid to set a perfectly centered registration point. Press OK.

Name the new movie clip **Full Airplane**.

Notice that the group of parts appears on the Stage inside a single bounding box; you can now drag and move the movie clips around the Stage as one unit. Keep in mind, though, that the original movie clips must remain in the library, as the new movie clip depends on them.

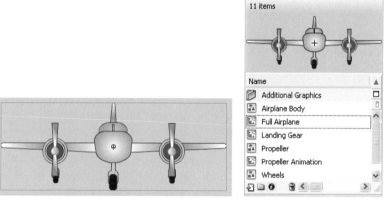

The new movie clip is now in one bounding box, while its pieces remain in the library.

3   Choose File > Publish Preview > Flash to view your movie in the Flash player. It should play just as it did before.

As the exercise demonstrates, movie clips can contain not only other movie clips, but graphics (such as the airplane body) and button symbols as well. This means that you can create entire animations inside movie clips without having to do anything on the Timeline.

4   Choose File > Save to save your work.

Movie clip facts, myths, and legends

Now that you're pretty deep into movie clips, it's time to review some rules, dispel some myths about how movie clips work, and pass on some important facts you need to know.

Dependencies: When you nest one symbol (movie clips, buttons, or graphics) inside of another, you create dependencies. In other words, the highest level symbol (for example, Full Airplane) depends on the symbols it contains (Airplane Body, Propellers, and Landing Gear, in this case) residing separately in the library. Placing other symbols inside a movie clip doesn't copy them, but rather references them. If you remove any lower-level symbol from the library, it will disappear from the larger symbol. If, for instance, you remove Landing Gear from the library, Full Airplane will no longer be able to find it and the landing gear component will disappear from the grouped movie clip.

Frame Rate: Although movie clip timelines are independent of the main timeline, they can't use a different frame rate. Frame Rate settings are global to a Flash movie (.swf), and can't be modified from movie clip to movie clip. Changing the frame rate for one affects the entire movie.

Timeline Length: Because a movie clip works from its own timeline, its length is independent from the main timeline's length or available space. You can place a 200-frame movie clip on the main timeline, even if there's no more than one frame there. The movie clip will still play as it should. Many movies are built using the main timeline as nothing more than a container for movie clips, and the main timeline sometimes contains no more than the first frame of each movie clip.

Timelines: Movie clip timelines work just as the main timeline does. Anything you can do on the main timeline, from tweens and layers to ActionScript, you can use on a movie clip timeline. Here's a little known fact: the main timeline is a movie clip in itself.

ActionScript: ActionScript on a movie clip timeline will have no effect on the main timeline or timelines of other movie clips (even included ones), and vice versa. ActionScript on a timeline, such as a stop or play action, affects only that timeline. This means you can use ActionScript across multiple timelines without a problem.

Adding ActionScript to movie clip timelines

When you preview your movie, you may notice that a few elements need some adjustment. The landing gear, for example, retracts but then shoots back out again (and again, and again) because nothing is directing the landing gear to stop when it has fully retracted. The nature of movie clips is to loop until told otherwise. The default behavior of the Flash Player is to make a movie loop. To override these two behaviors, you'll use a little bit of the ActionScript that you learned in Lesson 10, "Introducing ActionScript."

Controlling movie clip playback

Because movie clip timelines function just like the main timeline, placing ActionScript on a movie clip timeline is exactly the same as placing it on the main timeline. Prove this to yourself by modifying the Landing Gear symbol so that it doesn't loop.

1   In the Library panel, locate the Landing Gear movie clip symbol and double-click it to edit it. You should be in its Edit mode and see the tween you created earlier in the chapter.

2   With Layer 1 selected, press the Insert Layer button (⬔) to create a new layer, and rename it **Scripts**.

Although it's not required, separating ActionScript from frames that have content is a good practice.

3   Go to the last frame (Frame 30), and press F7 to create a new blank keyframe. Select the new frame, and choose Window > Actions or press F9 (Windows) or Option+F9 (Mac OS) to launch the Actions panel.

Create a new layer and blank keyframe for the ActionScript.

4   Before adding ActionScript, choose File > Publish Settings and select the Flash tab. Make sure the ActionScript version is set to ActionScript 2.0 for this lesson and press OK.

5   Press the Add a new item to the script button (⊕) to open the Actions menus. Choose Global Functions > Timeline Control > stop to add a *stop( )* action to the frame. This stops the animation and prevents the landing gear from looping. Close the Actions panel.

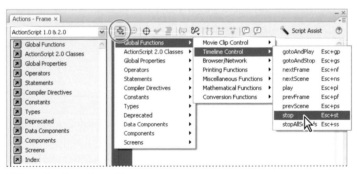

Add a stop( ) action to Frame 30.

A lowercase letter *a* on the frame indicates that the frame now contains a script.

6   Return to the main timeline by clicking the Scene 1 link below the Timeline.

7   Preview your movie, using File > Publish Preview > Flash. The landing gear should now retract and stay put without looping.

8   Choose File > Save to save your work.

Adding some variation to the propellers

To make your animation a little more dynamic, you can add two stages of speed to your propeller's rotation. All you need is some additional animation and a little ActionScript. At the moment, the propeller has a single tween that keeps it rotating. Simply add another rotation tween with a higher rate of speed right after the existing one to give the viewer the impression that the propellers pick up speed. To keep them from slowing down and speeding up repeatedly, you'll add ActionScript to animate it over a selected number of frames.

1 Locate the Propeller Animation movie clip in the Library panel and double-click it to edit it. You should see that the timeline for this movie clip contains a single tween.

You'll work with tweens to better animate the propeller.

2 Create new keyframes at Frame 21 and Frame 40 by pressing F6.

3 Create a motion tween at Frame 21 by choosing Motion from the Tween drop-down menu in the Property inspector.

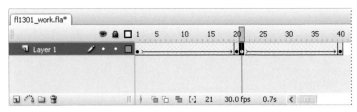

Create a second motion tween.

4 At the bottom of the Property inspector, set the Rotate direction to CW (clockwise), and enter **5** for the number of rotations. This will produce a very quick rotation, faster than the single rotation of the previous tween.

Adjust the Rotate options.

5   With Layer 1 selected in the Timeline, insert a new layer using the Insert layer button (⊒),
and rename it **Actions**. This layer will contain an action that forces the animation to loop.

6   Create a new blank keyframe on the Actions layer at Frame 40 by pressing F7. Select the
new keyframe and open the Actions panel (Window > Actions).

7   Make sure Script Assist mode is enabled and, using the Add a new item to the script button
(⊕), choose Global Functions > Timeline Control > goto. Flash will add the *gotoAndPlay( )*
function with the default of Frame 1.

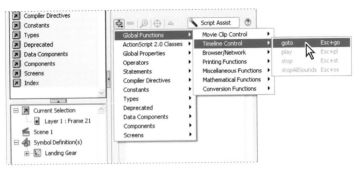

Add a goto script.

8   Use the Frame text-entry field above the script window to set the Frame to 21, so the
script reads: *gotoAndPlay(21);*. This will send the animation in a loop, but only from Frame
21, where the propeller is at full speed.

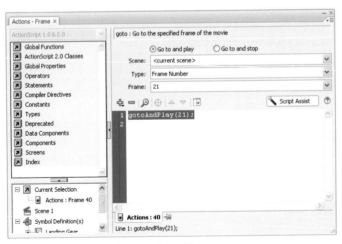

Add a gotoAndPlay( ) script that targets Frame 21.

The loop starts later in the Timeline because you want the speed increase to occur only once and then have the propeller maintain a consistent speed as it loops. After the propeller picks up speed through the two tweens, the animation will loop continuously from Frame 21, so the speed stays fast as the loop continues.

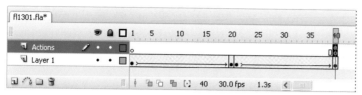

The finished Timeline.

9   Select the Scene 1 link under the Timeline. Preview your movie by choosing File > Publish Preview > Flash. The plane's propellers should appear to speed up and then rotate at a continuous rate. Because both propellers were instances of the same symbol, both automatically reflect the changes you made to the master symbol's animation.

10 Choose File > Save to save your work.

Tweening movie clips

To make your movie clips glide, transform, or change their color tint, you can apply motion tweens to them just as you would to other symbols. Creating a tween with a movie clip is exactly the same as for graphic symbols, and several movie clips can be tweened at the same time on separate layers.

You've already used a few tweens, and in this exercise you practice using motion tweens to make your airplane take off. Before you start, make sure the Property inspector is visible, and that you return to the main timeline by choosing the Scene 1 underneath the Timeline.

To tween your airplane and create a take-off sequence:

1   Select the entire airplane on the Stage (instance of Airplane Full). Use the Property inspector to set its position to X: 280, Y: 275. With proportions constrained, set the width of the airplane to 300. It should now be slightly smaller and sit on the bottom center of the Stage.

Reposition and shrink the airplane.

2   On the Propellers layer, create a new keyframe at Frame 30 (press F6). Select the new instance of the Airplane Full clip created at this frame, and use the Property inspector to set its position to X: 280, Y: 100.

3   Return to Frame 1 and create a motion tween from Frame 1 to Frame 30 using the Property inspector. You can also do this by right-clicking (Windows) or Ctrl+clicking (Mac OS), and choosing Motion Tween from the context menu.

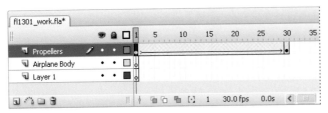

Set a motion tween on Frame 1.

4   To create the impression of gravity pulling down on your plane as it takes off, add an Ease of –100 on Frame 1.

Add an Ease on Frame 1.

5   Press Return to preview your movie; your airplane should now lift off and make its way toward the top of the screen with propellers and landing gear in full effect.

6   Choose File > Save to save your work.

Adding a second tween

Now that you have your airplane taking off, you can elaborate further on your animation by making the airplane come toward you as it continues to fly. This will require a second tween after the one you just created.

1   Create a new keyframe on Frame 31 right next to your new tween. Create a second new keyframe at Frame 60.

2   Select the instance of your airplane movie clip on Frame 60; its width and height are displayed below in the Property inspector.

3   With proportions constrained (make sure the padlock appears next to the W and H fields), enlarge the airplane by setting its width to 400 in the W (width) field.

Resize the airplane.

4   Using the Property inspector, create a motion tween on Frame 31.

5   Select Frame 1 and press Return to preview your animation; the airplane should now take off and appear to move forward right into your field of view.

As you've seen in these steps, tweening a movie clip instance is very much the same as working with a graphic symbol, so transformations, color effects, and motion can all be applied. Because movie clips can contain entire animations, however, you can fully explore more complex and dynamic animations.

Combining movie clips for complex animation

To make a movie as realistic and dynamic as possible, you can combine as many movie clips on the main timeline as you need to achieve the full effect. Because each movie clip is an independent animation of its own, multiple movie clips interacting on the Timeline will not interfere with each other. Keep in mind, however, that you may need to carefully orchestrate and sequence animation in different movie clips if one needs to interact with another.

Now that you've got your airplane up and running, to make the scene more realistic you'll add two things: a runway and some clouds. Both of these graphics will have their own motion, especially as your plane moves off of the runway and through the clouds. The movie clips for both of these have already been created for you in the library; all you'll need to do is place them on the main Timeline.

1   On the main timeline, with the Propellers layer selected, create a new layer and rename it **Clouds**. Make sure the new layer sits above the layer that contains your Airplane tween.

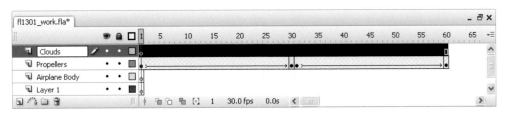

Create a new layer for the Clouds movie clip.

2   Locate the Clouds movie clip in the Library panel in the Additional Graphics folder and
    drag an instance to the Stage.

Drag an instance of Clouds to the Stage.

3   Use the Property inspector to position the new Clouds instance at X: 100, Y: 220.

4   While still on the main timeline, create a new layer and rename it **Runway**. Drag this layer
    below the layer that contains your airplane animation.

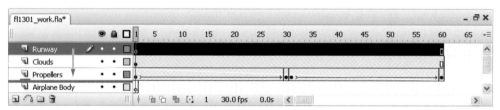

Create a new layer below the airplane tween to make room for your runway.

5 With the Runway layer selected, locate the Runway movie clip in the Library panel in the Additional Graphics folder and drag an instance of it to the Stage. Use the Property inspector to position it at X: 275, Y: 260.

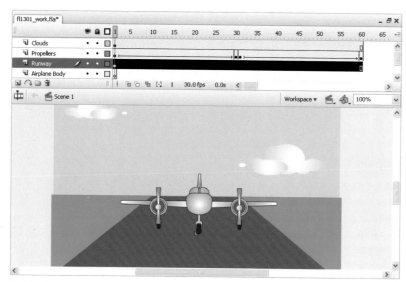

Position the Runway movie clip on the Runway layer.

6 Test your movie by choosing File > Publish Preview > Flash. The newly added clips animate along with the airplane you created; you now have a full animation scene.

7 Choose File > Save to save your work.

Exercise

To test your new skills, explore both of the provided movie clips in Edit mode to see how they were created. Try making modifications to them and see how your overall movie is affected. Because these movie clips were built to work together, major changes in length or animation style may require you to also adjust the other movie clips on the Stage.

Adding filter effects to movie clips

Movie clips have another advantage: they (and buttons) are the only symbol types to which you can apply Flash's built-in, high-quality filter effects, including blurs, drop shadows, and bevels. Because the filter effects are nondestructive, they won't permanently alter the pixel data in a symbol, meaning you can easily remove or edit filters, as well as apply unique filters to several instances of a movie clip.

Probably one of the coolest features to note is that Flash filters can be tweened, just like any other instance-specific property. For example, you can apply a blur gradually to a symbol to create realistic and artistic effects.

To try some of these effects, choose Window > Properties > Filters to launch the Filters panel, which is grouped with the Property inspector.

Some CS3 applications (most notably Adobe Photoshop) feature a variety of filter effects. If you're creating graphics in one of these applications, you may choose to apply filters then or directly in the Flash environment after import. Because Flash now natively supports importing Photoshop and Illustrator files, it will convert most common filter types to their Flash equivalent. The advantage of applying filters in Flash is that they can be easily edited without the need to switch applications and re-import updated files. In addition, you can manipulate Flash filters with ActionScript, which opens a world of dynamic filtering possibilities.

Using the Filters panel

In this exercise, you'll explore Flash filters by applying effects to the Clouds and Runway movie clips using the Filters panel. (The Filters panel is grouped with the Property inspector.) The Filters panel can apply and fine-tune such preset effects as blurs, drop shadows, and glows to movie clip instances. Before you begin, make sure the Property inspector and Filters panel are both visible; it's okay if they're either grouped together or separated.

1   Select the Clouds movie clip on the main timeline.

2   Bring the Filters panel forward so the filter list and Add filter button (⊕) are visible. Press the Add filter button and choose Blur from the pop-up list of filters. The sliders that appear to the right enable you to set the desired degree of vertical and horizontal blur.

Use the Filters panel to modify the appearance of your movie.

3 Enter 10 in the Blur X and Blur Y boxes; leave the padlock visible so the settings for width and height stay proportional.

Adjust the Blur in the Filters panel.

4 Under Quality, select Medium. This is a good choice for making sure the effect looks clean without putting too much strain on the Flash Player (filter effects are resource-intensive).

5 Preview your movie, using the shortcut key combination Ctrl+Enter (Windows) or Command+Return (Mac OS). Your clouds now have an interesting blur effect applied and, as a result, appear more realistic as the animation plays.

Creating a filter effect

Filtering an entire movie clip instance is a few clicks away using the Filters panel, but you can go a step further by combining tweens and filters to transition into a filter effect. Try this with your Runway movie clip by blurring the runway as the plane takes off and climbs above the ground.

1 Double-click the Runway movie clip on the Stage to edit it in place. You should see a basic motion tween that moves the runway down. The tween was created between two instances of a movie clip called Runway Graphics. (Graphics symbols cannot be used because you can apply filter effects only to movie clips or buttons.)

The Runway movie clip in Edit mode.

 You can apply filter effects only to movie clips, buttons, and dynamic text fields. If you want to apply a filter to a raw graphic, graphic symbol, or drawing object, you must convert it to a movie clip or button symbol first.

2 Select the instance of the Runway Graphics movie clip on Frame 30. Bring the Filters panel forward so the Add filter button is visible. Select Blur from the pop-up list of filters.

3   Using the sliders that appear on the panel, set the Blur X and Y values to 15. Set Quality to Medium. Because this instance of Runway Graphics now has a filter and the instance on Frame 1 does not, Flash creates a tween to gradually blur out the runway as it moves downwards, creating the effect that the airplane is moving farther away from the runway as it ascends.

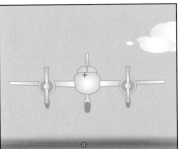

Apply Blur changes to your plane and runway.

4   Press Ctrl+Enter (Windows) or Command+Return (Mac OS) to preview your movie.

5   If you like, return to the main timeline and keep your airplane at cruising altitude by adding a *stop( )* action on Frame 60. Remember to insert a new layer for the *stop( )* action and create a new keyframe at Frame 60 before adding the action, to ensure it occurs in the right place. This will keep your movie from looping when you preview it in Test Movie mode, so you can enjoy your handiwork longer.

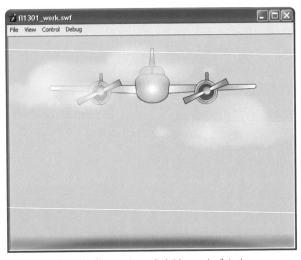

The preview shows the filters you've applied. Now you're flying!

6   Choose File > Save, then choose File > Close.

Wrapping up

Movie clips open a treasure trove of possibilities, and the best way to master movie clips is to use them—the more you do, the more ways you'll find to create innovative, complex, and eye-catching animations that far exceed what's possible on a single timeline. To get ideas for your next movie clip, explore ready-made clips, such as the Runway and Clouds movie clips in your library, to understand how they were created. Don't hesitate to modify the movie clips in this exercise by adding keyframes, experimenting with more filter effects, or adding some additional graphics of your own.

Self study

Choose a machine or object with two or more moving parts, then try to recreate it using movie clips. The subject doesn't have to be complex—get ideas from around the house, in the kitchen, or at the office. Chances are you'll find something worth recreating that's fun and lets you use your new skills.

Review

Questions

1   True or False: Movie clip timelines depend on the length and action of animation on the main timeline.

2   What type of symbols can be contained inside a movie clip?

3   How do you preview movie clip animation along with the main timeline and other movie clips?

Answers

1   False: movie clip timelines are fully independent of the main timeline.

2   Graphics, buttons, and other movie clips.

3   Use File > Publish Preview.

What you'll learn in this lesson:

- Understanding the principles of working with video in Flash

- Using the Video Import wizard to import and convert video files

- Controlling the playback of video on the Timeline

Working with Video

Video can greatly improve the quality and effectiveness of your projects by offering viewers a rich and immersive experience, whether you are creating a sales presentation, website, or animation. While Flash has long been able to work with video, Flash CS3 Professional has extended its capabilities, making Flash an even better platform for delivering web video content.

Starting up

Before starting, make sure that your tools and panels are consistent by resetting your workspace. See "Resetting the Flash workspace" on page 3.

You will work with several files from the fl14lessons folder in this lesson. Make sure that you have loaded the fllessons folder onto your hard drive from the supplied DVD. See "Loading lesson files" on page 3.

See Lesson 14 in action!

Use the accompanying video to gain a better understanding of how to use some of the features shown in this lesson. Open the DynamicLearning_FlashCS3.swf file located in the Videos folder and select Lesson 14 to view the video training file for this lesson.

The project

In this lesson, you'll import a video file into Flash and practice various methods of integrating it into your movies. Working through the exercises in this lesson, will introduce you to the different ways to work with video in your Flash projects. To view the finished file, choose File > Open and select the fl1401_done.fla and fl1402_done.fla files within the fl14lessons folder. Close the files when you are finished, or keep them open as a reference.

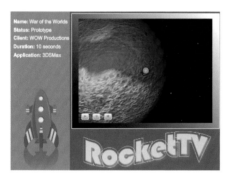
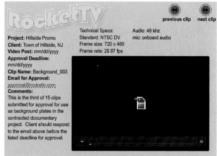

The finished files.

Video in Flash: formats and fundamentals

The first step toward importing video into Flash is to make sure you are equipped and ready. In addition to Flash CS3, you'll need either the QuickTime player on your system (at least version 6.5 for Windows or version 7.0 for Mac OS) or DirectX 9.0 (Windows). You'll also need a source video file to import and convert (video is provided for the exercises in this lesson).

Flash can import video in the following file formats:

• QuickTime (.mov)

• Windows (.avi)

• DV (.dv)

• ISO/IEC (.mpg)/(.mpeg)

The QuickTime player is available as a free download from http://www.apple.com. DirectX is available from Microsoft corporation at http://www.microsoft.com/downloads.

Videos are composed of a series of sequential still images. When played back very quickly, these images seem to form continuous motion. You need to remember two parameters when working with video: frame rate, which is the speed, measured by frames per second (fps) at which the video plays, and frame size, which is the size, measured in pixels, of each image.

Internal versus external video

There are two primary ways to import and display video within Flash: you can embed the video directly onto the Timeline (internal), or have your movie reference an external, or linked, video file.

External video files can be streamed from a Flash Media Server, a server solution optimized to deliver streaming or real-time media, or downloaded progressively from a Web server in Flash's own .flv video file format. Flash's .flv format can be created from several original video file formats from the Video Import wizard or by using Flash's standalone video encoder.

External video keeps the Flash file size fairly small, which makes assembling and developing Flash content easier, and is suitable for larger video clips and clips with synchronized audio. (For a comparison of the benefits of streaming versus progressively downloading, see the section "Working with linked video.") Embedded or internal video is placed directly on the Timeline, which significantly increases the .swf file size—potentially to unmanageable levels with longer clips. For this reason, embedded video is recommended only for short video clips.

With both methods, you can import video clips from your hard drive, converting them into frame-by-frame video on the Timeline or to Flash's .flv video format. Once you have completed your Flash project, embedded video is automatically be included when you upload your .swf file, while linked video must be uploaded separately.

Working with embedded video

Embedding video is the most straightforward method of adding video content to your movies. Because it can swell the size of your .swf file, however, it is best suited for adding short video clips, preferably without audio. In this exercise, you will import and embed a short video file into a prepared Flash document and use basic ActionScript to create play, pause, and stop buttons to control the Timeline.

Importing with the Video Import wizard

The first phase of the project is to prepare the document, bring the video clip into Flash with the Video Import wizard, and resize it to fit your movie. Before you begin, reset the Flash workspace to its default configuration by choosing Window > Workspace > Default so that your workspace matches the one used in the following exercises.

To begin importing video:

1   Open the file fl1401.fla from the fl14lessons folder and choose File > Save As. When the Save As dialog box appears, type **fl1401_work.fla** into the File name text field. Navigate to the fl14lessons folder and press Save.

You will be adding video to this pre-created interface.

2   Select File > Import > Import Video to start the Video Import wizard.

Access the Video Import wizard through the File menu.

3   Use the Browse (Windows) or Choose (Mac OS) button next to the File path text field to navigate to the fl14lessons folder, and select the QuickTime movie named fl1403.mov. Press Open to return to the wizard, then press Next (Windows) or Continue (Mac OS).

The two options in the Select Video section of the wizard allow you to select and convert video files that reside on your local hard drive or Flash video that is already deployed to a web server, streaming service, or Flash Media Server.

4   In the Deployment screen, select the Embed video in SWF and play in timeline radio button. This places the video directly in the Flash Timeline, which enables you to sync the video with other animation or add interactive elements to the video area. Press Next/Continue.

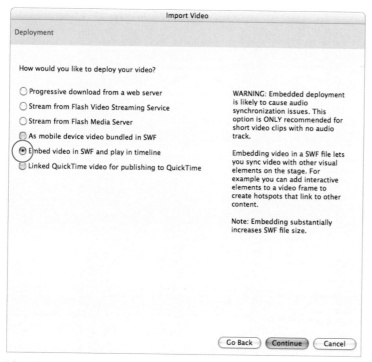

The Embed video in SWF and play in timeline option places your video directly on the Timeline.

5 In the Embedding screen, select Embedded video as the Symbol type. Embedded video is converted into a symbol, which can easily be controlled by the Timeline. Specify Integrated as the Audio track setting to keep the audio and video as one object.

Uncheck the checkboxes next to Place instance on the stage and Expand timeline if needed—these prevent the new video from being automatically added to the Timeline. Make sure the radio button next to Embed the entire video is selected. Press Next (Windows) or Continue (Mac OS).

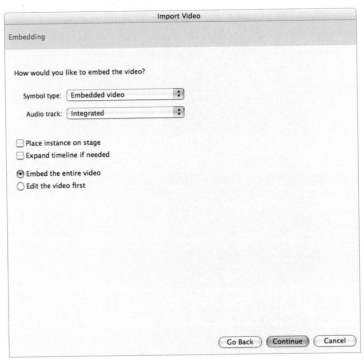

A number of options are available for embedding a video in your Flash file.

 Video symbols are very flexible. Their playback can be controlled by the main timeline (unlike movie clips, which are independent of the main timeline), and they can be targeted by ActionScript (unlike graphic symbols).

6 The wizard moves to the Encoding screen, which is organized into five tabs: Profiles, Video, Audio, Cue Points, and Crop and Resize. Press the Profiles tab, and select Flash 8 – High Quality (700kbps) from the drop-down menu.

Profiles are presets that have been created to encode video for playback in either Flash Player 7 or 8, using a variety of video and audio quality settings.

You can create and save your own custom profiles by clicking on the disk icon above the Profile drop-down menu.

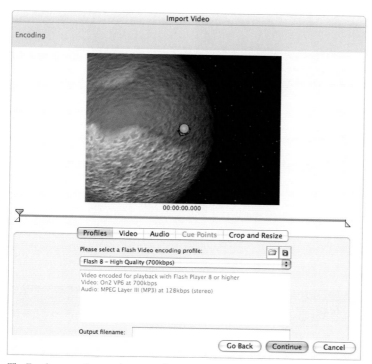

The Encoding screen lets you choose a profile, which determines the quality of the imported video.

7 Select the Video tab and make sure the Video Codec menu is set to On2 VP6 and Frame Rate is set to Same as Source. This ensures that your video plays back at the same frame rate at which it was originally created.

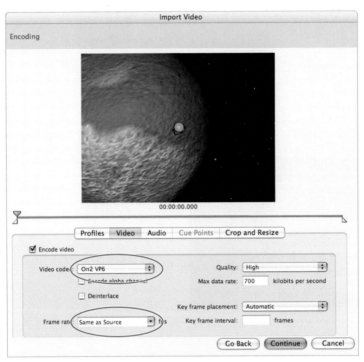

Check the codec and frame rate settings under the Video screen.

What is a codec?

Codecs are software routines that compress video files small enough to be emailed, viewed on the Internet, and burned to DVDs.

The viewer's computer then uses the same codec to decompress and play the video back. Flash and the Flash Player support two codec choices: Sorenson Spark or On2 VP6. The On2 VP6 codec is the default setting for videos encoded for version 8 and 9 of the Flash player because it provides higher video quality than the older Sorenson Spark. This higher quality video comes at the price of a slower encoding time and more use of system resources (RAM, connection speed, etc.) on the viewer's computer at playback time.

8 Select the Audio tab and uncheck the Encode audio checkbox. This video clip does not have sound.

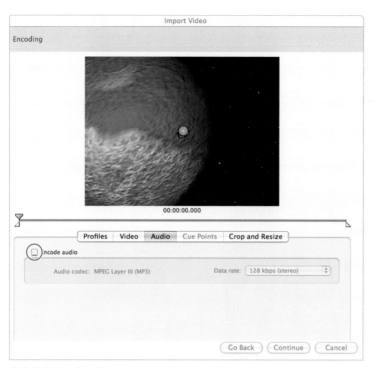

Uncheck the Encode audio checkbox.

9 Select the Crop and Resize tab, and click the Resize video checkbox so you can resize the incoming clip. Confirm that the Maintain Aspect Ratio is checked, and enter **480** in the Width field. The Height field should change to 360 automatically, maintaining the video's original proportions. Press Next/Continue.

10 The next wizard screen, Finish Video Import, gives you a summary of your choices as well as the location of the file to be converted. Because this is embedded video, it is placed in your document's library as a symbol. Press Finish to begin importing and rendering the video.

You may have to wait a bit while the video is encoded. The time required to render your new video file depends on your computer's available processing power.

11 Choose File > Save or use the keyboard shortcut Ctrl+S (Windows) or Command+S (Mac OS) to save the file. Leave the file open, as you will need it for the next exercise.

Adding embedded video to the Timeline

Upon successful import of your video, your new imported video should appear in your Library panel as a symbol, ready to be added to the Timeline. Give it a try.

1   Open your Library panel by choosing Window > Library, and locate the embedded video symbol named fl1403.mov.

2   Select the Video Here layer on the Timeline, and drag the fl1403.mov clip onto the Stage.

Place your new video on the Video Here layer on the Timeline.

3   Flash displays a warning message asking whether you would like to increase the Timeline to accommodate the length of the video. Press Yes.

Increase the size of the Timeline to accommodate the new video.

4 The layout of this Flash document has been set up so that there is a frame waiting to hold your new video. Click on the Selection tool (↖) in the Tools panel, and use it to position the video inside the gray frame on the right side of the Stage. The video snaps to the guidelines outlining the frame.

To make positioning the new video as easy as possible, make sure that snapping is enabled by choosing View > Snapping > Snap to Guides.

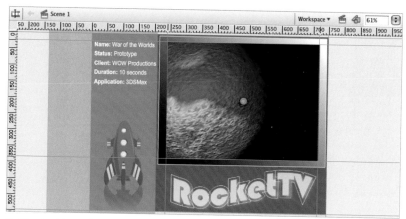

Position the video inside the gray frame.

5 As the Timeline currently stands, the video on the Video Here layer plays for 150 frames, but the theme, videoframe, and colorbar on the other three layers only exist at Frame 1. You'll correct this in the next few steps.

Click on Frame 150 in the Theme layer on the Timeline. Hold down the Ctrl (Windows) or Command (Mac OS) key, and click on Frame 150 in both the videoframe and colorbar layers to select them all at once.

6 Press the F5 key to add new frames to all three layers. This ensures that the content of the theme, videoframe, and colorbar layers remains on the Timeline until the video finishes playing.

7 Choose File > Save. Choose Control > Test Movie to preview your work so far.

8 Close the Flash player and leave the file open; you'll need it in the next exercise.

Building controls for embedded video

When you preview your work, you'll see that the video clip plays within your movie and then loops over and over again. It is standard behavior for the Flash player to loop .swf files, but in this case it's not the effect you want. To prevent this continuous looping, you will use ActionScript to control the Timeline and, in turn, the playback of the video.

1   Select the theme layer, and press the Insert Layer button (⬑) below the Timeline to create a new layer.

2   Double-click on the name of the new layer to edit it, and rename it **Controls**. On this layer you'll add the play, pause, and stop controls for the video clip.

*Add a new layer and name it **Controls**.*

3   Open your Library panel using Window > Library, if it is not already open, and locate the three button symbols named Pause_SilverRounded, Play_SilverRounded, and Stop_SilverRounded inside the buttons folder.

Locate the three pre-created buttons in the Library panel.

4 Make sure the Controls layer is still selected, and drag an instance of each of the three buttons from the Library panel onto the Stage. It doesn't matter when they end up; you'll precisely position them later.

5 On the Timeline, click the padlock icon (🔒) for the theme and Video Here layers to ensure that you don't accidentally move one of them. Use the Selection tool (🔖) to position the three buttons at the lower-left corner of the video clip in this order: Play, Pause, and Stop. Use the figure as a guide.

Position the Play, Pause, and Stop buttons in the lower left-hand corner of the video.

6 Use the Selection tool to Shift+click on all three buttons. Open the Align panel by choosing Window > Align.

The keyboard shortcut for the Align panel is Ctrl+K (Windows) or Command+K (Mac OS).

7 In the Align panel, turn off the To stage button if it is selected, and click on the Align vertical center button (🔘) to align the Play, Pause, and Stop buttons with each other.

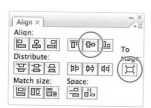

Deselect the To stage button and choose Align to vertical center.

8 With all three buttons still selected on the Stage, click the Distribute horizontal center (🔘) to make the spacing between the buttons equal.

9   Click on an empty area of the Stage to deselect your buttons. Select just the Play button on the Stage and, in the Property inspector, assign it an instance name of **play_btn**.

*Assign the Play button the instance name of **play_btn**.*

10 Repeat step 9 for the Pause and Stop buttons, giving them instance names of **pause_btn** and **stop_btn**, respectively.

11 On the Timeline, select the Controls layer and click on the Insert Layer button to create a new layer for your ActionScript above it. Name the new layer **Actions**. (It's always good practice to place ActionScript on its own layer in the Timeline.)

12 Select the first frame of the Actions layer and press F9 (Windows) or Option+F9 (Mac OS) to open the Actions panel. In order for the buttons to control the Timeline, you need to build three ActionScript functions, one for each button, and add instructions to activate them based on mouse events.

13 Place the code below into Script window on the right side of the Actions panel:

In the fl14lessons folder, the file fl1401_ButtonScript.as contains the code for this exercise. You can open it directly within Flash or a text editor of your choice, and copy and paste the code into the Actions panel.

```
stop( );
function playMovie(event:Event):void{
    this.play( );
}
function pauseMovie(event:Event):void{
    this.stop( );
}
function stopMovie(event:Event):void{
    this.gotoAndPlay(1);
}
play_btn.addEventListener(MouseEvent.CLICK,playMovie);
pause_btn.addEventListener(MouseEvent.CLICK,pauseMovie);
stop_btn.addEventListener(MouseEvent.CLICK,stopMovie);
```

Click the check syntax button (✔) at the top of the Script window. The check syntax button exists to make sure that you typed the code properly, following all the syntax rules that ActionScript requires. If a message pops up that this code contains no errors, go to the next step. If you are told that there are errors, check your typing and try again.

Written in ActionScript 3.0, this basic code uses the *stop( )* action on the first line to stop the Timeline so the video does not play automatically. The next three commands define the actions for each button: Play starts the movie, Pause stops the movie, and Stop returns to the beginning of the movie. Close the Actions window. The final three commands link their respective actions to a click of the mouse.

14 Choose Control > Test Movie to preview your movie. Click the Play button to start the video clip, and work with the Pause and Stop buttons. If you let the movie play until the end, it stops again on Frame 1. Choose File > Close to close the Flash Player.

15 Choose File > Save to save your work. Leave the file open; you'll need it in the next exercise.

Updating and exporting video

Look in the fl14lessons folder, and check the size of the fl1401_work.swf file created in the last exercise. It's a little large, approximately 900K. One possible way to reduce the file size is to reduce the quality of the video itself.

Using Flash's Update feature, you can change the video's quality without re-importing the footage. If the updating process doesn't reduce the file size sufficiently, you have a second alternative: export the embedded video and use it with one of the linked deployment methods.

1 On the Timeline, select the layer named Video Here.

2 Double-click the fl1403.mov embedded video symbol in the Library panel, which opens the Video Properties dialog box.

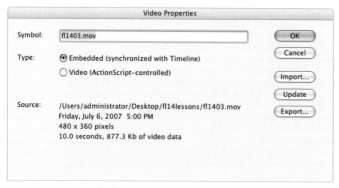

The Video Properties dialog box lets you update video you've already imported to the library.

3 Press Update on the right to open the Flash Video Encoding Settings dialog box.

4 In the Profiles tab of the Flash Video Encoding Settings dialog box, select the option for Flash 8-Medium Quality (400kbps) from the Profiles drop-down menu.

5 In the Audio tab, uncheck the Encode Audio checkbox. Remember, there is no audio included in this video.

6 In the Crop and Resize tab, select the Resize Video checkbox, and retype 480 in the Width text field. Flash automatically sets the Height to 360. Retyping the Width and Height ensures that the video encodes at that size; otherwise, the video encodes at its original size and you get different results. Press OK, and Flash re-encodes the video. When the video finishes encoding, press OK to close the Video Properties dialog box.

7 Preview the changes you've made by choosing Control > Test Movie. If you view the details for fl1401_work.swf in the fl14lessons folder, the file size should now be slightly smaller than 550K.

8 Choose File > Save to save your work. Make sure to leave your file open, as you'll need it for the next exercise.

If updating your movie didn't reduce its file size to your satisfaction, you'll discover how to greatly reduce the size of movies that include video by using linked, or external, video in your movie later in this lesson.

The Bandwidth Profiler

The Bandwidth Profiler is a useful tool that can help you measure the impact of embedded video on your movie. Even if your movie plays well for you, how does it perform for your target viewers? The Bandwidth Profiler enables you to test your movie's download time under a variety of conditions and gives you the ability to review the amount of data in each frame of your movie. Check how well your movies from the exercises stack up.

1 Preview your movie by choosing Control > Test Movie.

2 When your movie opens in the Flash player, choose View > Bandwidth Profiler.

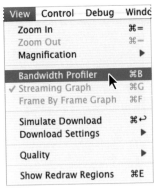

Access the Bandwidth Profiler through the View menu.

3 Choose View > Frame by Frame Graph to see a breakdown of your movie's parameters on the left and the size of each frame on the right.

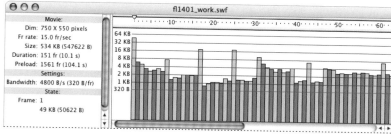

The Frame by Frame Graph displays the size of each frame in your movie.

4 Choose View > Download Settings > DSL (32.6 KB/s) to see how your movie is treated if viewed over a DSL connection instead of a 56K dial-up connection.

5 Choose View > Simulate Download to preview what viewers experience when they watch your movie at the currently selected download settings.

6 Choose File > Close to close the Flash Player, then File > Close again to close the file.

Working with linked video

If your video file is too large to embed into the .swf, you should consider importing it as linked, or external, video. Linked deployment gives you the choice of three approaches: web server, Flash Media Server, or Flash Video Streaming Service. Web server deployment enables you to use your current web server or hosting service plan to progressively download video into your Flash movie, using standard Hyper Text Transfer Protocols (HTTP). This allows users to begin watching a portion of your video while the rest of the file continues to load in the background.

Although progressively downloading a video clip from a web server doesn't provide the same real-time performance as Flash Media Server, this approach requires minimal overhead and works easily with the same server that currently hosts your website.

Video in the fast lane: Flash Media Server

For the fastest video delivery, consider deploying your video content to a Flash Media Server or Flash Video Streaming Service (FVSS).

The Stream from a Flash Video Streaming Service for your Deployment option (available from the Deployment Options screen on the Video Import wizard) enables you to upload your video to a Flash Media Server and stream it directly into your Flash movie.

Such providers are often called CDNs (content delivery networks). The Video Import wizard's Deployment Options screen also displays hyperlink to the Adobe website where you can find a licensed FVSS. Choosing Stream from Flash Media Server on the Deployment Options screen allows you to stream your Flash Video from a Flash Media Server that you host, and provides a hyperlink that takes you to the Adobe website to learn more about the Flash Media Server and how to license it.

For both linked approaches, you'll use the new FLVPlayback component or ActionScript to control video playback and provide intuitive controls for users to interact with the downloaded video.

Importing linked video

To explore the linked video approach, you'll add video to a sample layout for a client preview page. Because it is the most easily accessible method, this exercise focuses on progressive downloads from a web server.

1   Choose File > Open, and open the fl1402.fla located in the fl14lessons folder. This contains a pre-created layout for your new video preview page.

The pre-created layout for a video preview page.

2   Choose File > Save As. When the Save As dialog box appears, type **fl1402_work.fla** into the File name text field. Navigate to the fl14lessons folder and press Save.

3   Choose File > Import > Import Video to launch the Video Import wizard.

4   In the Select Video screen, select the Browse (Windows) or Choose (Mac OS) button, navigate to the fl14lessons folder, and select fl1404.mov. Press the Open button to return to the wizard. Press Next (Windows) or Continue (Mac OS) to advance to the next wizard screen.

Adobe has partnered with several CDN (Content Delivery Network) providers, such as VitalStream and Akamai, to offer hosted services for delivering on-demand Flash Video across high-performance, reliable networks. Built with Flash Media Server and integrated directly into the delivery, tracking, and reporting infrastructure of the CDN network, FVSS provides the most effective way to deliver Flash Video to the largest possible audience without the hassle of setting up and maintaining your own streaming server hardware and network.

5   On the Deployment screen, select Progressive download from a web server. With this option, you stream a local video file using a web server's standard HTTP protocols. Select the Next/Continue button to advance.

For the Progressive download from a web server option to work, you need to upload the Flash video to the same server as your final .swf file.

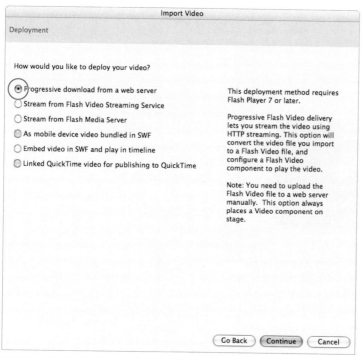

The Progressive download from a web server allows you to stream video using a standard web server.

6 On the Encoding screen, select Flash 8 – High Quality (700kbps) from the encoding profiles menu under the Profile tab. This high quality preset creates a Flash Video file (.flv) for playback in Flash Player 8 or later versions, and sets your video and audio settings.

7 Click the Crop and Resize tab, and check the Resize Video and Maintain Aspect ratio checkboxes. Enter **480** for Width, which automatically sets the height to 320. Press Next/Continue to advance to the next screen.

A deeper look at the Encoding panel

Although they're not used in this lesson, the Encoding screen features two additional useful controls:

The scrub bar below your video preview window lets you adjust the duration of your video. Use the triangular handles on the scrub bar to change your video's start and end points.

The Encoding screen's Cue Points tab becomes available when you choose external or linked video. Cue points are markers that you add to your Flash Video; you can then jump to these points using navigational controls or they'll trigger ActionScript-driven events in your Flash file.

8 In the Skinning screen, select ClearOverPlaySeekMute.swf from the Skin drop-down menu. Skins are pre-created face plates for your video component that feature different button configurations for controlling video playback. Flash ships with a variety of skins that you can use to customize the look and specific controls available for your video.

ClearOverPlaySeekMute.swf is one of many skins available in the skinning screen.

There are two additional options available from the Skin drop-down that are worth mentioning. The None option allows you to skip all play controls and just import the video. This is very helpful when you want the video to play in your movie without the user being able to interact with it. Custom enables you to specify a skin that you built yourself. For the Custom option to work, however, you must specify a URL so that Flash can find your skin file.

9   Press Next/Continue. The Finish Video Import screen displays a summary of the decisions you made in the Video Import wizard. It also explains that your video will be inserted into a Flash Video component with your skin copied into the same folder as your Flash file. Press Finish to begin the video rendering process.

Video rendering is a very intensive process that can take quite a long time. The video included in this lesson could take anywhere from 2-5 minutes to complete the process. For your convenience, we have included the pre-rendered Flash Video file (fl1404.flv) in the lesson14 folder.

10   When finished, Flash places a video component in the middle of the Stage. A component is a pre-created Flash object that can be used for a variety of functions. The FLVPlayback component is used as a display container for your linked video. Using the Selection tool (**k**), move the video into the Place Video Here frame.

 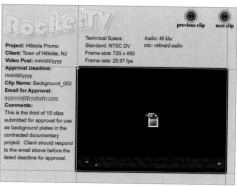

Use the Selection tool to move the new video component into the Place Video Here frame.

11   Choose Control > Test Movie to preview your movie. Experiment with the different playback controls on the skin's button bar.

You'll notice that the video plays automatically when the movie loads. A better effect would be for the video to pause at the beginning so that viewers could read the on-screen text and then play the video when they're ready. In the next exercise you'll edit the parameters of the component to do this.

Working with the FLVPlayback component

The FLVPlayback component is a special Flash object used to control the playback of linked video in Flash, and provide the user with an intuitive set of controls for interacting with your video. You interact with components a little differently than you do with other Flash objects—with components, you'll use the Parameters tab in the Property Inspector to control or edit its features and behavior. In this exercise, you'll use the FLVPlayback component to add controls for your preview page's linked video.

1 With the Selection tool (⬆) active, click on the video component on the Stage.

2 Click the Parameters tab of the Property inspector to view the FLVPlayback component's parameters.

With the video component on the Stage selected, click the Parameters tab on the Property inspector.

3 By default, the autoPlay parameter is set to true, which sets the video to automatically play when loaded. Click on the word "true," and select false from the drop-down menu that appears.

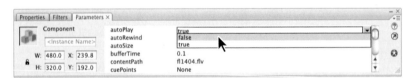

Change the autoPlay parameter in the Parameters panel.

4 Choose Control > Test Movie to test your movie. When the video appears, it should now be paused on the first frame; you'll have to click on the Play button for it to play. Close the Flash Player.

You may notice a slight delay between the time that the Flash movie loads and the appearance of the video. This is normal and varies by the speed of a user's Internet connection.

5 Choose File > Save.

6 Close your project by choosing File > Close.

In addition to the options you've already used, the Video Import wizard's Deployment screen offers two more specialized choices, which are usually grayed out. The As Mobile Device Video Bundled in SWF setting creates video content for deployment in FlashLite, the Adobe Flash solution for mobile content. Used to target Flash Player versions 3 through 5, the Linked QuickTime Video for Publishing to QuickTime feature creates linked video in the QuickTime format. If you click on either of these options when they are grayed out, a pop-up window directs you to the Publish Settings menu.

Flash Video Encoder

For video-heavy projects, Flash CS3 installs with the standalone Flash Video Encoder application for batch converting video files into the Flash Video (.flv) format. Because it relieves you of having to open Flash and importing each individual file to convert it, the Flash Video Encoder frees you to work on more important aspects of your project.

1   Open the Flash Video Encoder from the Program Files\Adobe (Windows) or Applications (Mac OS) folder on your computer.

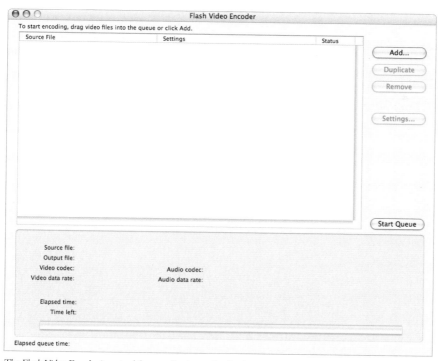

The Flash Video Encoder is a standalone application used to batch convert video files into .flv format.

2 Click the Add button on the right, and select both the fl1403.mov and the fl1404.mov files from the fl14lessons folder. Press Open.

You can select multiple files by holding down the Ctrl key (Windows) or Command key (Mac OS) and clicking on the files in the Open dialog box.

3 Both files should be selected when you return to the Flash Video Encoder. Press the Settings button on the right. An alert dialog box appears telling you that you are about to edit encoding settings for multiple files and that the previous settings lost. Press OK.

4 In the Flash Video Encoding Settings dialog box, select Flash 8 – High Quality (700kbps) from the Profiles drop-down menu. Press OK.

The Profiles menu is the same one that you saw earlier in this lesson when you first imported video into the Flash project. If you want to assign different settings to your video files, select and change the settings individually.

5 Press Start Queue to begin the encoding process. The files are placed into the same folder as the original video.

6 When the encoding completes, close the Flash Video Encoder.

A very useful source of information on working with video in flash is the Adobe website, adobe.com. Adobe offers a wide variety of articles, video tutorials, and white papers on Flash video and the ActionScript code used to control and manipulate Flash video.

Self study

1   Use the two Flash Video files you created in the last part of the lesson to create your own video player by embedding each of them into a Flash file.

2   Practice encoding your own video at various settings and compare the results of the different encoding options.

Review

Questions

1   What are the four standard deployment options with Flash Video? Briefly describe each.

2   Which linked deployment option is any Flash user with a website immediately able to use, and why?

3   Which ActionScript command is used in this lesson to completely stop the movement of the Timeline?

Answers

1   **a.** Progressive download from a web server: allows you to stream video, using a web server's standard HTTP protocols.

   b. Stream from a Flash Video Streaming Service: allows you to upload your video to a space on a Flash Media Server hosted by an Adobe licensed company.

   c. Stream from Flash Media Server: allows you to stream your Flash Video from a Flash Media Server that you host.

   d. Embed video in SWF and play in timeline: places the video directly in the Flash Timeline, which allows you to sync the video with other animation or add interactive elements to the video area.

2   The progressive download option can be used by any Flash user with a website because it uses a standard Internet protocol (HTTP) to load and display video.

3   The *stop( )* action can stop all movement in a Flash movie by stopping the playhead on the main timeline or any nested timelines from advancing.

Lesson 15

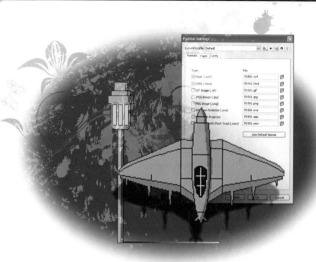

Delivering Your Final Movie

What you'll learn in this lesson:

- Publishing to the Web and CD

- Customizing Publish Settings

- Creating a standalone, full-screen projector

- Exporting to video

Although Flash is commonly thought of as a web design and development program, it's also a full-featured multimedia authoring tool. With Flash CS3 Professional, you can publish content for distribution to the Web, CDs, DVDs, and video.

Starting up

Before starting, make sure that your tools and panels are consistent by resetting your preferences. See "Resetting the Flash workspace" on page 3.

You will work with several files from the fl15lessons folder in this lesson. Make sure that you have loaded the fllessons folder onto your hard drive from the supplied DVD. See "Loading lesson files" on page 3.

See Lesson 15 in action!

Use the accompanying video to gain a better understanding of how to use some of the features shown in this lesson. Open the DynamicLearning_FlashCS3.swf file located in the Videos folder and select Lesson 15 to view the video training file for this lesson.

The project

In this lesson, you won't be creating a movie or even a piece of one. Instead, you'll be publishing existing movies to the Web and CD-ROM. You will also learn how to customize Publish settings to adapt Flash content for a variety of applications and, finally, you will create a Flash projector file to deploy your Flash movies as standalone files.

The publishing process

By now you should be very familiar with the Test Movie command. As you learned in previous lessons, the command generates an .swf file so that you can preview how your animation looks and how its interactive elements behave. Although Test Movie works very well as a preview and you can embed the resulting .swf directly into a web page, the Publish command gives you a much wider range of options. By default, the Publish command creates an HTML page with your .swf file embedded into it for display. It is important to remember that when you publish a file, you have to target a version of the Flash player to publish to. So, if you prefer, you can alter your Publish Settings to convert the .fla file to a GIF, JPEG, PNG, or QuickTime file. When combined with your .swf file, this option allows your Flash file to be displayed by viewers who have the targeted Flash player and the image file to be displayed by viewers who lack the correct version of the player. This alternative publishing format also includes the HTML needed to display the images in a viewer's browser window.

Publishing to the Web

For the best possible user experience, a Flash file must be embedded into a web page. If you are familiar with an HTML authoring program such as Adobe Dreamweaver, you could export an .swf file and then embed it into a page manually. An easier approach, however, is to use Flash's Publish command, which does all the work for you by creating an .swf file, an HTML file that has your .swf file embedded into it, and a JavaScript file that allows your Flash movie to automatically play in browsers that would normally block Flash content. Once you have the .swf, .html, and Javascript files, you can easily upload them to your web site.

Publishing a file is simple. With your .fla file open, select File > Publish. Flash then creates HTML, .swf, and JavaScript files, and saves them to the directory that contains the .fla file.

Customizing the Publish Settings

The default settings are fine for many situations, but you can customize the Publish Settings for better results. Give it a try:

1 From the fl15lessons folder, open the file named fl1501.fla, which is an animated footer for a website.

2 Choose File > Publish Settings to open the Publish Settings dialog box. The dialog box is initially composed of three tabs: Formats, which lets you choose the publish format; Flash, which contains settings for the .fla you're publishing; and HTML, which enables you to customize the associated HTML file. By default, Flash is already set to publish a Flash movie and embed it in an HTML page. If you choose another format in the Formats tab, additional tabs related to that format appear. For now, keep the default Format settings.

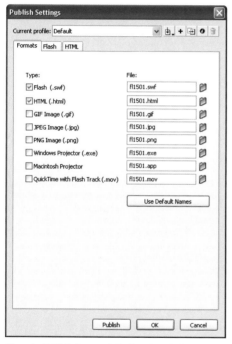

Open the Publish Settings dialog box through the File menu.

3 Click the Flash tab. The settings here control how the Flash movie you publish is created. They are grouped into three general sections: swf file options, image options, and audio options. Make sure that Version is set to Flash Player 9, and ActionScript is set to ActionScript 2.0. By default, the Flash Player version is set to the most recent version available. In addition, Flash automatically sets the ActionScript version to match the choice you make when you choose Actionscript 2.0 or 3.0 when first creating a document.

4   In the Options section, click to turn on the Protect from import checkbox and click to turn off the Export hidden layers checkbox. Protect from import prevents a user from downloading your Flash movie and re-importing it into Flash to reuse. Deselecting Export hidden layers makes sure that layers that are hidden are not included in the published file.

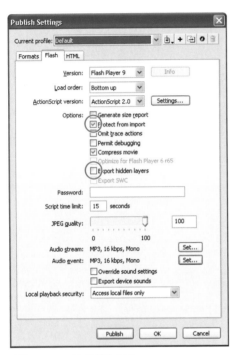

Adjust your movie's Publish Settings.

You can set three additional options for the Flash file export. Omit Trace Action and Permit Debugging are specifically geared toward working with ActionScript, while Generate Size Report creates a text file that breaks down the size of each scene and symbol in your movie.

5   Raise the JPEG Quality slider to 100 to ensure the least amount of compression on the bitmap images in your movie.

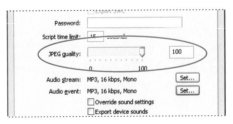

Drag the JPEG quality slider to 100.

Although the example file does not use any audio effects, the last section of the Flash tab enables you to set a movie's audio quality. By clicking on the Set buttons to the right of Audio Stream and Audio Event, you can open up dialog boxes that control how those types of audio objects are compressed. The default MP3 setting is very efficient in most situations.

6   Click the HTML tab to view the options for the HTML file that you are publishing. By default, Template is set to display Flash only. Click the Info button to the right of the Template drop-down menu to view the description of the current template. For Flash Only, the Info pop-up explains that this template is intended as a container for your Flash movie, and that the publish operation creates a file named AC_OETags.js, which is an external JavaScript file that the HTML page needs to display the Flash content correctly. Close the pop-up after you have reviewed the description.

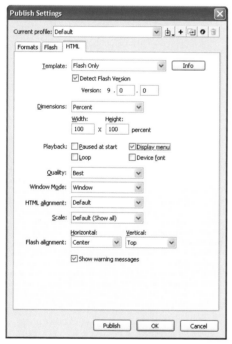

Review the descriptions on the HTML tab.

7   Click on the checkbox for Detect Flash Version, which configures your document to detect the user's version of Flash Player and sends the user to an alternative HTML page if the targeted player isn't present.

8   Select Percent from the Dimensions drop-down menu. The Dimensions menu sets the display size of the Flash movie in your HTML page. Make sure Width and Height are both set to 100% to ensure that the movie scales to fit the size of the browser window.

9 In the Playback options area, click the Display Menu checkbox. The playback options control how the Flash movie acts when loaded into the browser. With Display Menu on, the user can display a context menu by right-clicking (Windows) or Control-clicking (Mac OS) on the Flash movie in the browser.

Because the example movie uses a nested movie clip symbol, the HTML tab's Paused at Start and Loop Playback options would have no effect; they target the main timeline only. Device Fonts is a Windows-only solution that substitutes system fonts for fonts used in the Flash movie that are not loaded on the user's computer.

10 Choose Best from the Quality drop-down menu to ensure that the Flash movie displays at its highest possible quality setting. Be aware that this setting has a downside: the processing time needed to achieve Best quality is greater than for lower settings.

11 Leave HTML Alignment, Window Mode, and Scale at the default settings. HTML Alignment controls the position of the .swf file window in the web page. Window Mode controls the appearance of the box in which the .swf file appears; you can use it to create an .swf file with a transparent background. Apply Scale only if you changed the .swf file's original dimensions.

12 Next to Flash Alignment options, set Horizontal to Center and Vertical to Top, which places the .swf file in the upper-middle portion of the browser window.

Choose Center from the Horizontal fiield and Top from the Vertical field.

13 Press OK to keep these settings. They save when you save the Flash document.

To publish the file with your new settings, you can choose File > Publish while the file is open, or you can publish directly from the Publish Settings panel by clicking its Publish button.

CD-ROM delivery

The Web is not your only option for delivering your Flash content. You can distribute it offline, as well as via CDs and DVDs by creating projector files. A projector file is a standalone executable Flash document that can be downloaded or delivered on a CD or DVD. Projector files are often used to deliver games and presentations that are deployed locally on the viewer's computer and not through the Internet. Because the Flash Player is included in the projector, users can display the Flash content without a web browser.

Creating a standalone projector

Like publishing to the Web, the process of publishing an .fla file to a projector file starts in the Publish Settings panel. The difference is what you set in the Formats tab.

1   Open the fl1502.fla file from the fl15lessons folder. This file contains the beginning stages of a game called Dodge 'Em that you will publish as an executable projector file.

2   Choose File > Publish Settings.

3   In the Formats tab of the Publish Settings panel, turn off the Flash and HTML checkboxes. Turn on the checkbox next to Windows Projector (.exe). Unlike Flash and HTML files, there are no editable options for the Projector format.

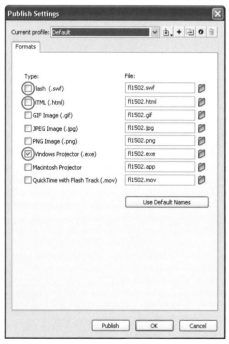

Deselect the HTML and Flash checkboxes and choose Windows Projector.

The File fields to the right of each output type allow you to specify a name for your file and an output location. By default, the output name and location are the same as that of your Flash .fla file.

4 Click the Publish button in the Publish Settings panel to produce a standalone Flash projector. Press OK.

If the Publish Settings panel is closed, you can publish a file by choosing File > Publish or pressing Shift+F12.

5 Minimize Flash, and, from your desktop, navigate to the fl15lessons folder. Double-click on the fl1502.exe file to launch it. The Dodge 'Em game that you just published should open and play inside a window on your desktop. The window is the same size as the Stage was in Flash. Close the file and return to Flash.

Making a full-screen projector

The projector's ability to deliver standalone Flash movies makes it an ideal choice for delivering content, such as interactive portfolios, marketing materials, and presentations, but watching a presentation on-screen surrounded by all the other icons and applications that may be running on your desktop is distracting. With a little ActionScript, however, you can set a Flash projector file to launch as a full-screen application.

1 If the fl1502.fla file is not already open, reopen it now. Select the first frame of the Actions layer in the Timeline.

Select Frame 1 in the Actions layer.

2 Choose Window > Actions to open the Actions panel.

3 The first line of code is a *stop( )* action to stop the movement of the playhead at Frame 1. Place your cursor at the end of the first line, after the semicolon, and press the Enter (Windows) or Return (Mac OS) key.

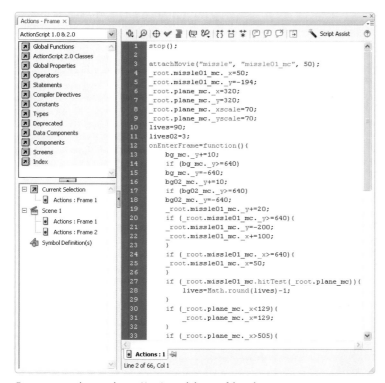

Open up a space between the stop( ) action and the rest of the code.

4 With your cursor now on line 2, enter in the following line of code:

```
fscommand("fullscreen", true);
```

Fscommand is an ActionScript function that enables the .swf movie to communicate with the container that is holding it, whether that container is a web browser or the standalone Flash Player, as it is here. The command tells the Flash Player to display at the full-screen resolution of the viewer's monitor, thus ensuring an immersive experience.

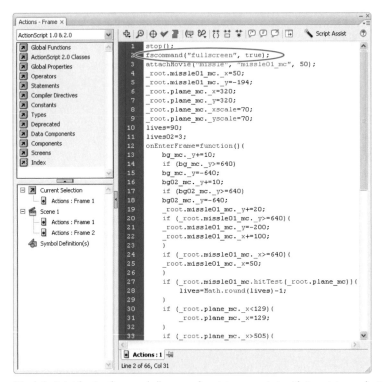

The ActionScript function fscommand allows a .swf movie to communicate with its container application.

5 Save your file, using File > Save, and publish it using File > Publish.

6 Minimize Flash, and, from your desktop, navigate to the fl15lessons folder and double-click on the Flash Projector file to open it. The file should now appear at the full-screen resolution.

If your Flash movie is not sized proportionally to the viewer's screen resolution, the fscommand reveals the area outside the Stage to make up for the different ratio.

7 Close the file, return to Flash, and close the project.

The fscommand folder

CD-ROM developers can take advantage of the fscommand folder to have Flash launch other applications. For example, you could use Flash to create an installer application or an interactive form. For security reasons, Flash cannot connect and run applications on your local hard drive. Instead, you must create a folder named fscommand and place your executable files there. The fscommand folder must be in the same directory as your Flash projector File.

Using Export Movie

You can extend your range of output formats by using the Export Movie command. In addition to creating .swf files, Export Movie can export the content of the main timeline to AVI and QuickTime video formats, or as a sequence of still images for editing in applications like Photoshop, Premiere, and After Effects. In addition to the extended options you have for saving in different formats, the main difference between the Export command and the Publish command that you have worked with previously is that the Publish settings are stored in your .fla file when you save your document, export options are not.

1   In the fl15lessons folder, open the file named fl1503.fla, which is a variation of the animated Web site footer you worked with in the first exercise. The main difference is that here the animation takes place on the main timeline instead of in a nested movie clip. This is a very important distinction when exporting Flash content to other formats, as the majority of the exportable formats lack interactivity and simply display the content of the main timeline as it appears in Flash.

2   Choose File > Export > Export Movie.

This exercise covers exporting the entire movie from the Timeline. If you would rather export only a single frame, select that frame, then choose File > Export > Export Image.

3   In the resulting dialog box, choose the fl15lessons folder in the Save As drop-down menu, if it is not already listed there.

4   Select QuickTime (.mov) in the Save as type pull-down menu to create a standalone QuickTime movie that can be played using the free QuickTime player, converted for display on such mobile devices as PSPs and iPods, or imported into video editing or motions graphics programs, such as Adobe Premiere or After Effects. Press Save. The QuickTime Export Settings dialog box appears.

5   In the QuickTime Export Settings dialog box, confirm that Render width is set to 1024 and Render height is 100. Ensure that the Maintain aspect ratio checkbox below the Render boxes is unchecked.

Below the Render height field in the QuickTime Export Settings dialog box are two checkboxes. The first, Maintain Aspect Ratio, simply ensures that if you alter either width or height, the other value changes proportionately. The second, Ignore Stage Color, generates a QuickTime movie with an alpha channel that you can then import into a video editing or motion graphics program, such as Adobe Premiere or After Effects.

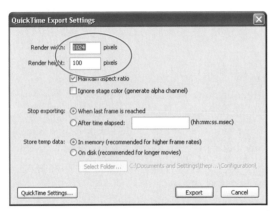

Set the Render width and height in the QuickTime Export Settings dialog box.

6 Leave the Stop Exporting and Store Temp Date radio buttons unchanged. They allow you to control how much of your movie is rendered to video and whether you want to use either your system's memory or hard drive space during the rendering process. The defaults work fine for this animation. Press Export. Flash builds your QuickTime movie.

You may receive a message informing you that Flash has finished building your movie. Press OK.

7 Minimize Flash and navigate to the fl15lessons folder. Double-click on your QuickTime movie to play it, and view the animation you have just exported.

An overview of FTP (File Transfer Protocol)

FTP is an acronym for the phrase File Transfer Protocol. These are the set of rules that allow different computers to connect to each other over the Web. Once you have created and published your Flash movie, you need to upload it to a web server in order to allow people to view it online. Whether this web server is one that you maintain yourself, one set up for you by your company's IT department, or space you rent from a web host, the publishing process is basically the same. While there are standalone FTP applications that allow you to connect to a web server, Abode's industry-leading web design application, Dreamweaver, comes complete with an internal FTP engine that integrates very well with Flash content. The basic steps to follow when uploading Flash content for the Internet are:

1   Create a Flash movie and publish it to your local hard drive.

2   Upload your Flash movie to your web server, along with any secondary content (.html and javascript files) created by the publishing process. Your web hosting service or IT department can provide you with information on where to upload your files, as well as the login and password information you need to connect.

3   If you want to make any changes to the movie, edit the file you published to your local hard drive, not the version on the server.

4   Re-upload the edited version of your Flash movie to the web server, including any secondary content you may have modified.

Using Adobe Device Central in Flash

Adobe Device Central is a new tool available within many of Adobe's CS3 applications. It is a simulation platform useful for developing content for mobile devices. Device Central allows you to preview the appearance and performance of Flash content on a variety of mobile devices. You can access Device Central when you start a project, or later in the development cycle. You use Device Central by targeting one of the Flash Lite players in the Publish Settings dialog box. Flash Lite is Adobe's standalone application for playing Flash content on mobile devices. In this exercise, you'll explore the steps used when creating content for mobile devices using Device Central.

1   Choose File > Open. Navigate to the fl15lessons folder and select the file named LampPost.fla. Press Open.

This Flash file was designed to play on the type of small screen found on a mobile phone or PDA. You must now direct the file to play in the Flash Lite player.

2   Choose File > Publish Settings to target the Flash Lite player as your publishing environment.

3 In the Publish Settings dialog box, click the Flash tab to bring it forward, then select Flash Lite 2.1 from the Version drop-down menu. Leave all other settings unchanged. Press OK to close the Publish Settings dialog box.

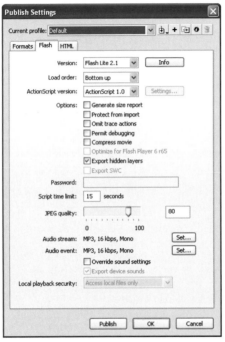

The Publish Settings dialog box controls the options for your published .swf files.

4 Choose Control > Test Movie to preview your Flash file. With Flash Lite set as your player, the movie opens in Adobe Device Central.

When you test the Flash movie, you will receive an error message in the Output panel that states, WARNING: This movie uses features that are not supported in the Flash Lite 2.1 Player. This message is caused by an image created in Adobe Illustrator that was embedded in this file using an older version of Flash. You can ignore this warning message; it does not prevent you from previewing the file using Adobe Device Central.

5 From the list of available devices on the left side of the window, click the plus sign to the left of the Kyocera option, then double-click the Kyocera W43K to preview your Flash animation on this Kyocera phone. The list of available devices is based on the version of the Flash Lite Player that you selected in step 3. Device names that are dimmed are not available using the selected version of the Flash Lite Player.

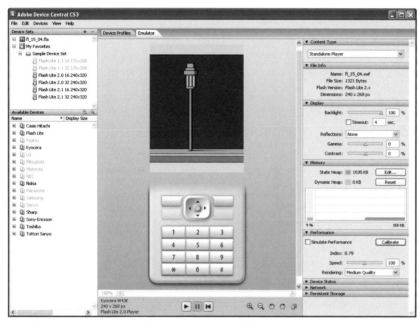

Adobe Device Central previews your Flash movie on a variety of phones and mobile devices.

The device emulator in the center of your screen allows you to see your project. If your project uses ActionScript, you can also interact with it. On the right side of the interface are controls you can use to evaluate the display and performance settings. These controls are based upon the mobile device you have selected.

6 In Adobe Device Central, select File > Return to Flash to return to the Flash authoring environment. You can continue to develop your Flash file and switch back to Device Central whenever you want to preview your changes.

Some ActionScript is not supported by Flash Lite. If you are using ActionScript in your Flash movie that is not supported by Flash Lite, you will be notified of this in the Output panel when you test your movie.

Self study

1   Open the LampPost.fla file in the fl15lessons folder and add the *fscommand* to the Actions layer so that the file can display full-screen. Publish the file as a Flash projector.

2   Open the masthead.fla file in the fl15lessons folder, and publish it as a Flash movie embedded in an HTML document. Experiment with different JPEG quality settings to see the effects on the resulting .swf file's size.

Review

Questions

1   What is the advantage of using the Publish command instead of the Test Movie command?

2   Why would you want to export a QuickTime Movie or AVI file?

3   When using the standalone Flash projector, where must you store any executable application that you want Flash to launch?

Answers

1   **a**. The Publish command can create a playable .swf file and automatically embed it into an HTML page.

  b. The Publish command offers a wide range of exportable formats in addition to standard .swf creation.

2   **a**. To display your Flash animation on video devices such as iPods and PSPs.

  b. For import into a video editing or motion graphics program.

3   Inside a folder named fscommand, which must be in the same directory as your Flash projector application itself.

Index

Where innovation, creativity, and technology converge.

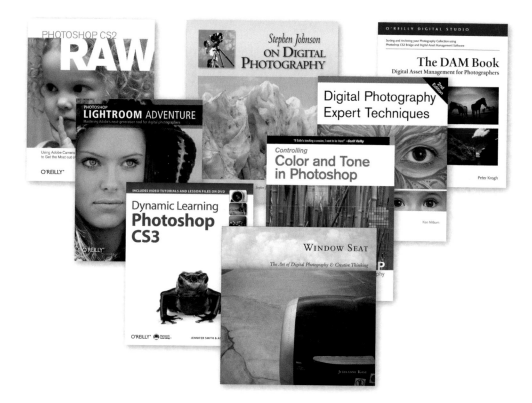

There's a revolution in how the world engages ideas and information. As our culture becomes more visual and information-rich, anyone can create and share effective, interactive, and extraordinary visual and aural communications. Through our books, videos, Web sites and newsletters, O'Reilly spreads the knowledge of the creative innovators at the heart of this revolution, helping you to put their knowledge and ideas to work in your projects.

To find out more, visit us at digitalmedia.oreilly.com

O'REILLY®

Want to learn
Adobe Creative Suite 3?

Don't just get a book.

Introducing O'Reilly Dynamic Learning—a comprehensive, self-paced training system that includes books, video tutorials, online resources, and instructor guides. Written by product experts and trainers who have produced many of Adobe's training titles, the books are organized into practical, easy-to-follow lessons that cover everything you need to know about the applications in CS3.

Look for the complete Dynamic Learning series at your favorite bookseller, or online at www.oreilly.com/store

 oreilly.com/store/series/dynamiclearning